Goldmining in
Foreclosure Properties

Testimonials

Your "between-two-houses" ideas for finding deals is one of the best ideas in any real estate book I've ever read.

Sarah Lopez, Houston

We bought our first home with only option money (that was refunded by our mortgage) using your ideas.

E.M. Strand, Chicago

My brother and I are doing this part-time and so far we've made over $100,000 apiece in a little over two years.

Edgar Cole, Hartford

We made money on our first Goldmining deal to take care of all the costs on our second Goldmining home (which we are living in). Thanks.

Stan Londski, Colton

Using your Goldmining system, there seems to be no end to the deals I'm making. You're making me a very rich man. Thanks.

H. Marcus, Costa Mesa

The people we helped (using your Goldmining book) are real close friends now. They're much better off than they would have been without both of us.

H.C. Chen, San Francisco

I followed your advice to the letter and made over $12,000 on my first deal and over $15,000 on my next. Your forms and checklists are worth a fortune to me.

N. Dooley, Los Angeles

Goldmining in Foreclosure Properties

Fifth Edition

George Achenbach

WILEY

John Wiley & Sons, Inc.

Published by John Wiley & Sons, Inc., Hoboken, New Jersey.
Published simultaneously in Canada.

For general information on our other products and services please consult our Customer Care Department within the United States at (800) 762-2974, outside the United States at (317) 572-3993 or fax (317) 572-4002.

Wiley also publishes its books in a variety of electronic formats. Some content that appears in print may not be available in electronic books. For more information about Wiley products, visit our web site at *www.wiley.com*.

Library of Congress Cataloging-in-Publication Data:

Achenbach, George, 1928–
    Goldmining in foreclosure properties / Geroge Achenbach, Sr.— 5th ed.
        p. cm.
    Includes index.
    ISBN 0-471-46485-6 (pbk.)
    1. Real estate investment. 2. House buying. 3. Foreclosure. 4. Real property. I. Title.
HD1382.5.A27 2003
332.63′243—dc21

                                                                    2003049653

Printed in the United States of America.

10 9 8 7 6 5 4 3 2

Contents

Introduction

The more changes, the more chances for profit.
—*Jay Adler*

In my twenty-five-year career as a builder-developer, I built and sold over 7,000 single-family homes and apartment units. During this period, I learned to understand buyers, lenders, and market fundamentals. I also saw home buying change drastically. In the sixties, a family could buy an average 3 bedroom, 1.5 bath home (on half an acre of land) for about $20,000. They only had to put down $1,000 in cash, and their monthly payments were around $150.

Today's home prices and terms are 10 to 20 times greater. For a large number of people, owning a home today is an unaffordable luxury. Many households depend on two (or more) incomes to cover their expenses.

Many of the people who bought houses a couple of years ago are now in trouble. They are overextended financially and behind in their loan payments. Some take out second, third, fourth, or even fifth loans just to make payments on prior loans.

When the payments stop, the legal process begins. Notices of default are filed, and more often than not, the property is taken away. Foreclosure sales could soon be more common than ever.

In nearly thirty years in the real estate business, I have been involved in hundreds of foreclosure transactions. I have repeatedly seen buyers (myself included) step in early in the process and work deals with the troubled owners, the lenders, and the creditors. I have been at over 150 auctions where buyers (myself included) bought foreclosure property that was quickly resold for a good profit. I have also seen dozens of properties change ownership in foreclosure-type transactions that give the new buyer a large, almost instant profit.

This book contains many examples of properties I bought from troubled owners. These case studies detail each step along the way, from the first notice of default to the foreclosure sale or auction to the final disposition of the profit-making property.

I've always taken a personal interest in troubled owners, because in the past I've been a troubled owner myself. I know firsthand how it feels to lose a home you cherish through foreclosure. I know that anyone in such a situation looks at help as a godsend. Usually, when foreclosure is threatened, nobody wants to touch the property. Potential buyers back away, figuring that foreclosure proceedings wouldn't have started if the deal was salvageable. But this is not necessarily the case. Sometimes a situation arises that the homeowners can't control. The least you can do as a prospective investor is to make a careful analysis of the possible opportunities. My experience is that nine times out of ten the opportunities are there—not only to make a profit on the investment, but also to save the owners' credit and property.

Make no mistake about it, many owners threatened by foreclosure are going to lose their home because of their terrible financial position. But under the right conditions, you can help them save their credit. That's what helps them recover and resume their regular economic life. You can make a good deal that helps them, too.

A Working Handbook for Making Money

Goldmining in Foreclosure Properties tells you what happens during the foreclosure process, why it happens, and exactly what to do when it happens. Specifically, this guide includes:

• Statistical information and facts

• Sample forms, worksheets, and checklists

• Procedures for locating distress properties

• Recommendations on negotiating with troubled owners

• Complete financial analysis techniques to help you evaluate each property and make the right offer

• Insight into creating deals once legal action has started, bidding successfully at auction, and dealing with lenders who get the property if the property is not sold at auction

• Details on how to resell the property quickly if that is in your best interest

• Information on negotiating with a new purchaser and transferring title in the most profitable way

• Suggestions on leasing the home and beginning a process that could create rental income, capital appreciation, and tax savings

- Information on pitfalls and problem areas, allowing you to benefit from the experience of those who have done this in the past

The book also includes many examples of deals I have made, both good and bad. To protect the privacy of the people involved in these case studies, I've changed the names and a few details, but the lessons of each deal come through clearly. This edition includes a new chapter covering the pros and cons of bankruptcy and highlights the latest proposed changes in the law such as homestead exemption and needs-based rules.

The appendix consists of a selection of California Civil Codes that apply to home equity sales contracts, mortgages, and mortgage foreclosure consultants. In other states the headings and content of the codes may be different, but the subject matter will be similar. (You may want to consult an attorney, an accountant, or a loan broker if you have technical questions, because their expertise in certain areas is greater than mine.)

At the end of the book is a Glossary of Real Estate Terms, with over 120 of the key words and phrases used in this business, and an index to help you quickly find the specific information you need. In this edition, a new chapter has been added, "Dealing with Bankruptcy Cases."

If you carefully study this book, you can become a specialist in the field of distress properties. Read with a pencil or marker handy and underline the ideas or techniques that have special meaning for you. Use the margin on each page to add your own thoughts and plans. On the inside front cover, list the page numbers you may want to refer back to at some point in the future. There are definite advantages to using a computer and the Internet for whatever functions it may now and in the future provide—but it is not necessary for success in the distress property business. Some possibilities for using a computer would be to keep all your information about properties in disk files, to search for information about codes and regulations, police information, and sources of default and foreclosure filings on the Internet, to print out maps from Internet sites, and to search classified ads and perhaps legal notices in newspaper listings on the Internet.

Hundreds of people are "goldmining" in distress properties right now. No magic or mystery is involved. For investors with even a little money, this is a good time. You just have to make up your mind to take advantage of this unique situation. You can acquire one, two, five, or ten good properties if you spend some time doing so. You just need to be creative and work hard.

This type of goldmining need not be limited to investors, either. The market is wide open for first-time home buyers. Instead of responding to ads for new or existing homes, you should be responding to the opportunities in distress properties. These homes will find their way to the marketplace sooner or later, anyway. As a prospective buyer, you probably already have some knowledge about the homes in your area. With the information in this book, you can jump into the distress property market and do some good for everyone concerned. Quite often you save the credit rating of the troubled owners and help them leave with self-esteem and a few dollars. You restore a neglected property to its full value and win the respect of the neighbors. And you find yourself a good deal on a first home that you can someday sell at a profit.

This book does not say that you can accomplish your goals overnight. You can't just sit back, relax, and think about being rich. But in today's real estate environment, if you work only a few hours a week, you can acquire your first piece of distress property within three months and, depending on your effort, another one every month thereafter. Just implement the simple techniques presented here to take advantage of today's circumstances. You might also help some troubled owners save their credit rating.

CHAPTER 1
Your Place in the Distress Property Cycle

Techniques only work when you do.
—*Carlos Royal*

Goldmining in Foreclosure Properties deals with homes, condos, and smaller rental units that have fallen into the "distress" category, meaning that the owners are in a hurry to sell. These people may be prompted to sell by personal problems or financial problems, but in either case the result is the same. They need to get out with some financial arrangement tailored to their needs and with at least a shred of dignity intact.

As a private party, you are better able to help the troubled owners (and yourself) than the experts are. You know the consumers' problems. You can take the time and make the effort to work on one deal at a time, whether it's for your own home or for an investment. If you're really motivated, you might even undertake "goldmining" as a small part-time business. It could bring you between $40,000 and $100,000 a year, depending on the energy you expend.

A Unique Opportunity

Human nature being what it is, there is always someone who wants to get rid of a property because of a personal situation—a divorce, a falling-out with partners, a job transfer. By staying alert for cases like these, specialists in distress property should always be able to find deals. Case Study 1.1 is an example of such a deal.

But the time has never been better for aspiring real estate investors. Today the real estate industry is saturated with overfinanced properties. The economy is threatened with slowdowns due to overseas problems which could create havoc in home building

Case Study 1.1

Mr. and Mrs. Saybrook were the first buyers in a new subdivision (in the early 1950s). Because sales were slow, they were able to purchase their home and receive a building lot free. But after 10 years of an unhappy marriage, they had agreed to separate. I was living close by at the time and noticed their For Sale by Owner sign.

After a few visits, I learned the following:

Market value of home	$60,000
First loan	23,400
Other liens	0
Net equity	$36,600

We had no way to determine the value of the extra lot, so we included it as part of the house package. Property was plentiful at that time.

Because the Saybrooks' parents had loaned them the money to purchase their home (without security), the Saybrooks felt obliged to repay the loan only if they received a large cash payment. I asked if they would take $1,000 cash apiece as a down payment and let me pay the balance over twenty years at 5 percent interest, with half going directly to each of them. After deducting the $2,000 down payment from $36,600, we had a balance of $34,600. At 5 percent interest, amortized over twenty years, the monthly payment would be $228.34, or $114.17 per month each. This deal seemed custom-made for them, so we agreed to an option period of about sixty days.

I knew I could interest a local builder in buying the adjacent lot if the terms were right. He was always interested in "no down" deals. I offered the lot to him for $10,300 with no money down but with monthly payments of $229.12 (based on a five-year term at 12 percent interest). This amount worked in well with his plans (most of the purchase price was deductible interest charges), so he readily agreed. He knew that in five years a lot with sewer and water in an established neighborhood could be worth many times the price he was paying.

When we concluded the deal, I had solved the troubled owners' problem and acquired a beautiful rental property with a small but growing cash flow for only $2,000 down.

and construction. But in chaos there is opportunity, and the real estate industry is no exception. In current conditions, people with skill, capital, and vision can make great profits. The existence of these opportunities is no secret. There is a shortage of capable real estate entrepreneurs, however, so this field is ripe for the taking.

Because of the inflated real estate prices over the past several years, buyers have had to take out larger loans than ever before, with extremely large monthly payments. The lenders are all too willing to help. In fact, lenders' actions seem calculated to overload borrowers. If the lenders repossess and sell a property, they could increase their profits dramatically, unless the loan is greater than the value of the property. But the borrowers will lose everything—home, equity, and credit. In many cases, even a small financial reversal can get the borrowers in trouble. A tremendous flood of distress properties seems all but inevitable.

In 2002 the rate of mortgage foreclosures reached the highest rate recorded in 30 years. In one three-month period, the proportion of loans on which foreclosures were started reached four per 1,000. Mortgages in the foreclosure process at any one time rose to more than 12 per thousand. The trend has stirred concern among industry leaders, fearing that the industry has been weakened by over-financing of homes.

Now is a very good time for knowledgeable investors to step in and enrich themselves while helping troubled owners and lenders resolve their problems. Why? Because properties could soon be in more trouble than ever before. More default notices are filed today than at any time in the past ten years. More borrowers and owners of property cannot make payments on their first, second, or even third or fourth loans. The current estimate of delinquencies is well over 3 million per year. The estimated number of foreclosure actions started in court is about 400,000 per year.

What's happening to the other 2.6 million delinquencies? Some are resolved by the owners before foreclosure takes place. But lots of deals are being made, too. If you want to buy a home to live in or to invest in, you should try dealing in distress property. Whether you are male or female, single, married, or living with someone, senior citizen or youngster, this is a great opportunity. With the forms and procedures provided in this book, you can help yourself and save the credit rating of the troubled owners.

The Distress Property Cycle

The life cycle in distress properties has four distinct stages:

- **Stage I:** Before Legal Action Begins. This is when the owners first stop making payments on the loan (or loans). Financial setbacks, personal changes, and family pressures may all play a role.

• **Stage II:** After Legal Notices Are Filed. At this point the foreclosure clock starts to tick. Only a limited number of days are left for the owners to pay up, sell, or make other deals with creditors.

• **Stage III:** Auction Time. This is how the court legally sells the property to satisfy the unpaid loans.

• **Stage IV:** REOs and Repos. When no one bids the amount owed, the property reverts back to the lender. It becomes an REO (real estate owned) property. When it reaches this stage, you must deal directly with the lender (who is now the owner).

Most specialists in distress property work in all four of these stages eventually. As a beginner, you'll probably want to choose one. The Distress Property Cycle chart in Figure 1.1 can help you decide. Then you can go on to consider a number of other important areas.

Analyze the Deal's Advantages and Disadvantages

Each prospective deal has advantages and disadvantages. You have to determine, in light of your own situation, what's most important for you. Plenty of deals are available. You just have to pick the one you'll be most comfortable with.

Start by analyzing your reasons for seeking title to a distress property. Are you after income from property management? Appreciation of capital? A tax shelter? More cash flow? Profit from resale of the property? A home of your own?

Once you've identified your motives, you can focus on the distress property itself. Each investor has a different way of analyzing values, but several key factors will have to be addressed:

• The total amount of investment necessary
• When the funds will have to be invested
• How much of the return will be in "hard" dollars and how much in "soft" dollars
• When the investment dollars will be returned

Obviously, before you can make a profit dealing in distress properties, you have to understand the details of any transaction. You are concerned with the same basic questions as the original mortgagee of that property.

In conjunction with your own economic review, you will probably ask the lending institutions certain threshold questions: Are additional funds available from the original lender? Will the

Stage	Players	Your Role As "Specialist"	Minimum Cash Required
I: Before Legal Action Begins	Troubled owners, lenders, creditors, broker, escrow company, title company, buyer	Understand problems, get correct facts, create solutions, make deals, rehab property, market for profit	$500 for options (in some deals, 10% down for temporary financing)
II: After Legal Notices Are Filed	Same as Stage I, plus trustees, lawyers	Same as Stage I, plus know foreclosure process	Same as Stage I
III: Auction Time	Trustees, lawyers, auctioneer, broker, escrow company, title company, buyer	Investigate much more, take higher risks, take quicker action	Usually full amount of bid in cash
IV: REOs and Repos	REO officers, appraisers, VA and HUD offices, broker, escrow company, title company, buyer	Develop awareness, develop contacts and working relationships, understand values	10% or less down (negotiable); financing available from source

Figure 1.1   Distress Property Cycle

lender indemnify you, as the new buyer, against any unforeseen claims against the property?

Avoid the Excessive Cost of Banks, Lawyers, and Realtors

This book does not and cannot give legal or professional advice. It does show how, with the right research and information, you can avoid all excessive professional costs associated with taking over existing property. For the most part, you just have to be aware of the applicable local, county, and state laws and be alert to some of the economic fundamentals. Although the procedures outlined here will not work in every county or every state, they provide enough basic information so you can consummate these transactions at minimum cost. You need only think a little and perhaps consult occasionally with an attorney or local professional.

Avoid Leverage Tricks

Leverage is advocated by most books with titles like "How to Make a Million Dollars in Thirty Days." Leverage is fine in a hypothetical example on paper. In real life, however, leverage works both ways. Prime rates go up and down (from 4.35 to 15.75 percent in the past 20 years or so). The banks and other lenders continually pressure the consumer to pay the piper. When you use other people's money ("OPM," as it's called in most get-rich-quick books on leverage), you invite total ruin. A better, safer way to operate is as an individual investor, handling only what you can manage.

When you use your own money (meaning yours, your family's, or your business's), you eliminate a variable factor that could upset your planning. If all the money is yours, nobody can call your loan and ask for the money back.

It is never a good idea to rely on other people's money, except when buying a property subject to an existing mortgage. Unnecessary risks are foolish. To accomplish the ends presented in this book, you do not have to use leverage in the speculative sense, nor do you have to borrow other people's money.

Observe the Laws That Apply in Your State

Although the ideas included in this book have been shown to work in most areas of the country, you must carefully check your local laws. It is impossible in a book of this kind to interpret the real estate laws of all fifty states and set down one group of rules that will work for all of them. For instance, some states have mortgages; others have deeds of trust. Even if the terms are essentially interchangeable, you would be well advised to consult a trusted attorney or accountant for the answer to any specific question concerning a specific area.

Critical Success Factor

The basic economic principle behind this program is the law of supply and demand. But other factors that contribute to its success are under your control:

- Intimate knowledge of a particular location
- Ability to maintain the property you acquire in such a manner as to increase its value
- Sincere concern for the welfare of troubled owners

- Willingness to work outside the regular nine-to-five hours of most professionals
- Willingness to deal directly with the sellers and the buyers
- Knowledge of how to buy property subject to existing mortgages and thereby avoid red tape

Remember, you probably know more about the territory than the experts do, and you can react more quickly. Your unique position as a specialist and your interest in helping owners who are in trouble will be your greatest advantages.

Where Do You Fit In?

The number of distress properties available changes when business conditions change. During times of full employment and low interest rates, there probably will be fewer. During bad times, when unemployment and high interest rates present a problem, the number of distress properties increases. But this issue is really beside the point. What's important is where you'll operate. What will your area be? How many housing units are in this area? How many properties do you want to buy per year? What are your personal goals?

One of my friends is content with one deal per year. His "farm" area consists of about three tracts right around where he lives. He gets all the information he needs from a small newspaper that comes out twice a week. It lists divorces, deaths, and trustee sales. He is very selective. He lists the suspect properties. He develops prospects and easily gets his one good deal per year.

I know another fellow who operates in three large counties in California—Orange County, Riverside County, and San Bernardino County. He and his two partners go for one deal a week. They haven't reached that level yet, but they have been averaging about two to three deals per month.

Once you have full knowledge of how the process operates, you have almost unlimited opportunities. The important thing is to get the knowledge and then develop a system for yourself. Pick a market large enough to accommodate your personal goals. Of course, another limiting factor is the amount of cash you have. I always recommend starting small. If you can get one good deal a year, you can expand to two deals or more as your skills expand.

Each stage of the distress property cycle has its own opportunities and its own problems. But they are all solvable, practical, bread-and-butter problems. There is nothing esoteric about them (like having to put a man on the moon). As long as you know where to go and who to ask for answers to these problems, you will be alright.

The Value of a Positive Mental Attitude

As you read this book and make preparations to go into the field, bear in mind that you are doing several people a favor. Your acquisition of distress property will stabilize or improve the credit rating of the struggling owners. You will help the people in the neighborhood by turning a property that is starting to run down into a property that has some dignity and potential value. Finally, you will help yourself (if you move into that home) or the people who lease or buy the place by providing a decent residence at a reasonable price.

Maintain an "I know what I am doing and I am doing something good" attitude. You need to approach every situation with a positive manner and a desire to make good things happen. The sellers need to feel that their problems are receiving sympathetic consideration and that you are offering personal service as well as service to the neighborhood. This whole endeavor should be a source of pride and confidence for you and everyone else involved. A positive attitude is your most valuable resource.

I remember one particular deal that started out so poorly I felt like quitting real estate over it. It was only my positive attitude that finally caused the bad deal to yield a big profit. A real estate agent called to say his broker wanted to sell an investment condo she owned. The broker needed cash for another investment. The condo was a 4 bedroom, 2.5 bath, two-story townhouse in very bad condition but in a good location.

After days of meeting with the agent, the broker, and the tenant (who turned out to be the real owner), I realized the deal was too confusing. The original buyer had sold the unit to the broker, who sold the unit to the present owner under a long-term contract of sale, very much like a lease with an option to buy. The buyer was making lease-type payments to the broker. The broker had obtained additional loans on the unit, as had the buyer.

By the time I decided to back out, the broker had committed herself to another deal using the money she was expecting to receive from me. In fact, all three parties had planned a chain of purchases. When I told them I wanted out, their cries of anguish could be heard halfway across the state.

This was a classic case of misunderstanding upon misrepresentation upon mistake. No one had really lied or intended to defraud. The problem was just that no one had presented all the facts in a normal way.

In response to the reaction, I guess, I stepped back and reviewed all the facts. Actually, the numbers did work. A good profit was possible on a sale one to two years down the road. All I had to do was be sure that all the liens and encumbrances were included and that I had safeguards. My positive attitude prevailed. I met with all three parties at a lawyer's office, and a few hours later we had a deal.

Everyone, except me, was in a hurry to make the deal. So I got all the safeguards I wanted and a few extra price concessions besides. I agreed to refinance the unit, replacing all financing with a new first loan. The agent, the broker, and the owner all got their money, and I got a choice property that eventually earned a neat profit—because I kept a can-do, positive attitude.

CHAPTER 2
Where's the Gold?

There are acres of diamonds (and tons of gold) in your own backyard.
—*Lee Crown*

Most people will agree that the real estate market is very different today from what it was only 15 years ago. There have been changes in the way real estate is sold and in the way it is purchased. Perhaps, too, there has been a change in our philosophy or manner of living. Today homes are usually not bought to be lived in for a lifetime. As each year passes, the rate of turnover in the ownership of homes reaches new highs.

There's also been a change in the way real estate is financed. People are borrowing more money than ever before to buy homes. Properties are more overmortgaged today than during the Great Depression.

Major lenders for single-family homes, like other good business people, have always tried to charge as much interest on their loans as possible. Five to ten years ago they encouraged people with home equity to refinance either with second mortgages or with larger first mortgages at higher interest rates. This is a good deal for the lenders, because they receive greater returns on their money. But it's a tremendous load on owners of single-family homes. Now the "chickens" are coming home to roost. Homeowners' financial plans are breaking down, and people are discovering they're not able to pay for the borrowed money.

Warning signs of this overborrowing are turning up in recorders' offices all over the country. The present volume of foreclosure and default notices indicates that, by the middle of the 2000s, we may well have an avalanche of foreclosures and defaults. Moreover, distress property sales prompted by imminent foreclosure will likely increase substantially.

Today lenders are quick to file default notices the first time a mortgage, tax, or escrow payment falls past due. They once waited up to three months and then called the borrower in to discuss the past-due payments. But today, with second and third loans so prevalent, most first-mortgage lenders move as quickly as possible to protect and improve their position.

For the most part, these troubles stem from two changes in the American lifestyle:

• Too large a percentage of our net income is needed to cover housing expenses (more than 50 percent in most families).

• Most families depend on two or more incomes to support themselves.

The tax law changes in 1986 and 1997 encouraged homeowners to take out second or third loans against their property to finance other purchases. Even though the interest payments were tax deductible, the loans still had to be paid off. But people went ahead and borrowed freely, because they thought the value of their home would go even higher.

If you look at Figure 2.1, Consumer Debt as a Percentage of Disposable Income, you can see how much consumer debt has risen in ten years. In 2001 it was a staggering 94 percent of disposable income, compared to 76 percent in 1989. This 24 percent increase comes at the expense of all other needs of the consumer. Less than a tenth of a family's net disposable income is left for

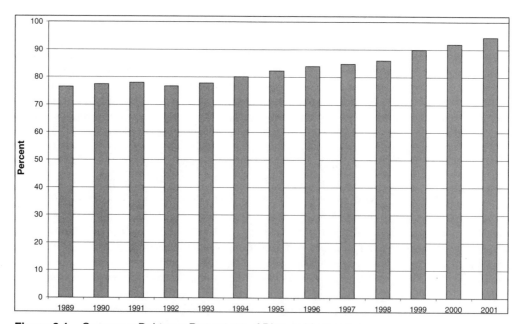

Figure 2.1   Consumer Debt as a Percentage of Disposable Income

food, clothing, education, transportation, health, fun, and anything else, compared with about 25 percent left in 1989.

Even bleaker days are ahead for the beleaguered consumer. Some of those who took out second and third mortgages reasoned that, if they ever had a problem making the loan payments, they could always sell their home for a profit. Then values peaked and, in some cases, went down. But the payments remained the same and had to be met.

Sadly, nothing is on the horizon that will help the average owner of a single-family home who is being hurt by abnormally high monthly housing payments. Certainly no help is coming from local and state governments. In almost every jurisdiction, 55 to 65 percent of the voters are homeowners, which ensures that nothing will be done to lower the quality or the standards involved in home construction. Indeed, more restrictions and higher standards are likely, meaning higher prices.

Most Financially Troubled Homeowners Will Not Recover

Monthly mortgage payments generally consume a larger part of family income than before. Thus homeowners have more trouble catching up when they are in arrears. Out of funds that have already proven insufficient, they have to keep up with current payments and come up with back payments plus extra charges for late payments, legal fees, and other expenses.

Most financially troubled homeowners will surely lose their property to the lenders unless they can secure additional funds. But the high cost of borrowing money and all the other obligations that these homeowners have already incurred probably mean that they will not be able to obtain the additional funds that can forestall foreclosure.

Statistics have shown that a financially troubled homeowner will not only end up losing the home but will probably lose a good credit rating as well. This is the point at which you can step in and help. If you diligently follow the rules presented in this book, you will help out the homeowner and be able to buy one, two, or three properties with little or no money down, subject to the existing mortgages.

The Opportunities to Help—and Profit— Are There

There will always be distress properties for sale. There will always be problems like overfinancing and 125 percent of value home loans. There will always be credit binges and shortages. People will always have family, personal, and job problems. Government will keep trying new trouble-solving (and problem-creating) programs. There will always be periods of feast or famine for real estate. Thus there will always be opportunities for "goldmining" in distress properties.

Anyone with an interest in real estate, a special knowledge of an existing territory or neighborhood, a good credit rating, and some money and time to invest can take advantage of the tremendous potential in this field.

It's interesting to compare the investment in single-family homes and condos with some other popular investment alternatives:

• *Savings account.* The average saver now has over a dozen different ways to invest savings. As always, guaranteed savings pay less than nonguaranteed savings. Most savings accounts have yields between 3.5 to 7 percent; the rate of inflation varies from 1.5 to 4 percent. Obviously, a saver cannot even keep up with inflation. Remember that the money you deposit in a savings account is reinvested at a return high enough to pay the account's interest and to give the lender a fat 3 to 6 percent gain for profit and overhead. Often the lender reinvests in the real estate market.

• *Stock market.* The average person does not have the time or knowledge to fully understand the stock market. Thus, for most people, the stock market is a very big gamble. Experience and inside contacts are necessary to make money. Brokers can help, but they reap some of the profits. It's nearly impossible to determine how well the stock market has done in the past twenty years, and even by checking the averages, it's difficult to make true comparisons between this form of investment and the others. The average person would be hard-pressed to get the expertise needed to make good profits in this area.

• *Gold, silver, and precious metals.* Investing in precious metals is highly speculative, and it pays no dividends. The metal must be stored until sale, with the risk of robbery, and the price varies more than in almost any other investment alternative.

• *Other real estate investments.* In this category are vacant land, commercial property, income property, and special investment situations. Most of these require considerable expertise and a great deal of time to manage. People make—and lose—money every day in such dealings. But those who make the money have the special expertise to do so. That expertise is rarely available to the person just starting in real estate. If you don't even own a single-family home of your own, this is not a good area to concentrate in.

The surest and fastest way to make money in real estate today is to buy and sell single-family homes and condos and small multifamily rental units. Almost anyone can begin an investment career this way. Neither a great deal of capital nor extensive experience is needed. You live in either an apartment or a house, so you already have the basic knowledge to begin investing. The investment return can be $40,000, $50,000, or even $100,000 each year. The profit is not realized until the property is sold, of course, but it is there and it does accumulate. (See Case Study 2.1.)

Although investors have been acquiring single-family homes and other properties in this manner for the past twenty or thirty years, changes in the law and the economic environment have created a totally new ball game. Today the opportunities are in favor of the individual, small investor. Larger investors who have been picking up 20, 30, or more houses now find themselves overwhelmed with unmanageable problems.

There is a practical limit to the number of single-family homes that one person should hold at a time. Probably 10 is a good number. On the other hand, millions of people have not even purchased their first investment home. For them, this book provides a shortcut to success. You can succeed, too, and you do not need experience. You just need to follow the procedures outlined in this book, perhaps supplementing the information with an attorney's or accountant's advice.

Statistics Are on the Side of Homeownership

According to 2002 Bureau of the Census data, approximately 68 percent of Americans own their own residence. That percentage is increasing daily, partly because of the increase in condominium conversions and the decrease in apartment construction. The result is that a solid majority of the voting public are homeowners. These people are going to pass more legislation favoring homeownership at the expense of everyone else. Lenders will help the cause, because they benefit from the appreciation of single-family homes. In fact, it's possible that lenders will benefit the most. This two-pronged attack—by voters and lenders—will keep the value of single-family homes rising over the long term.

It is interesting to note that approximately 6 percent of Americans own a second home that they use for vacations, a retreat, or a family getaway. Another 7 or 8 percent own and lease out single-family homes.

The demand for single-family homes extends to the young. Nearly half of those buying real estate are under the age of 45, a third under 40. Of those below 30, approximately 12 percent purchase single-family homes.

About 20 percent of all home buyers are single. Divorces and separations add to the trend, by creating two households where one previously existed.

Statistics like these are leading more and more people to invest in homes. These are the main reasons:

• *Ease of understanding.* Since most of the people in this country already own their own home, they can easily understand the basic principles involved in investing in single-family homes.

• *Increasing value.* Over the long term, say twenty or thirty years, single-family homes will become more valuable. Fewer homes are being built, but at the same time more people want them. Values do go up and down with changes in business conditions, but the long-term trend is definitely up.

• *Safety.* Buying a single-family home is considered a safe personal investment. If you buy the property right and take good care of it, you will have a sound investment that can likely be sold for a profit.

• *Supply and demand.* It's important to reemphasize that fewer single-family homes are being built each year. The scarcity of land (especially land with sewers and water) is the main factor, but development is also hampered by the increasing costs of land, lumber, other building materials, and labor. Building codes and regulations protecting coastal and wetland areas are becoming more rigid, also making construction more costly. The result is fewer available homes. With more family formations, more people living alone, and apartment building declining, the need is greater. Thus the investment potential of single-family homes is enormous. As more people grow aware of the opportunity, the demand on a very short supply will help increase the price.

Patience Pays Off

If you're convinced that it makes sense to become a specialist in distress property, think now about what the endeavor requires. Time and effort are required to research targets. Diligence and

Case Study 2.1

This new home, located in Connecticut, had never been lived in when I bought it. Phil and his family were building it themselves, using a construction loan for financing. They were providing the sweat equity needed to finish the home. When they were almost finished, Phil lost his job with a law firm because of a falling-out with one of the senior partners. He then decided to open an office and practice independently. But when it came time to pay off the construction loan with a permanent mortgage, Phil could not find a lender. Everyone declined because Phil did not have a record of earning outside his previous job. Thus Phil had no first loan, and the construction lender was threatening to foreclose.

The market value of the home was about $85,000 at that time. The construction loan was for $50,000. Phil and his family had created equity of about $35,000, but at that moment the real estate market was very soft. They didn't know what to do.

Rental rates for homes in this neighborhood were about $550 monthly and rising, so this looked like a good opportunity for me to help. Phil's costs at that time were less than $50,000, so we agreed to a deal whereby I would buy the home from him for $85,000, secure a first loan of $60,000, and give him a three-year straight note for $25,000 at 10 percent, all due and payable at the end. We agreed I would manage the unit and make all negative payments. At the end of the three-year period, I could sell the home and give Phil 25 percent of my net profits.

I used the $60,000 in new money to pay off Phil's construction loan and give him $10,000 in cash, which would help him while he started his new practice. In three years, after he was sure where he really wanted to live, he would have a lump sum to buy a new home. His participation in any profit on this home compensated him for all the hard work that he and his family had put into the effort.

For my part I had a rental unit with no money down. And as it happened, the loan payments I had to make exceeded the rent I collected for only a very short time. I ended up selling the home before the three years were up for $129,000. So Phil collected an additional $10,000 of profit, and I had over $30,000 for my management time and effort.

energy are necessary to make a deal. But the most rewarding virtue is patience. Everything you do will bring results of one kind or another, whether or not you actually close a deal on every property that interests you. With every effort, you'll gain a bit of knowledge that will add to your strength and your ability to make a better deal. (See Case Study 2.2.)

Remember that your goal is to be the most informed real estate person in the area you choose to concentrate on. Arrange your files so they can easily be updated. When properties in your area are listed, record them. When properties are sold, draw up comparable tables so you can keep abreast of trends and values. As mortgage rates fluctuate, you will need to chart the volatility of the market and observe its effects on supply and demand. Being knowledgeable is the best preparation for acting quickly when opportunities present themselves. Others may be scratching their heads, wondering what to do, but you will know the correct values instantly and make the best deals.

There's No Time Like the Present to Start

To the specialist in distress properties, it makes no difference whether we are in a buyer's market or seller's market. Don't delay your start in this business by saying, well, it's a buyer's market, too many properties are on the market, and it's impossible to get a good price on a purchase. Or it's a seller's market, not enough properties are available, there are too many buyers, and it's too hard to make a good deal. The truth is really the opposite. You can make a good deal in either market.

The only factors that make a good deal are troubled owners and a knowledge of the territory. If you know the territory well, you will be able to respond quickly enough to help the troubled owners and yourself. The kind of market does not matter in the slightest. There are always deals, and people make money in both types of markets. The only limit on your success is the initiative you bring to the process.

If you don't believe it, ask yourself what the curve of real estate activity is across both buyer's and seller's markets. Prices may not always be rising, but the overall trend is always up. Over time, homes will continue to climb in value.

No matter which direction the immediate market is moving in, you can offer a better deal to troubled homeowners. When you resell the property in an "up" market, the buyers' eagerness to take part will help you close the deal. In a "down" market, you can point out that every valley has a peak and, although the market is down now, the buyers can look ahead to tomorrow's rising prop-

Case Study 2.2

One day I noticed a For Sale by Owner sign on the front lawn of a house on Pepperill Street, which was across the street from a park I liked. It was a one-story house in a tract of large lots and mostly two-story homes. I stopped by, and the son of the owners, a teenager, told me his dad had deserted them and was divorcing his mom. He showed me around the house and took my card, promising me someone would call.

After two weeks (and no calls) I stopped by again. This time the For Sale sign was gone. The teenager said that his mother had gone to Seattle to marry someone there and that his older brother was moving in to keep the family going.

Apparently, no deal was possible. So I forgot about Pepperill until about three months later, when I noticed that legal action had started against the owner (the father). The holder of a second deed of trust had filed a notice of default.

I called the father several times, but he didn't return my calls. I sent him a letter. Then another one. Then he called me. He wanted me to make him an offer. We met, and I did an analysis. I made him an offer that would allow him to leave the property with his credit intact and some extra cash besides. He said he'd consider it.

About a month later I noticed that an auction date had been set for the house on Pepperill. I called the owner, and his secretary told me that he was filing for personal bankruptcy for reasons related to leaving his wife and family.

The auction date was postponed twice, but by this time I was well prepared to act. I'd had time to arrange some big advantages. By working with the troubled owner prior to the auction, I knew a lot more about the property than the other six bidders did. Plus I had already found a buyer who would buy the house from me without listing it through a broker.

So I did all my homework, showed up at the auction, and bid more than anyone else to win the property. It turned out to be a profitable purchase. And it proved that you never know for sure exactly when in the distress property cycle you will make your deal. All you know is that, by starting with the problem property at the earliest possible point and patiently going after it, you have a great chance to make a good deal.

erty values. The new buyers are buying on the ground floor. Simply by understanding the basic economics of supply and demand and the basic rules for business cycles, you can continue to arrange good deals. Just use the forms, checklists, and procedures described in this book, and show a little initiative. Stay alert, and you can continue to make good deals on a regular basis.

CHAPTER 3

Some Commonly Asked Questions

Knowing the right question is half the answer.

—*Ed Cole*

Before we get into the details of "goldmining" in distress properties, let's consider some often-asked questions. The answers are short and direct. The purpose of this chapter is to set up a frame of reference to help you understand the detailed information that follows.

Is This a "Get-Rich-Quick" Book?

You've got to be kidding! The procedures described in this book work well and make me (and others) a good deal of money, but following through is hard work. It takes time. It takes intelligence. It takes a real understanding of the whole process.

I have always made large profits and never lost money using the techniques described in this book. Every person I've helped get started in this business has also done well.

You, too, can find a profitable niche and make money, but it won't be quick money. This is not a "get-rich-quick" scheme. You'll need to make an effort, and you'll need smarts.

If the Troubled Owners Can't Solve Their Loan Problems, How Can I?

Because you're in a different financial position. When troubled owners are in arrears, they need money to catch up on their payments. They usually have a long list of other debts, too. With a little work and a lot of knowledge, you can make a mutually profitable deal.

Never before have so many negative factors been working against so many homeowners. Conversely, the opportunities for someone like you are unprecedented.

However, when the property is in the foreclosure stage (or going to auction), then you join a group of other people who want to buy the property at a bargain price. The person who does the best job should be able to make a profitable deal. This is happening hundreds of times every day in your state and mine.

Are Troubled Owners Hard to Deal With?

Yes and no. But you will work only with the ones who want to be helped. They are usually frightened people who will cooperate to save time. Look for these people, and avoid the owners who are hard to deal with. This book includes many ideas for making contact with the right owners.

What's more, at auctions you almost never meet the owners. They may even be out of the area. The bad part is that often you haven't seen the inside of the property.

What Factors in Our Society Are Creating Trouble for Homeowners?

Each case is different, of course, but the most frequent factor is overuse of debt. People borrow more than they can repay.

Unexpected divorce, deaths, and other problems also cause major financial strains that can lead to loss of a home.

Drugs are still a factor in some households, but lately they seem to be less so.

More frequently now, depression and lack of confidence in the future are affecting many households. Ever-present national and world crises knock the "will to earn" out of a lot of people.

Is This a "Good" Business for "Bad" Times Only?

It's better in bad times, but it's also good in good times. There are fewer deals when the economy is humming and real estate values are going up. It's easier for troubled owners to solve their own problems. But, and this is important, by anticipating changes in the economy, you can always stay ahead. You can even make a lot more money by holding properties if you see a big upswing coming. And when you feel a drop is coming, you can use those feelings to get better prices from everyone.

Is There Anything Wrong with Making Money This Way?

No. In fact you're doing everyone a big service. Remember, you didn't cause troubled owners any of their problems. You didn't sell them a house that was more than they could afford. You didn't raise their rent. You never knew them. You're coming onto the scene after the fact—on a "white horse," in a way.

And at the auction sale, you're just one of thousands who have the opportunity to bid. If you're the only one there, as I have been many times, it's because you did your homework better than the rest of the crowd.

And when you take a repossessed property off the hands of a lender, you make a friend who usually brings you more deals.

Everyone is happy if you're able to turn problem properties into profitable deals.

How Profitable Can This Business Really Be?

It's just like buying wholesale and selling retail (with practically no overhead). That's because you make a conscious decision not to get involved with any other type of deal. I won't waste time on any property that won't make me a profit of at least 10 percent of the final selling price. And that's after including a return of prime plus 2 percent on any money I have to invest.

Your strategy might be different. You may want more, or you may settle for less. Because there are so many opportunities at each stage of the process, you can pick your parameters.

How Do I Know Which Stage to Start In?

You start by learning more about each stage. By following the suggestions for each group of troubled owners, you'll get firsthand experience. Then you'll find that you feel more comfortable working with one group than with the others. This is how you develop a niche. But you'll probably be involved in all stages in one way or another from time to time.

Incidentally, business conditions may affect the way you start. During bad times, you may favor working directly with troubled owners. When the economy is better, you may feel you have more chance for profit at foreclosure auctions.

At What Stage Is It Easiest to Buy Distress Property for Large Profits?

Buying at an auction sale is the easiest. For one thing, you don't have to deal with the homeowners, whose situation requires some patience and understanding on your part. All you need is advance notice of the sale to start your work. Then you need ready cash for the bidding process. However, although it's easiest, this stage also presents the most risks. Usually you can't examine the inside of the property (in trust deed states), and you need more up-front cash.

You might think buying repossessed properties would be easiest. It would be if you weren't interested in making a profit. Most REOs are taken back by the lender because the lender reduced the price to less than the amount owed. Thus there probably is little or no profit left for any investor.

Do I Need a Real Estate License to Start?

In most states, people who buy and sell property for their own account don't need a real estate license. Whether you buy one property or twenty-one, as long as they're for your account, you don't need a license.

Do I Need a Corporation or Office Setup to Start?

Not at all. I advise starting from wherever you are now. Don't add unnecessary overhead. But also never let troubled owners come to your home. Always transact business at their place (or at the lender's offices or escrow, insurance, or title company's offices).

Incorporation, to limit your liability, may be a good idea. But there are other ways to do the same thing, so ask your accountant for advice. You could certainly do one or two deals personally under your own insurance policies (include a business liability umbrella). Then make changes as you go along.

How Much Time Should I Spend on This Business?

I recommend starting part-time. That means ten to twenty hours a week. You'll need one to four weeks to get acclimated to the business—or possibly less if you have experience in real estate.

The real question is how much time and energy you want to spend. There are many ways to make profits by becoming a specialist in distress properties. At first they all depend on knowledge and technique. Then your personal qualities of persistence and hard work come into play. When you become a pro (even a part-time pro), you should be able to average one deal every ten to fifteen working hours. Time should not be much of a limiting factor.

How Much Cash Do I Need?

Again, it depends—on the type of deals you choose to specialize in. If you become a problem solver for troubled owners, you may be able to get by with between $500 and $15,000 in cash to start. You can always find partners to provide the cash if you can originate profit-making deals.

If you have more (or have access to more), you can buy properties at auctions and make bigger profits. And if you can make a deal with a lender for repossessed properties, you won't need much money at all. Most lenders are so anxious to unload their REOs (real estate owned properties) that they provide maximum financing.

Is There Much Competition?

Yes. And there always will be. But only a handful of people in this business do their homework. These few do most of the business.

The three keys to beating your competition are to (1) select a personal "farm" area or neighborhood, (2) stick to the procedures recommended in this book, and (3) work smarter on every new deal.

Should I Start by Working with a Pro?

No. Spend the time it takes to learn all there is to know yourself. Then the business will truly be yours. You'll find ways to improve on almost everything. You'll be able to make decisions faster. This route may take a bit more time, but it will be worthwhile.

Financial partners (family members or close business associates) are another matter. Most people don't have enough money to do all the business they can generate. It's always good to have access to more cash. At first you may have to pay more to borrow (as much as one and a half times the prime rate). But after a few successful deals, you'll be borrowing at no more than prime plus two points.

What Are Some of the Biggest Problems I'll Face?

Besides not having enough time and cash, the biggest problems have to do with gathering the correct information. How much is really owed? Whose name is on the title? What's wrong with the property? What's the neighborhood really like? Are there any title or insurance problems? Any liens on the property? Is the IRS or any other taxing authority involved?

The good news is that all these problems (and a lot of other little ones) are covered extensively in this book. They all can be solved easily.

If Owners Declare Bankruptcy, Will My Work Be Affected?

Important question. The answer is a tricky yes and no. It all depends on the laws in your state and the timing of the bankruptcy. But a troubled owner going bankrupt is one of the most important acts to watch out for. Many sections of this book talk about it.

The no part of the answer concerns a bankrupt owner whose property is up for auction. When the bankruptcy court releases the property for auction sale, in most cases you're in a better position as a buyer. See Chapter 19 for details.

What About Problems at the Auction Itself?

If you follow the rules of the state you're in, you should have no problems. Most states require certified checks. Most trust deed states have procedures to prevent fraud or rigged bidding. This book tells you where to get detailed information about the auction process.

Because our society is so oriented toward consumer protection, the real problems could come from illegal things you might do. The biggest problem is conspiring with one or more bidders (at the wrong time) to be partners in the bidding process. If you go with partners as a group to an auction, and no one else is bidding, working together may be alright. But if a group of you at the auction agree that one should make the only bid, you'll have big problems. If what you're considering doing in such situations seems wrong, it probably is also illegal.

Each state has its own list of dos and don'ts, which is readily available to potential bidders.

Will I Need Help in Selling the Property?

You should always try to sell the property yourself. Start as soon as the property looks good, but limit yourself to three weeks maximum. If nothing else, this attempt to sell the property yourself will give you valuable knowledge of the market in your area.

If you don't have a sale at the end of three weeks, turn the property over to the best real estate broker in the area. The best is probably the one who's already contacted you three or four times trying to get the listing. Usually, however, it's best to interview two or three before giving the listing to anyone.

Is It Worthwhile to Attend Seminars on This Subject?

Absolutely—providing the speaker has had at least five years of actual experience in all stages of the distress property cycle. Too many speakers simply read about someone else's experiences and put together a seminar to teach others.

Probably the best way to learn is to set your own schedule for reading, listening to tapes, and doing. You know your own best speed. Sometimes seminars give you a quick burst of knowledge and enthusiasm that leave you almost as quickly as they come. But with a book and notes in front of you and no one racing ahead (or talking about matters that don't interest you), you can get a lot more done.

The best way to learn is to follow the procedures in this book as closely as possible. Select a farm area, develop a rhythm, have a time-line, use checklists—and get your own experience.

What Is the Number-One Secret of Success in This Business?

It's the same here as in any other business. The secret is simply to be ready to act when your opportunities come. The more ready you are, the better your chances. You simply must know what's really going on: What's happening in your area? Who's most likely to have trouble? What caused all their problems?

This book is all about preparing you to act. If you're prepared to act, you have the best chance at success when the right deals come along.

What's the Biggest Mistake Beginners Make?

It's assuming your information is correct. Everything must be checked and verified. Distress property is loaded with problem points. You must remember that Trouble (with a capital T) happened. Make sure you don't take any of it with you when you buy the property.

The good news is that there are only so many Trouble areas, and you can check into them all. Just don't assume anything.

How Do I Get Started?

Simply turn the page.

CHAPTER 4
The Rules and the Players

So many deals are lost by making the right move with the wrong people.

—*Bill Levitt*

The most important point to remember about the rules of the game is that they are local. No two regions in our country are exactly the same.

So the first research you'll have to do is to find out the rules in your own backyard. You probably know most of what you need to know already. Are you in a trust deed state (like California) or a mortgage state (like Connecticut)? Where are deeds recorded? Where can you get information about foreclosure postings? About notices of default? You get the picture.

The appendix to this book includes some of the most relevant parts of the California codes; the codes in most other states are similar. In addition, you can ask your local realtor, title officer, accountant, attorney, or escrow officer where to find specific information about your area. They stand to benefit if you create business and include them as supporting players. They may know how to do things faster in your area. They may know other people who can help you. They may even be sources of information about potential deals.

People in government offices can also help you. Each level of government involved in a typical transaction has information you may need:

- *Federal government:* IRS liens pending

- *State government:* All-encompassing real estate laws (title, lending, foreclosures, and so on)

- *County government:* Lien procedures, recording rules, and so on

- *City government:* Lien procedures, recording rules, CC&Rs (codes, covenants, and restrictions in a tract), information about water, sewer, and so on

Many government agencies have pamphlets or circulars that summarize the laws and procedures of interest to you. For instance, the state real estate department may have a written summary of the foreclosure process in your state. As a general rule, you'll learn the most by going to the source, asking your questions, and looking for written material to take home with you.

At the bottom of everything are local neighborhood conditions. You'll be buying a specific piece of property in a defined area. You must know all there is to know about that area—anything that could affect the fair market value—or risk heavy losses. (See Case Study 4.1.)

This business presents a great many possibilities, and laws and procedures are always changing. It's up to you as a specialist to always know what's going on.

The Players and Their Interests

Those who become involved during each of the four stages of the distress property cycle and during the investment phase of the game are listed in Figure 4.1. The only important person that the chart does not list is *you*. As the specialist, you are the central player. You will be interacting with these major players and many minor ones.

By beginning with Stage I, before legal action begins, you may be able to lay a better foundation for dealing with the other stages. It's during Stage I (covered in detail in Chapter 7) that you have the most opportunity to really help the owners. Once notices of default are filed, the expenses begin to add up. Helping the owners then is tougher because another layer of people get into the act.

After the start of legal proceedings, Stage II (covered in detail in Chapter 8), you still work with the same group of people, but your direction may shift. You may become a lender yourself. You may decide to buy out the loan of one of the creditors (at a discount, of course). Or you may sense that the owners cannot be helped. In this case you might then consider waiting and bidding for the property at the next stage (the auction).

The auction stage, Stage III (covered in detail in Chapter 13), is vastly different from state to state. Even counties within the same state may have special requirements. But your basic duties are the same: Get lots of information and patiently follow through.

Case Study 4.1

One day I noticed that a trustee sale was scheduled for a home in a neighborhood I liked in the hills near Upland, California. I lived high in the hills near Upland, California.

The house was located on Mountain View Road. According to the published information, it was a 3 bedroom, 2 bath, two-story home with 1,250 square feet of living space. It sat on a 12,900 square foot lot. the second deed of trust, which was the one foreclosing, was about $99,000. Its original amount (originated in April 1985) was $90,500. The first deed of trust was also listed as $90,500, and it too was originated in April 1985.

These key facts didn't make sense to me. First of all, I knew the area and I couldn't remember any 1,250 square foot, two-story homes. They all seemed twice as large. Second, it didn't seem logical that two lenders would each lend $90,500 on a 1,250 square foot home in that area back in 1985.

I decided to track this trustee sale. I called two days before the scheduled date and was told that the sale had been postponed for sixty days. About sixty days later I called again. This time the borrowers had filed for bankruptcy, so the sale was postponed another sixty days.

Postponements tend to reduce the number of bidders who show up at auctions. So I went to my computer to pull up the assessor's information on this property. Sure enough, the house was not 1,250 square feet; it was 2,510 square feet. A big difference. I put a note on this file to review it again in sixty days.

After one more postponement, it appeared that the property was really going to auction in about a week. I ordered an updated title for this house because I was still concerned about the two loans. The title report solved this problem but added a new one. The two loans for $90,500 were actually the same. The second loan mentioned in the notice of default was a re-recording of the first. This sometimes happens because of local procedures and because the lender wants to be sure of its position. I felt such might be the case in this instance.

The new problem had to do with IRS liens. These were filed after the date that the first default notice was filed, so normally they wouldn't be a problem if the IRS was properly notified of the auction. But whenever the IRS is on record regarding a property you want, you must be extra careful.

Rather than spend the extra time on IRS details, I called the utility companies to get more information on the occupants. Both the power and the telephone had been disconnected. The house must be vacant. These are very good signs for a bidder, because seeing the inside of the house before the auction is easier when nobody's in it. Also, there's no thirty- to ninety-day delay evicting the occupants.

Feeling sure that all the factors were in place for another successful bid—and what looked like a big profit—I included this house in the tour I was making the next day. If everything was still OK, I'd be all set for the auction the following day.

My tour was interesting, and I lined up two good possible deals. But all during the day I kept thinking of my last stop, the house on Mountain View Road.

What luck! The house was on a corner, and it did have several good views. When I drove into the driveway, I noticed large cracks in the driveway and in the walkway leading to the front door. I made a mental note about them and looked through the windows at a home in reasonably good shape. So far so good, but I always try to talk to the neighbors to get more information. I walked next door with great expectations.

When I left the neighbor, I felt completely different. The ground around the corner had slipped badly. The town had condemned the property as unsafe. The owners had fought the action and lost. That's why they filed for bankruptcy and left.

continued on next page

Case 4.1 Continued

In other words, the house was nothing but trouble. I know many bidders who never go into detail when checking property. If any of them had been tracking this house on Mountain View Road and went ahead and bid on it without doing all their homework, they were going to lose a lot of time and money. That's why it's so important to check specific local conditions. I didn't make any money on this deal, but I also preserved my record of never losing any money on a deal.

If no one bids on a property at auction, it usually reverts to the lender. This is Stage IV (covered in detail in Chapter 14). If you're still interested, you run into a new set of players. In the lender's REO (real estate owned) department, you may deal with loan officers, appraisers, real estate agents, property managers, and other real estate professionals.

The Investor Game

After you buy a property and become an investor, you must know several new sets of rules and players (see Figure 4.1). You should bring your insurance agent into the picture at this point. Most properties require some rehabilitation work, so you'll need to know local contractors and the building codes. When you're ready to sell, you'll select the best broker in the area—after attempting to sell it yourself. All this is covered in detail in Chapter 15.

If you decide to keep the property as a rental, you must know all about the tenant-landlord laws in your area. Besides the fair-rent and rent-control laws, you must know about late payment and eviction rules. If this is your first experience as a landlord, join a local landlord group for help. This subject also will be covered in detail in a later chapter, Chapter 16.

Before We Begin

The purposes of this chapter are simple:

• To warn you that local knowledge is the key to success in this business

• To remind you that you can't get local knowledge by reading this book, you can get it only by doing your homework

• To reassure you that the overall procedure in each stage of the distress property cycle is basically the same

Stage	Players	Interests
Distress Property Cycle		
I: Before Legal Action Begins	Troubled owners	Want to solve home problems
	Divorcing owners	Same as above, only more problems
	Neighbors	Want neighborhood improved
	First lender	Wants all of its money back
	Other lenders	Want most of their money back
	Creditors	Want some of their money back
	Escrow officer, title officer, real estate brokers	Want business, will help
II: After Legal Notices Are Filed	All Stage I players	Same as Stage I, except everyone is more cooperative to meet deadlines
	Trustee	Wants timely action
	Attorneys	Want business, will help
III: Auction Time	All Stage II players	Want to make deal, will help
	Neighbors, utility companies	Want property to be occupied, will help with information
	Title officer	Wants business, will provide information on liens, ownership, financials
	Local officials	Want any problems solved and taxes paid, will help uncover problems
IV: REOs and Repos	REO officers	Want to unload properties, will start you on your quest
	Appraisers, realtors, property managers	Want business, can help with offer
	VA and HUD officers	Want to unload properties, can provide information about repo bargains
Investment Phase		
Property Ownership	Rehab contractors, insurance agents, property managers	Want business, will help
	Tenants	Want place to live
Property Sales	Escrow officer, title officer, real estate brokers, attorneys	Want business, will help
	Buyers	Want place to live

Figure 4.1   Players in the Distress Property Business

For instance, in several of the stages you need to deal with troubled owners. A whole chapter, Chapter 9, is devoted to negotiating with troubled owners. Chapter 10 is all about negotiating with lenders and creditors, which again is a skill that you can apply in several stages. Chapter 11 has to do with inspecting and evaluating the properties being considered for purchase. There's a whole chapter, Chapter 12, about the problems of closing the deal with troubled owners.

Although most of these basic techniques can be used in more than one stage, each area has its own special set of circumstances that can make lots of profit for you or kill you—if you don't do your homework. The next two chapters will get you started.

CHAPTER 5
Overall Strategies and Procedures

But you gotta know the territory!
—*from* The Music Man

At this point, knowing of all the rules and players involved in the distress property business, you may be feeling a little overwhelmed. It is a complex business. But the steps, taken one at a time, are relatively easy. And the end result is ownership of profitable properties, with some extra cash along the way. Just make the decision to get organized, and then follow the step-by-step procedures recommended in this chapter. Later chapters expand on all these topics.

1. Decide on a special territory.

Nobody can have all the available information on all neighborhoods in a local area. You would do better to concentrate on one territory, where you can more easily become familiar with trends, market values, and events that affect property values. Specializing in one territory also helps you meet and deal with the specific people in government and the real estate industry who can be most helpful.

2. Know the value of properties within your territory.

After you've decided on a territory, you can easily get to know the value of properties in it. Look at everything you can get your hands on, such as real estate circulars, that lists the prices and features of nearby properties.

Just keep in mind the difference between asking price and sales price. Realtors and brokers usually list properties at considerably more than they expect to get. They do this in part so the buyer can have the pleasure of negotiating with the seller. Acquiring the property at less than list price gives the buyer a lot of satisfaction.

To you, the important value is the actual sales price, what the buyer paid, not what the seller originally asked. This is the "comparable value" that you use as a benchmark for the property you're interested in.

If you concentrate on a particular territory and have a ready understanding of the property values, you will be able to make quicker decisions about acquiring and selling properties. You won't have to consult middlemen, and you will know immediately when a price is out of line and by how much. Buying at the right price is the basis for profit in real estate.

3. Keep informed on all real estate transactions.

Once you have chosen a territory and started becoming familiar with it, make arrangements to get complete information regularly on all distress properties within that territory. You'd be surprised how much information you can tap into to find out about things like foreclosure notices and default notices.

4. Look for signs of opportunities.

Published legal notices are easy to find, for you as well as your competitors. What may be more difficult, especially for someone from out of the area, is to spot subtle signs of distress before legal action begins. By reading the local newspaper and keeping in touch with your network of contacts, you will be the first to hear of new opportunities.

Information is power. Be on the lookout for these sorts of events:

• *Divorces.* A divorce usually leads to a broken household and the sale of a home. In most cases, the real value of the property is the furthest thing from the mind of either party. They just want to split and get the whole thing over with as soon as possible. Their preoccupation with personal problems may also lead to neglect in making payments and the sort of financial problems that only a third party can solve.

• *Deaths.* When someone in a family dies, the remaining members often want to leave the area. They are either troubled by memories of happier times or unable to maintain the property. After a reasonable time, the property is likely to be offered for sale. Sometimes a death also causes unusual financial hardship, which turns into a distress situation that an outside party can help alleviate.

• *Growing families.* Families with new babies might be looking for a larger home. They may also be unable to keep the home they are in because of the added financial strain of supporting another child.

• *Out-of-state landlords.* Rental property is very difficult to manage when you don't live in the area. Communication between tenant and owner is much slower. When things need to be done, the owner has trouble getting the right price and quick service. Within a very short time, the rental property becomes a real drag and a cash-flow loser. The out-of-state owner then grows anxious to dispose of the property. Keep a complete list of local rentals owned by people who live out of state so you can be helpful if this situation arises.

• *Relocating sellers.* Another thing to watch for is property that has been up for sale but has not been sold before the owners have to move out of the area. Many people are transferred quickly by their employers. In some cases the broker is unable to sell the home equally quickly. Rather than renting out the property, the owners may prefer to continue trying to sell it. Situations like this require fast action and may be handled by dealing directly with the property owners.

• *Plant closings.* If a company decides to close a plant, it usually throws a good many people out of work. Those who decide to move to areas where there is likely to be work have to sell quickly. Those who remain may find themselves unable to meet the payments on their home because they are unemployed.

I have been able to make deals in all these situations. By far, most troubled owners seem to have marital problems. Without commenting on which came first, the financial trouble or marital trouble, I would point out that the head sometimes cannot function well in matters of the heart. So in negotiating with owners who are splitting up, you need to take extra care.

5. Set up a "suspect" file.

Whenever something turns up that might be interesting, fill out a Suspect Information form (Figure 5.1). This is a technique for gathering in a convenient place basic information about properties that might come onto the market and could be a good value. The form lists the name of the owner, the address and type of the property, the reasons for the distress, and other vital points. It also

SUSPECT INFORMATION
B.T.H.* NO. _____
                    (Lot) (Block)

Name: _____ Date: _____

Location: _____

Description: _____

Reasons for Distress: _____

_____

_____

_____

QUICK ANALYSIS

Location Factors: _____

Upside Potential: _____

_____

Reasons to Make into Prospect: _____

_____

_____

Downside Potential: _____

_____

Reasons to Stop: _____

_____

_____

Conclusions (Include Preliminary Financial Information): _____

_____

_____

_____

_____

_____

*B.T.H.—Between Two Houses (See Chapter 6)   *(Save for Future Use)*

Figure 5.1 Suspect Information Form for Evaluating a Possible Distress Property

includes space for noting the good and bad points about the location and the potential for making money on the deal. The purpose of the form is to help you analyze whether this "suspect" should become a "prospect."

Remember that, for you to make any deal, the property must have equity. With equity, there is usually a great deal of room for you and the troubled owners to negotiate. But even when all the conditions are right, not every property will end up as a purchase. Only the best of the lot will even become prospects. Remember as you fill out your Suspect Information forms that you want to maximize your chances of working on deals that can pay off.

6. Set up a "prospect" file.

Prospects are the people you want to see and meet for negotiations. The first step in determining which suspects should be prospects is to collect the information needed to make a financial evaluation of the suspect's situation. The Financial Analysis form is designed to help you do this. Think of it as a starting point for further inquiry. Use it as a guide, and develop your own form if other questions occur to you. The preliminary financial information that it calls for will come from many sources, including the suspect, your knowledge of the territory, and your network of friends.

After you have done this basic analysis, you can decide whether it is advisable to go any further with this particular property. If you conclude that you should, then immediately pull out a Prospect History form (Figure 5.2), which you will use as you continue pursuing this property. This form lists more detailed financial information, such as the date of the default notice and the final date to correct. In addition, it has space for noting specific information that you will acquire on your first visit to the house.

If you decide you should not pursue this deal, don't throw away the Suspect Information form or the Prospect History form. Save them for future use. Strangely enough, properties have a way of repeating themselves. Many are distressed more than once. The next time one in your territory is, your response may be quicker if you have all this information at hand.

7. Contact the owners.

Your goals at this stage are to let the owners know that you may be interested in helping, to get a very clear picture of the condition of the house, and to get any other information that will help you analyze the potential for a deal. Because this is such an

PROSPECT HISTORY
B.T.H. NO. _____
            (Lot)   (Block)

RECORD
1st Call
2nd Call
3rd Call
4th Call

Name: _____
Location: _____
Phone: _____
        (Home)   (Work)   (Relative)

Trustee: _____
Lender(s): _____
_____

Default Action
Date of Default Notice: _____
Final Date to Correct: _____
Other Financial Details: _____
_____
_____
_____

House Size: _____ Lot Size: _____
No. Bedrooms: _____ No. Bathrooms: _____ Garage: _____
Interior Conditions (Summary): _____
_____
_____
_____

Exterior Conditions (Summary): _____
_____
_____
_____

Location Factors: _____
Lot Location: _____
Shopping: _____
School Details: _____
Parks & Other: _____
Freeways: _____
Other: _____

Figure 5.2   Prospect History Form for Evaluating a Potential Distress Property Deal

important step, later chapters provide many suggestions for establishing a relationship with prospects—including introducing yourself, breaking the ice, and beginning the negotiating dialogue. By keeping in mind that one of your goals is to help the prospect, you will find it easier to go through this whole exercise.

8. Make a detailed financial analysis.

After you collect the prospect information and meet the owners, it's time to pull out the Financial Analysis form (Figure 5.3). You need to determine accurately the dollars needed to make the property healthy again. The analysis sheet asks for details about the first loan and about the second loan, if there is any. It states the amount required to pay off the first and second loans. It also lists the extra expenses—delinquency late charges, default and foreclosure fees, and the like—that would have to be satisfied before the banks would release the property. (See Case Study 5.1.) On the second page is a section for estimating the total cash you would need to buy the property, as well as a space for summarizing your proposed deal to the owners.

9. Explain the procedure to the owners.

After you've completed the Financial Analysis form, you must show it to the owners and discuss it thoroughly. They must see that their situation has deteriorated to the point that there is a real financial burden on the property. They must realize that a lot of risk capital is necessary to buy the property and understand how the cash will be distributed in various categories.

Make sure the owners understand that this form is not an offer. What you are showing them is probably the maximum that could be arranged if a purchase is intended. Let them know that you have to do more analysis before you can extend a specific offer.

You should also explain that your next step is to check out the title to the property, the comparables in the area, and the loan details. Tell them that you will return in twenty-four hours with a final offer. Ask them for all the documents regarding the house: the payment slips, the loan document, the title insurance, every piece of paper they may have that will help you make a final analysis. (See Case Study 5.2.)

10. Contact the lenders.

To proceed, you'll need some additional information from the lenders—senior lenders, junior lenders, and other creditors. You

FINANCIAL ANALYSIS
B.T.H. NO. _____

Page 1 of 2

        (Lot)   (Block)

Name: _____

Location: _____

Date of Default Action: _____ End Date: _____

First Loan

Lender's Name:_____ Loan Number: _____

Type:_____ % Interest _____ Original Amount _____

Monthly Payments: _____ Yearly Taxes _____

Balance as of _____ is _____

Second Loan

Lender's Name:_____ Loan Number:_____

Type: _____ % Interest _____ Original Amount _____

Monthly Payments: _____ Yearly Taxes _____

Balance as of _____ is _____

Other Liens (describe)

  1. _____ As of _____ Total owing is _____

  2. _____ As of _____ Total owing is _____

  3. _____ As of _____ Total owing is _____

(Be sure to include all penalty payments, etc.)

Delinquent Payments

1st Loan _____ Months @ _____ = _____

2nd Loan_____ Months @ _____ = _____

Delinquency Late Charges   _____

Default and Foreclosure Fees   _____

Other Lien Payments   _____

  1. _____ = _____

  2. _____ = _____

  3. _____ = _____

Total Delinquency as of_____ = _____

Figure 5.3   Financial Analysis Form for Evaluating Costs in a Distress Property Deal

Preliminary Estimates   Page 2 of 2

    Cost for All Delinquencies   = _____

    Approximate Escrow and Title Expenses   = _____

    Approximate Loan Transfer Fees (1%)   = _____

    Approximate Origination Fees (1%)   = _____

    One Month P.&I. & Taxes & Late Charges   = _____

    Approximate Cash for Other Liens   = _____

    Approximate Refurbishing Costs   = _____

Total Cash Needed to Update   = _____

Market Value Comparables

    1. _____   + _____

    2. _____   + _____

    3. _____   + _____

True Market Value   + (_____)

Minus

    Total Cash Needed to Update   - (_____)

    Real Estate Commission 6% of Value   - (_____)

    Equity Remaining   (_____)

Proposed Deal to Owner

Cash to Owner $ _____

Deed to Buyer   (date) _____

Property Vacated by   (date) _____

Figure 5.3 *Continued*

want to get them on your side, working with you to make a deal, and there are many easy ways to do so. All they want is most of their money back. You may be the only person who can help them.

11. Inspect the subject property.

Real estate is loaded with possible problems. You want to make sure you know about all of them before you buy a property, so you

Case Study 5.1

The owners of this lovely old modified Cape Cod in Connecticut called me directly. Mr. Owens had lost his job, and they had decided to leave the area. A banker told them I might be able to purchase their home quickly if I was interested.

A special problem here was liens on the property. One had been filed by the subcontractors who installed the septic system. Another lien and a lawsuit were pending by the carpenter who had added the back porch. One was due to a furniture purchase. Another problem was a three-month delinquency in loan payments. But no notice of default had yet been filed.

Using the Financial Analysis form, I summarized the information:

Market value	$72,500
First loan	$42,500
Second loan	0
Lien (septic)	12,500
Lien (carpenter)	18,000
Lien (furniture)	10,000
Mortgage delinquencies	1,200
Total owed	$84,200
Deficit remaining	$11,700

Usually an $11,700 discrepancy between the value of the property and the amount owed would have me worried. But because the first loan was at 8.75 percent (and the going rate was about 11 percent), I became very interested.

I optioned the property for thirty days for one dollar and full assumption of all debts. Immediately I spoke to the lender, who agreed to rewrite the loan for $60,000 at 9.5 percent if I would assume it and make it current. This plan would create about $16,500 in new dollars. I then contacted the creditors and got them to agree to a net settlement of $15,000 cash if I paid within ninety days.

When this series of deals had been concluded, I was in a position to buy the property for no money down, to pay off the liens and delinquencies with the proceeds of a new first loan, and to cover with the few dollars left any negatives that might arise due to delays in renting.

The former owners were happy, too, because they left the area with clean credit instead of having $11,700 in debt hanging over them.

All this was accomplished within the thirty-day time frame of my option and with only two meetings per creditor and banker.

Case Study 5.2

Once I responded to an ad offering a "lease-option" on a house in Southern California. A lease with an option to buy is one of the best deals an investor can make. For very little down, an investor can lease out a home for one to five years at a fixed monthly cost, with an option to buy the home at a fixed price. Then the investor subleases the unit for three to six months at a time, steadily raising the rent to reduce the negative cash flow. The big gain comes through inflation and appreciation. A home could appreciate in value from 5 to 15 percent a year. So with a lease-option to buy a home for $100,000 at the end of three years, the investor could realize much more.

In this particular case, the seller (Dave Dabble) was anxious to make a quick deal. He was asking $800 per month on the lease and set a price of $125,000 on the house. My comparables showed that houses like this one were selling for $120,000 to $122,500. They were renting for about $600 a month. Dave wanted a lot of cash up front: $10,000 down on the house and ten months in advance on the lease, a total of $18,000 cash.

After a high-powered negotiating session, I got Dave to extend the lease term to five years and reduce the final price to $122,500, but he now wanted $20,000 up front. We agreed to draw up the papers.

Because it was a lease-option and not a purchase, Dave suggested that we save the attorney's fees and conclude the transaction outside of escrow. I agreed, providing I had time to check the title. The next day I found that title to the property was indeed in Dave Dabble's name.

But by that time I had a bad feeling about the deal, which just looked too good. I kept remembering an old business axiom: "The man who doesn't intend to pay will promise you anything." And yet the deal was too good to simply walk away. I decided all I really needed was assurances from a title company that, if I performed under the terms of the agreement, Dave Dabble would also have to perform.

I called an escrow and title company, gave them the full information, and asked them to rush a regular closing. They would prepare a "holding escrow" and have a properly executed grant deed in escrow, subject to completed performance on the agreement.

Dave Dabble exploded when I told him what I had done. He was completely unwilling to pay escrow fees, nor would he entrust the escrow company with holding the documents. He tried to convince me to go ahead without this protection. When he offered to reduce the sales price even further, I knew something was drastically wrong. I finally picked up all my papers, made my last offer (including a proper closing with a holding escrow), and left.

The deal fell apart. The title company found that the Dave Dabble who owned the property was not the Dave Dabble trying to sell it. The seller was the nephew of the owner and was living in the house free "to get a new start." His new start would have included a big rip-off of other people's money in the form of a bogus lease-option—had I not remembered my business fundamentals. I passed all this information along to the owner of the unit, and it ceased being offered for sale.

can accurately assess its fair market value and be sure you're not buying trouble. There's a right way and many a wrong way to inspect a property, all discussed later in the book.

As important as the comparable value of a property is its value after you've fixed it up. There are many ways to maximize the value at lower-than-expected costs.

12. Prepare the Profit Action Plan.

After looking over the owners' documents and carefully inspecting the property, you're ready to fill out the Profit Action Plan (Figure 5.4). This confidential analysis is based on an estimate of the property's true market value, which comes from studying comparable properties. The rest is an analysis of the total cash requirements for buying the property, including the estimated costs of keeping it until it is sold or leased. Remember that the longer it takes to refurbish the property and the longer you hold it before selling, the higher your costs and the lower your profit will be. After taking all this into account, the Profit Action Plan tells you how much spread or profit, if any, is available in this transaction.

If you have limited working capital, you need to set an option period that will give you just enough time to consummate the purchase and possibly even resell the house before the former owner leaves—and stops making payments. Your goal is to reduce the amount of cash you need to put into the property.

Note that the form has two columns for you to fill out, one for figuring out your minimum profit and another for figuring out some options that could increase your profit. Your greatest opportunity is in the area of expenses. For instance, you may be able to reduce the escrow and title expenses and the loan transfer fees. Prior to your final negotiations with the owners, simply ask the escrow, title, and other people for a reduction in your costs. Tell them you won't proceed with the deal unless you can shave a certain number of dollars off their portion of it. Since they're usually competing vigorously for business, especially in a slow market, they are likely to agree. You may even be able to pass along to the new buyers the negative impound balances, such as unpaid taxes, insurance, and assessments against the property.

Another area for potential savings is the refurbishing costs. As you gain experience and contacts, you'll learn ways to reduce these.

PROFIT ACTION PLAN (Confidential)
B.T.H. NO._____
              (Lot)   (Block)

As of _____

	Presented to Owners	Alternative Possibilities and Reasons
Market Value		
1st Loan Balance	+ _____	+ _____
1st Loan Payments Due	- _____	- _____
1st Loan Penalties	- _____	- _____
2nd Loan Balance	- _____	- _____
2nd Loan Payments Due	- _____	- _____
2nd Loan Penalties	- _____	- _____
Escrow Fees	- _____	- _____
Title Expenses	- _____	- _____
Loan Transfer Fees (1%)	- _____	- _____
Origination Fees (1%)	- _____	- _____
One Mo. (P+I+T+Ins.+Late Charges)	- _____	- _____
Cash for Other Liens	- _____	- _____
Refurbishing Costs	- _____	- _____
Real Estate Commission (6%)	- _____	- _____
Cash to Owners	- _____	- _____
Other	_____	_____
Impounds (Reserve Accounts)	Zero	+ _____
Total Expenses	- _____	- _____
	Minimum	**Maximum**
Net Profit	_____	_____
Action Check Points		

Figure 5.4   Profit Action Plan Form for Evaluating Expenses and Profit in a Distress Property Deal

13. Make an offer, make a deal.

After you've done the Profit Action Plan analysis, ask yourself whether the profit potential is commensurate with the risk involved. If you feel strongly that it is, then make an offer to the owners. Remember that you are seeking mutual gain. Remember, too, that you're dealing with troubled owners, so you'll need to negotiate with some sensitivity. But all negotiating skills come from experience. As you practice, you will develop yours.

14. Transfer the title, and close escrow.

No real estate transaction is complete until the property changes hands. To buy the title and receive the deed on the property, you must correctly fill out and record certain forms. Although the details may vary from state to state, the basic requirements are essentially the same.

15. Resell—or keep and lease—the newly purchased property.

In many cases you will elect to resell the acquired property. In these situations you will be dealing with new buyers. Another set of procedures is necessary to transfer your interest in the newly acquired property to them.

In other cases you will elect to keep the new acquisition and lease it out for income. This is a great way of building net worth. The value of your property will increase yearly because of the narrowing supply and the growing demand. However, you need to be aware of the many pitfalls in leasing single-family homes.

Whichever you choose to do, you will again benefit from your growing skill in negotiating and your growing knowledge of market values in your territory.

CHAPTER 6
Between Two Houses

You can observe a lot by watching.
—*Yogi Berra*

Making a business investment without knowing all the facts you can gather is the best way to lose money. It's like shooting in the dark or guessing a number from one to a hundred. Conversely, the more you know going into a business transaction, the more dramatically your odds of succeeding increase. If you learn to operate in areas where you have a knowledge advantage over everyone else, then the chances are that you will succeed.

Strangely, it usually takes less time to be adequately informed about a business deal than it takes to make a decision without information. When you don't know the facts, you usually spend a lot of time guessing or worrying about your decisions. You think about the best and worst possibilities; you ask yourself endless questions you can't answer. And even at the moment when you are taking the plunge, you worry about what you are doing. You go over earlier opinions and re-question many of the assumptions you made. And often you know that you could have avoided all this worrying if you had gotten all your facts in the first place.

If you follow the recommendations in this book, you will always be able to enter a business deal with information you consider accurate. When you see a deal materialize, you will be able to recognize it. You will have very strong feelings about comparable sales prices and about future appreciation possibilities of the property. You will be well aware of competitive financing rates and your ability to negotiate special conditions to make the deal work.

The basic information for you to have as a specialist in distress property is an extensive knowledge of the values in your territory. In fact, I can state categorically that you cannot succeed unless you really know your territory. The trick is to pick a good one that you can get to know very, very well.

Choose a Good Territory

In general, it's better to look for an area that is showing signs of growth. In any area of growth, prices are improving and demand is increasing. Thus you have a better chance of making a successful deal. If you're in an area that people want to move into, even a less-than-average deal could be profitable.

Finding growing areas is easy. For example, many local newspapers regularly publish information supplied by government bureaus about the traffic flow on various roads in every area of your county. By tracking data like these, you can spot growth trends. Watch out for these revealing factors as well:

• *New construction and rehabilitation.* Builders, developers, and investors are more than willing to put their money and effort into areas that show signs of improvement. These business people usually spend much of their time on market research. Plus, before they can get funds, they have to prove to lenders that the areas in which they are investing show signs of growth. The lenders themselves have market research departments and accurate information about which areas are worth investing in. If you see developer money going into an area, you can assume that research has shown it to be growing.

• *New branches of major banks and retailers.* Banks, supermarkets, discount stores, and major retailers are usually a step or two ahead of the rest of us. They call in demographic consultants before they invest in any major addition. Whenever you notice that any of these outfits is remodeling or building a new office in an area, you can assume that it's an area you also might want to be investing in.

• *Neighborhood spirit.* Usually growing neighborhoods have associations and clubs that are always in the news with some activity—block dances, parades, special money-raising activities, and the like. These sorts of events show that the people living in this area like it and have made up their mind to do everything they can to improve it. Neighborhood spirit tends to be a self-fulfilling prophecy. The more people do to celebrate their lovely neighborhood, the lovelier it becomes.

• *Negative news items.* A major fire, disturbance, or crime usually gets lots of space in the newspapers. If you see that one area consistently has more negative coverage, you can mark it down as an area to avoid. On the other hand, if the area you are considering very rarely has any problems, you can confirm your decision to consider this area your territory.

Once you've selected a handful of interesting areas, it's time to compare them. Narrow your choices to two or three different neighborhoods. Then visit these finalists often. List the friends and other contacts, especially relatives, that you have in each of them. You might even list each neighborhood's positive and negative points. You can assign numerical weights to these characteristics and then add the totals to see which neighborhood comes out on top.

Now it's time for your personal "smell test." Walk through each of your top-choice areas and ask which one you feel most comfortable in. Which area do you like the most? In which one do you feel the best "vibrations"? A "smell test" is the opposite of numerical judgment; it isn't based on rational thinking. It is based on all the input your mental computer has received and the feelings it generates for you. Ninety-nine times out of a hundred, your own personal judgment will be correct.

Take the time you need to make this important decision. Your territory is where you will be spending most of your time as a specialist in distress properties and where you will probably be making a lot of money.

Stake Your Claim "Between Two Houses"

You would be wise to choose as a territory the neighborhood where you live. You already know this area well and feel comfortable in it. You're there all the time anyway. A little extra trick, called "between two houses," can help you get to know it even better.

The trick is to stake out a territory between two houses that you know well. The idea is actually to operate between these two houses. The first house is usually your own. The second should be one you know equally well and often visit. In between should be, preferably, about 500 buildings, but never more than 700. You don't need to confine yourself to single-family homes. With knowledge of the territory, you can also appraise raw land or commercial property offered for sale. What you want is a good-sized territory that will offer plenty of prospects but will still be manageable. If you work "between two houses," you'll be able to keep an eye on your territory without a lot of extra travel or effort.

As I've already said, it's advisable to go in the direction of growth and prosperity, because in such an area property values usually increase. If your own neighborhood doesn't meet this criterion, then it might be better to select two houses in an area that has growth potential.

Here's a handy way to organize your between-two-houses plan. The key is to define your territory's boundaries and then to accumulate useful and accurate information about as many properties as possible.

1. Get the largest possible map (or maps) of your special area. Usually you can get it from the assessor's or county clerk's office.

2. If the map isn't laid out in lots and blocks, mark them in. Every lot and block should be shown separately.

3. Set up a BTH (for "between two houses") numbering system. For ease of reference, it should be similar to the block and lot system used by your local government (see Figure 6.1).

4. Mark major favorable and unfavorable information right on the map in pencil, so you can see the area's trends at a glance.

5. Keep two files for newspaper clippings, one for the important favorable news and the other for the important unfavorable news.

6. Keep a file on each property in your territory as you learn about it (see the between-two-houses information form in Figure 6.1). Insert both favorable and unfavorable information. Keep this information in a safe place, because it soon will become your most valuable asset.

7. Keep up to date on comparable values in the area. Make graphs, tables, and notes on sales. If you keep track of how many dollars per square foot the properties are selling for, you will have an idea of which streets are worth more.

By following this plan, you will soon become a first-rate appraiser who can determine the approximate value of a property in your area as soon as it is put on the market. Then, with a few quick phone calls or a visit to the recorder's office, you can determine a price range that you will accept as the fair market value of a property you're interested in.

Keep Track of the Values in Your Territory

Keeping track of the ever-changing values in your territory is mostly a matter of knowing where to look for information and

BETWEEN TWO HOUSES

B.T.H. No. _____

(Lot)   (Block)

Location: _____

Description: _____

House Size: _____ Lot Size: _____

Amenities: _____

_____

Other Features: _____

_____

_____

Recorded Information

Owner			
Purchase Date			
Purchase Price			
Sales Date			
Sales Price			
$ Gained			
Months Held			
Annual % Gain*			
Special Factors			

$$* \% \text{ Gain} = \frac{12}{\text{Months Held}} \times \frac{\text{Gain}}{\text{Purchase Price}}$$

Figure 6.1   Between Two Houses Information Form

having a system for storing it and making use of it. Any system that works for you is fine.

Your goal is to be well aware of present values and to have an idea of future values. Stay up-to-date on the economic trends in your area. Is employment increasing or decreasing? Are industries moving in or out? Does the state have any special plans for the area that would affect it one way or another? Is anything else happening that could affect the property values? Major economic events have a way of telegraphing themselves in advance. People generally buy at yesterday's prices and sell at yesterday's prices. You'll profit only if you buy at yesterday's prices knowing—not just hoping—that tomorrow's prices will be higher.

More specific, current information about your territory usually comes from these sources:

• *Your own tours of the area.* Try to schedule a regular time every day for walking or driving through your area. Note the properties that are for sale and the ones that have been sold. These regularly scheduled tours are the best and most revealing source of up-to-date information. You can see which real estate agencies do the most business in sections of your territory. You can regularly note what property is for sale by owners. You can track new construction and rehabilitation. You'll know which roads are being improved and which ones are deteriorating. All this information will help you quickly analyze a new property when it comes onto the market.

• *For Sale ads.* Scan the classified ads to get an idea of market trends. For example, if you notice that the number of homes listed for sale in one part of your territory either expands or contracts dramatically, you will know that substantial change is occurring. In addition, these ads usually contain such information as necessary down payments, sales prices, and conditions. You may find ads for distress sales or ads placed by people who are being forced into foreclosure. Check every kind of paper in your area, including the advertisers, the local throwaways, the hometown newspapers, the regional papers. They are all good sources of information.

• *For Rent ads.* Knowing what properties rent for is an important part of your financial analysis. After you go through the financial information on a particular property and before you conclude any purchase, you should know what you can rent a property for if you decide to keep it. A wrong guess of $50 to $150 per month would make a substantial difference.

• *Model homes and open houses.* Most areas generally have a running stream of open houses conducted by real estate brokers. Usually the agent has a printed information sheet telling what the asking price and terms are for that particular property at that time. Files of these information sheets are a ready guide to what the better real estate brokers believe property is selling for. You can compare these to the actual sales prices you read about in your local financial newspaper to get a good idea of comparable values. In addition, visiting open houses and models will give you a feeling for how quickly property is selling. By talking to the agent on the site, you will get a lot more information—such as whether the market is better for buyers or for sellers.

• *Your network of friends.* Everybody likes to talk about real estate, so when you are talking with friends who live or own property in your territory, let them tell you what they know about the current situation. Ask them pointed questions about people who may be moving out of town and selling their property. Also ask if they know of anyone who is having a problem that might cause a precipitous move. Don't hesitate to tell your friends that you are looking for good real estate investments. Friends like to help each other, and that will work both ways.

• *Properties for sale.* To keep in touch with the current market in real estate, one of the best things you can do is to call for information about properties for sale. You are in fact a serious buyer, so you can freely ask questions regarding values, sales prices, and sales terms. Inquire about as many of these properties as you have time for, not only to look for prospects, but also to get a good feeling for market values. This information on comparable properties will help you react instantaneously to any good deal you might find.

Systematically gather and store all this information. If your area is served by a good weekly financial newspaper, keep and file the copies for future use. Clip and file both positive and negative news stories. They'll help you remember the developments that may affect your decisions about a property. And someday, when you're negotiating to buy a property, you'll be able to pull out your bad-news file and remind the owners of all the negative occurrences in the territory. When you're selling a property to another buyer or investor, you can use your good-news file and emphasize all the good things happening in the area. The information you retain in your files will be a source of constant help.

Develop Your Network of Friends and Acquaintances

As I've already pointed out, friends and acquaintances within your territory are a valuable resource. They can keep you informed of any changes that might affect market values and of any property being put on the market. I've had the help of family members or friends on more than half the deals I've completed. You'll find it a great help to have people you trust giving you information.

Sources of information are all around you. Surveys state that each of us averages over 200 personal contacts per week. Not all these contacts can be lingering or meaningful, but many of them may give you more information. Some may even result in specific leads for new business contacts.

Always keep this list of potential contacts in mind:

• *Family members.* Tell everyone in your family what you are doing. Ask them all for specific information and help.

• *Business contacts.* Select a few close associates and ask them for specific information. If your job is outside your between-two-houses territory, your business acquaintances who live in the territory may be able to help.

• *Friends.* Since the topic of real estate usually comes up at least once in most social conversation, you can easily get feedback from any of your friends who may know about your territory. In addition, I always buy charity tickets from people who come to my door trying to sell them, providing they're from my area. I keep track of these donations, and I don't hesitate to ask the sellers for information and favors when I need them.

• *Service people.* It's a good idea to buy goods and services within your area. Then make friends with these business people. You're providing them with business income, so it seems reasonable for them to provide you with information. Some of your best inside tips may come from business people who may also be lenders to and creditors of troubled owners in your area.

• *Religious and civic contacts.* These may be added sources of information, in much the same way as many of the above.

The hardest part of relationships like this is repaying their help. At first I tried a finder's fee. I developed an elaborate formula: 1 percent of the sales price or 10 percent of the profit or 0.5 percent of something else. Nothing worked well. When I had to explain why I was paying what I was, there were always questions—and the potential for bad feelings. Finally I stopped paying according to any precise formula. I began giving gifts, their value based on how helpful my finders were. The gifts were better appreciated and helped me sidestep the problem of paying for the help of friends and relatives. Another alternative is to help your informants select or acquire properties of their own.

The important thing is for you to become the most knowledgeable person in real estate in your selected area. The better you know the territory, the more profit you can make.

Advertise in Local Newspapers

If your territory has a small weekly newspaper or local throw-away featuring classified ads, insert a small ad on a regular basis. The ad should simply state that a private party would like to buy a 3 bedroom or 4 bedroom house immediately. Mention that cash is available, and give a phone number. When you get calls, you can honestly explain that you're looking for a bargain and can respond quickly.

A sample ad might look like this:

Real Estate Wanted

Cash paid for well-located 3 or 4 bedroom home. Immediate occupancy. Phone for fast action: [your telephone number].

When you start getting calls, at all times remember that you are providing a useful service, that you're giving special help to the owner. Also keep in mind that you won't want every house you'll be offered. You're looking for the right combination, the situation where your interests and abilities match the needs of a troubled owner. The only way to find that situation is through exposure to as many troubled owners and other contacts as possible.

Seek "For Sale by Owner" (FSBO) Properties

The people trying to sell their own home are the ones to contact on a regular basis. They usually have a very special reason for taking this route. Perhaps they want really fast action because they are in foreclosure or are having problems meeting their payments. Or maybe they want to save on real estate commissions and other expenses. This is where you come in. Many of your "suspects" will come from the For Sale by Owner group.

When talking to FSBO people, tell them you are looking for a home, are willing to pay cash, and are thus an acceptable prospective buyer. Clarifying these facts right at the beginning will allow negotiations to continue in a fruitful manner.

One thing you can be sure of is that the right price will be apparent to both you and the owners at the right time. Usually, troubled owners have the same comparable pricing data that you have. But they are more negative than you are about expenses and the final outcome. Nothing seems to be going right, so *their* right price sinks quickly to a point met by *your* right price. On the other hand, a deal that is mutually beneficial will happen more smoothly and quickly, and satisfied parties will probably generate more business for you. Both parties want a deal, and so the right price is likely to be reached through bargaining. (See Case Study 6.1.)

Do Not Buy the Very Best

No, you shouldn't buy in a depressed area. But also avoid buying the best house in any neighborhood. Property values are set by the most expensive home. When the most expensive house is the one in trouble, values may go down throughout the neighborhood. Also, buying at the top leaves little room for profit. There are always more buyers for less-expensive homes in a neighborhood of higher-priced homes. So concentrate on the lower end of the spectrum.

When you're buying a lower-priced home in an area, the neighbors will often cooperate with you. Their homes are usually worth more than the home you're thinking of buying. They'll do everything they can to increase the value of the property you're interested in. If you buy it and turn it around, you improve the value of the entire neighborhood. The neighbors' property can only appreciate.

Other Factors in Location

Be aware of location but not obsessed by it. Other factors are equally important to the overall value of a property. For instance, the quality and enthusiasm of the neighbors is an important point. If you choose an active area that people are interested in upgrading, the location will be better in the future.

The price range of a neighborhood is not the most important thing either. Obviously inflation will continually raise prices over-

Case Study 6.1

I bought this unit for no money down from a seasoned investor because he had gotten "sick and tired" of dealing with tenants.

I answered a "lease with option to buy" ad. The unit was a 1,600 square foot, 4 bedroom, 2.5 bath condominium in a lovely community. I called the owner and learned that he was a wealthy, seasoned investor who had owned this unit for several years for rental income, but his health was deteriorating. When I met him, he looked terrible. He talked more about his high blood pressure than about the property. He hated tenant relationships and wanted to sell the property on a lease-option, but he was uncertain about the future price.

His proposal was as follows:

Market value	$94,000
First loan (9 percent, principal and interest $514.96)	64,000
Second loan (15 percent, interest only $187.50)	15,000

With property taxes and association fees, the monthly outgo was $817.46.

The owner asked for $2,000 down and $600 per month on a three-year lease-option. The kicker was that he wanted to split the profits at the end of three years. For instance, he suggested, if the inflation rate was 6 percent, the property would be worth about $112,000 in three years, so we would split $18,000 in profit.

I explained that it would be far better for me to buy the property outright, with him financing the deal. Then I would be paying him a monthly cash flow that would be positive for him (rather than negative, as he proposed). I agreed to pay him $94,000 plus $10,000 assumed profit now, or a total of $104,000 for the unit. After subtracting the loans on the property, he would have equity of $25,000. I would pay him 12 percent, interest only, per month ($250 cash). In three years I would pay off his equity.

He gladly accepted the deal. Besides getting rid of tenant problems, he would have a sale and a note receivable that would look very good on his balance sheet.

It was a quick and simple deal. I bought the property for a $25,000 third note and trust deed. My total monthly costs were the original $817.46 plus $250.00, or $1,067.46. Within a few days I had rented for $650.00 per month. Although my cash flow started at minus $417.46 per month, by the end of the first year I had raised the rent to $750.00 per month.

continued on next page

Case Study 6.1 Continued

More importantly, four months after I closed the deal, a similar 4 bedroom unit was sold for $114,500. Three months later, another one just like mine sold for $124,000. Then there were three more sales of comparable units, averaging $135,000.

What happened? Unknown to both of us at the time of the purchase, there was a pent-up demand for large 4 bedroom units in this area.

I sold this unit before my three years were up at a net profit of over $30,000, with only a small cash investment. The entire transaction took three short meetings with the owner, plus the usual escrow and closing time.

all. The important point is to find a neighborhood where the increase in price will be the greatest. You must consider the resale values four or five years hence. For the most part, properties that back up to shopping centers, apartment complexes, freeways, or industrial areas are undesirable.

The freeway or shopping center may not be there today, but what about tomorrow, when you go to resell the property? It is of great importance that you realize what the planning department has on the boards for tomorrow. This is another reason I recommend concentrating on one area. Only real familiarity with a specific area can help you gather enough knowledge to predict future directions.

CHAPTER 7
Stage I: Before Legal Action Begins

There is nothing new under the sun, just newer ways to look at it.

—Lee Crown

Because of increasing debt and the tremendous pressures on the average homeowner today, more and more people are unable to keep up their mortgage payments. The first indication of distress is a property that is beginning to look shabby. People begin to lose interest in maintenance when they know they may lose their home in a short while. You, of course, because you are plugged into your own information network, recognize the signs of possible distress early on.

What follows are some sources of information about properties that are either in, or close to, distress. They are arranged in order of reliability, from the sources you should be checking first to those you may fall back on if the others aren't bringing you any leads. With experience, you may discover that your priorities are different.

• *Publications dealing in financial matters.* Every county in every state has journals (published weekly or even daily) that list pending foreclosures. You may need to do a little research to find these publications, but usually every area has at least one that will satisfy your needs. In some areas, you may also subscribe to a special service that will supply these data on a regular basis. As usual, the yellow pages of your local telephone directory can also be of great assistance. Look under Publishers, Newspapers, or Financial Data and Foreclosure Services. Under these headings, look for companies publishing legal filings from the county recorder's office. If you live near a university with a business department, you might check the library there for this information. If the county law library is nearby, you might visit it.

- *Title insurance companies.* In some cases, title insurance companies might supply the information directly. On the assumption that they could get valuable extra business from you, most of them will be very cooperative.

- *County clerk's office.* Quite often the county clerk's office can help—if the inquiry doesn't take up too much time. Be organized and ask for information in a precise manner. Ask where the notices of default are filed. Ask how you may scan the general index to learn of pending foreclosure sales. Ask if they know of any easier way for you to accomplish your business. Someone there may offer to help you analyze the records and to notify you of any properties that have been put on notice of default.

- *Families suffering divorce or death.* In either case, a change of residence may be in store. It's easy to keep informed when you concentrate on a particular area. Keep a tickler file of people who are going through these major upheavals so you can contact them at an appropriate time. At some point, they may well be putting their property up for sale.

- *Out-of-state owners.* Stay alert for properties that are continually rented out. (See Case Study 7.1.) You may find that the owners live out of state. In most cases, these owners are anxious to sell their holdings to avoid the constant hassle of being an absentee landlord. Once out of state, they may have found that they need the money more than they need the investment. Contact such people as soon as possible so they know you're available to help them.

- *Disappearing For Sale signs.* When a real estate broker's sign has been on a house for several months and then comes off without the house being sold, chances are that the broker's effort to sell the house has been unsuccessful. Inside the house are probably owners willing to make a quick deal.

- *Ads in your local newspaper.* Remember that another source of leads is your own ad in the classified section, under Real Estate Wanted. Also, most jurisdictions require some kind of public notice in local newspapers at some point in the default-foreclosure process. The lenders are supposed to give sufficient and timely notice to the borrowers that legal action is being taken. These ads, under Legal Notices, can usually be found either at the beginning of the classified section or on the page preceding it. Try placing your own ad as close to the legal notices as possible so as to attract the attention of more people who might be "suspects" for you.

Case Study 7.1

My interest was piqued by the For Rent sign that had been on the unit for several months. I became even more interested when I learned that the rent was only $480 per month, although comparable rates in the area were at least $600. Another interesting point was that the telephone number of the owner was in another county, over a hundred miles away. Clues like that led me to believe there was a real opportunity for me to make a deal on this house.

Making an appointment to see the property was like getting in to see the President. I called the listed number several times during the week, but nobody answered. Then I called again on the weekend with similar results. Finally, two weekends later, I reached the owner, Mr. Adams, and asked him if I could see the property.

Mr. Adams was sour on tenants. He and his wife had lived in the house when he was working in the area. Since they had moved, over three years ago, they had had only two tenants, but both had been problems. In fact, the unit had been vacant for more than twenty months since they moved. It was now a financial drain, although in the beginning the Adamses felt the tax shelter more than compensated for the negative cash flow.

Now the Adamses had decided that they wanted to build a fourplex for themselves and other members of their family. They were shopping for a building lot and were allowing themselves two to three years to finish the building.

I proposed a lease-option on the house that would give them some cash right away and a lump-sum payment in eighteen months, just in time for them to build their fourplex.

Market value of unit	$86,000
First loan	36,000
Equity	$50,000

We agreed that I would pay $480 a month for the lease, the same as the rent they were asking, and $50,000 cash for their equity in eighteen months. They also agreed to let me have an extra six months to cash out their equity, at an increased lease rate of $600 per month, if I still needed it at the end of the eighteen months.

Immediately I had a positive cash flow, because I rented the unit for its market rate of $600.

continued on next page

Case Study 7.1 Continued

As it happened, I needed the extra six months to complete the deal. I finally sold the unit for $116,000. The new buyer put down $16,000 cash, assumed the first mortgage, got a second loan of $34,000 at 17.5 percent, and gave me a third note for $30,000 at 18 percent, interest-only payable monthly for five years, with a balloon payment at the end.

Thus with no money down I purchased a unit that paid my $450 monthly interest and made a profit of about $30,000 in one balloon payment.

The Adamses very happily got rid of a headache, made a fair profit, and received a large amount of cash just when they needed it.

The new buyer has a property that is still appreciating at over 6 percent per year. He also had enough time left to refinance under favorable conditions so he could repay the second lender and me.

- *For Sale by Owner ads.* Call the advertisers directly and say that you are willing to make a cash deal. This is a good way to discover distress properties while getting insight into the prices asked for comparable properties.

- *For Sale by Owner signs.* Tell these owners that you are interested in living in the area and that you will pay cash if things work out.

- *"Bird dogs."* You'll develop more leads if you tell friends, neighbors, and relatives about your business and ask them to help you. (See Case Study 7.2.)

Property Available in Probate Court

Another valuable source of property leads is the probate court of most counties. Between the obituary column and the county clerk, you may find out about two kinds of opportunities: when the deceased has heirs out of state and when the estate must be liquidated.

When you find out about such a situation, you should contact the executor of the estate to determine whether the terms of the will allow the property to be sold through a private sale. If the permission of the court is not required, you may be able to examine the property quickly and negotiate a deal faster than any of the competitors. If your offer is within 10 percent of the executor's appraisal and the estate can save the broker's fee, you have a good chance of making a deal.

A word of caution: Most states have a waiting period of thirty to sixty days before the deal is set to allow for higher bids or written objections. Usually a bid less than 5 percent higher than yours would not be considered. Thus you will need to gauge your bid very carefully.

I have not personally been involved in a probate court deal, but

Case Study 7.2

This beautiful home was one I fell in love with and wanted to live in if I could buy it. But it turned into a deal that did not work because one of the officers at the bank holding the mortgage had the same idea.

The owners were a professional couple named Mary and John (both doctors). But both were compulsive spenders, and soon they had debts and liens in excess of the fair market value of their home:

Fair market value	$120,000
First mortgage	$ 60,000
Second mortgage	30,000
Third mortgage	20,000
Liens	37,000
Total debt	$147,000

I knew this couple through mutual friends. When their financial adviser suggested they file for personal bankruptcy, they asked me for a second opinion. I refused to get involved in their overall affairs, but I told them I could help them sell their home in an advantageous way. I also offered to let them rent the home from me, after the sale, for up to two years. This would give them enough time to gracefully exit the neighborhood (and would give me enough time to sell my present home at a maximum price).

I outlined my plan of action to the couple. I would leave the first loan intact (it was fully assumable). I would renegotiate the second and third loans and settle the liens for as little as possible. Any costs over $114,000 (fair market value less 5 percent for expenses) they would owe me on a personal demand note, paying monthly only the interest, which we set at the prime rate plus 2 percent.

We never had a chance to go much further with this plan. Our friend at the bank was at that time negotiating an extension of a very large commercial construction loan on a medical building that the doctors and their parents were building. When the banker learned that

continued on next page

Case Study 7.2 Continued

Mary and John were seriously considering selling their home to someone else—a real estate professional who would probably live there forever—he made them an offer they couldn't refuse. He would arrange the extension of their multimillion-dollar loan in consideration for their selling him their home. There was no way I could have anticipated this development.

The ending to this story is rather sad. The banker is living happily in this home, and it has appreciated dramatically. Unfortunately, the doctors finally went bankrupt, and the lenders took over the new medical building, which is now fully rented and doing well.

I have been told by people with experience that it requires extreme patience and thoroughness. They say that all details must be accounted for and great care must be taken to provide full information to all parties at all times. In your planning, you must take into account the possibility of extra delays and expenses due to the protections built into the judicial procedures.

My own suggestion would be to consider this route only if it concerns property with which you are very familiar or property in the hands of your family or close friends. In this case, you would know more about the people involved. You also would have a better feel for the time required to complete the process.

Suspects and Prospects

I categorize my possible deals as "suspects" and "prospects." All leads start out as suspects. This classification means I may be interested in buying the property. It means I have to do some more work before the property graduates into a prospect. If I classify something as a prospect, the deal looks promising. There's a good chance that I can make the deal happen.

It usually takes 20 or more suspects to get one good prospect. It takes 10 or more prospects to actually make a deal. So the more suspects you gather, the more prospects you'll cull, and the more deals you'll make.

You might find that a calendar will help you keep track of the critical dates involved with each suspect. The important dates include the dates of the notice of default, the foreclosure notice, and the foreclosure sale. You will have other critical time factors to include also. The important thing is to leave enough time between your initial contact and these deadlines to work out a deal.

Before going out to see a property for the first time, you should determine whether it falls within your specified territory or satisfies your investment interests. Start filling out the Financial Analysis form (found in Chapter 1) and the Suspect Information form (found in Chapter 5). Compare what you know about the sales price and the location against your file of information about the territory. Is the property in a neighborhood that is continually troubled with distress properties? Remember, a depressed neighborhood should be avoided. Do the figures appear too high, based on what you know of sales and purchases in that area?

Gradually you will develop a feel for the kind of property to put on your suspect list. The more time and effort you spend at home with your collection of information about the territory, the faster you will be able to operate out in the field, where the deals are made.

The Best Deals You Can Make Before Legal Action Starts

Many of the distress properties you look at will be in very bad shape. You may be inclined to pass them up. Just remember, though, that a run-down house is always a great opportunity for a deal. The more problems, the better.

Every problem can be solved at a price. First, catalog the problems; then, estimate minimum and maximum prices for correcting each one. Your deal with the owners should be based on your maximum estimates for repairing the house—and still include a good profit for you. If you get estimates from contractors, you'll be pretty safe. They will allow enough money and enough time to do the work. Use these estimates in evaluating the pros and cons of fixing the house's problems. However, after you've decided to go ahead with the deal, do everything possible to speed up the repair process and to reduce the actual cost. One thing you can do is to tie payments to the speed with which the subcontractors perform. In other words, pay $100 for a job done within ten days, $90 if it takes twelve days, and so forth. You win both ways. If the project takes longer than planned, you pay less. If it goes quickly, the lender's carrying charges are less.

To make money rehabilitating a house, you do not have to be handy at fixing things. But you do have to be able to accurately estimate the range of the repair costs. And you do have to be thorough in finding and analyzing the problems. Be systematic, like a computer. The more thorough your evaluation, the higher the price can be when you resell the property. You will be able to speak with certainty about the condition of the roof or foundation because you will know what has been repaired and how.

Most importantly, you need to know what a completely refurbished house would sell for in that neighborhood. It is foolish to purchase a property if the cost of buying and rehabilitating it is greater than its value.

Financing: A Very Important Part of Buying

One of the factors requiring the most attention in purchasing a home is the existing financing. It's usually to your advantage to keep the existing loan, for the following reasons:

• *No need to get a new first mortgage.* When you are dealing with an existing loan, you don't have to apply and qualify for a new mortgage. If you have a good credit record, job history, and income, you should have no problem. You'll save time, and you might even get an added bonus if lower interest rates were in effect when the original loan was placed.

• *Lower closing costs.* When you get a new mortgage, everybody gets in on the act. Lenders impose points, service fees, origination fees, finder's fees, and other charges; there is always a new device on the horizon. Real estate brokers appear for their 6 percent commission. Then the attorneys come up with all kinds of other expenses. You can minimize these charges by buying property according to the procedures outlined in this book. When you resell the property to the new buyers, you can use the same procedures to save them money and increase your profit at the same time.

• *Low or no prepayment penalties.* If the existing mortgage is over six months or a year old, much of the prepayment penalty (if there is one) usually has expired. Thus, when you go to resell the property, the new buyers can either refinance or take over the existing mortgage with little or no worry about a prepayment penalty. Taking over the existing loan will not trigger a prepayment penalty unless the lender can and does call the loan under a due-on-sale clause and is not otherwise restricted by law. Some states, for example, prohibit a prepayment penalty on an owner-occupied single-family dwelling where the owners have lived for five years or more.

When you plan to buy a property, it pays to know as much as possible about the existing financing. Obviously, the lower the interest rate and the more years until maturity, the lower the monthly payments and the better the deal.

You have two basic choices for taking over existing financing: (1) to assume the mortgage or (2) to buy the property "subject to" the existing mortgage. A buyer who assumes an existing mortgage takes over responsibility for the loan from the seller and pays the lender directly. Buying the property "subject to" means leaving responsibility for the loan with the seller and paying the seller, who in turn keeps up payments to the lender.

In most cases, assuming the loan is better for the buyer. These are the advantages:

• No uncertainties about the status of the loan, because the buyer makes direct payments to the lender

• Improved credit standing, because the buyer is building a track record with the lender

• More control over future disposition of the property, because the former seller doesn't have to be involved

A loan assumption does have a couple of disadvantages as compared with a "subject to" purchase: one-time transfer fees imposed by the lender (usually 0.5 to 1 percent of the loan) and liability for any deficiency judgment, if a legally enforceable judgment is ever granted to the lender.

However, most lenders have taken steps to limit the assumability of loans. With gyrating interest rates and rapidly inflating real estate prices, they've been reluctant to lock themselves into the same terms with a new buyer. Thus buying a home "subject to" the present mortgage has become the alternative of choice when the loan can't be assumed. Because the seller technically remains the borrower, this method allows you to avoid the hassles and costs of reapplying for a new loan, and it allows you to sidestep deficiency judgments if the payments aren't made. On the other hand, you could end up with a foreclosed property yourself if the original borrower doesn't pass along your payments to the lender.

A special note about FHA and VA loans: When buying property with an existing FHA or VA mortgage, be especially careful. There is enough literature on the problems and requirements of both these loans to alert any investor. However, one point not stressed enough is that, when assuming a VA loan, you should make sure the property was held by the veteran for at least a month, because it takes at least a month to have the lender receive the official VA guarantee. If title passes too quickly, you may not have what you thought you were buying. In other words, the low-interest, long-term loan may not be part of the sale. When you buy the property "subject to" the existing conditions, you are far less likely to run into trouble of any kind.

How to Buy a Home with Little Cash

If, like many people today, you don't have enough money for a down payment and you can't readily get the money from a friend or relative, you may still be able to buy a home. The secret is timing. The little cash you do have must buy you enough time to sell the same property to someone else.

Here's how it works: You give the sellers an agreed-upon amount of cash, from $100 to $500, to execute an equity purchase agreement (discussed in more detail in Chapter 12). Between the time the agreement is executed and the time the owners leave the residence, you resell the property and thereby raise enough money to pay off the cash requirements and obtain a little cash yourself. If the deal requires a second mortgage or a second trust deed, you also have to use the time to find someone willing to invest in a new loan. You can use this device to get money to keep a second home or to raise the capital needed to move into one or more new deals.

Many people do this sort of thing every day. It depends on the right timing, but it can be accomplished with a little hustle. Choose a deal with a wide spread between the debts outstanding and the market value of the property. Write the papers in such a way that there is no risk on your part. Use an action calendar so that every day counts. As soon as the equity agreement is executed, place a For Sale by Owner ad in the paper and begin attracting people who might be interested in buying the property. Here's a sample:

For Sale by Owner

Newly decorated [or charming or sweet investment], 3 [or 4] bedroom, 2 bath home in value neighborhood. Take over old existing mortgage [details]. Total sales price [details]. No bank qualifying. Move in quickly. Principals only. [Address of property. Your telephone number.]

This approach works best for property that is vacant or owned by people who are out of state or recently deceased. In fact, over half of these opportunities involve properties belonging to absentee owners. If the sellers are still living in the home, do not arrange to sell the property before you and they have signed the final papers.

The most to be lost, if the property does not sell during the "option" period, is your deposit. It is possible, therefore, for you to lose the dollars and not complete the deal. However, if you follow all the steps outlined in this book, you are likely to execute the transaction, sell the property, and make enough money to cover the sale and earn a profit. This profit makes it a little easier to swing the next deal.

It isn't the low cash deposit that makes a deal like this work. It's your personal knowledge and your enthusiastic response to opportunities. The profit you make is your pay for countless hours of preparation and many days of negotiating with the troubled owners and the lenders.

CHAPTER 8

Stage II: After Legal Action Begins

Mortgage, a legal conveyance of property to a creditor for security (from the Latin meaning death pledge)
—*American Heritage Dictionary, 2nd edition*

All along I have stressed my belief that it is best to make a deal with troubled owners before a notice of default is filed, before any foreclosure action or court proceedings. Experience has proven to me that only lawyers profit from court proceedings. Since the net proceeds to the sellers are much greater before the additional expenses of foreclosure are added, they usually make a much better deal before legal action is taken. I've found that telling troubled owners about the details and consequences of a typical court action helps us wrap up a fair deal as quickly as possible. Having the facts gives me more leverage before the default notice is filed.

Troubled owners don't always think this clearly, however. They often believe they'll be able to figure out a way to keep up their payments. Even after they default on a loan and receive notice of legal action, they are usually hoping against hope that something will bail them out before an actual auction occurs. Many feel in the back of their mind that they can always file for bankruptcy (although, as explained in Chapter 19, that is probably the worst thing to do). Many of them figure somehow they can remain in the property a little longer. When you come along, offering a way out of their dilemma, they're often relieved and grateful.

By and large, lenders and creditors also prefer to avoid court action. Many uncertainties arise from legal proceedings because of the many safeguards built into the system and the variable opinions on procedures. The risk is that court action will transform equity into expenses, benefiting few of the original parties to the deal.

Sources of Information

You'll make more deals if you start looking for them before legal action begins. At the same time, you must be completely aware of when action starts on properties in your territory because this stage does offer opportunities. (See Case Study 8.1.) You want to be ready to act at any point in the distress property cycle.

As a specialist working on problem property, you must know exactly what is going on in Stage II. You have to know when lenders file notices of default. You have to know how much time you have before the auction sale. States and localities vary considerably in the amount of time they allow, but they all require that notices of default and of trustee sales (auctions) be published someplace. Fortunately, we are a very consumer-oriented country. We want to give people who are in trouble as much opportunity as possible to get out of it. Therefore, in most areas you have three or four sources of information regarding legal action.

You can follow the notices of default in your local paper. However, it probably is best to get a commercial paper or a paper that specializes in foreclosure notices. Every area of the country is covered by one of these. Many people think they should just go down to the courthouse or wherever notices are filed and keep track of them that way. But I think it's better to spend some money and rely on a professional organization that will send you copies or notices of all legal actions that are filed. The best of these publications list the notices of default, tell when the loan in trouble was originally placed, give the amount of the default, and tell when the default began. Ideally they even tell you something about the property, such as how many stories it has, how many square feet, how many bedrooms and bathrooms, and when the property was built. Specializing in distress properties is a business like any other business and it's pretty competitive, so I suggest that you shop for the best and least expensive source of information.

In many areas of the country, particularly in the larger metropolitan areas, special private newsletters cover foreclosure properties. The newsletters I have seen provide some very good ideas and techniques for "goldmining" in a particular area. I would not count on them, however, for the actual legal and filing information. It's better to go to a large commercial newspaper that is sold to lenders, insurance people, real estate people, and escrow people—as well as to investors looking for deals in this area.

Mortgages, Trust Deeds, and Land Contracts

Legal actions proceed from three types of instruments: the mortgage, the trust deed, and the land contract. All are used to

Case Study 8.1

Martinvale Court was a lovely, long cul-de-sac in a good neighborhood. The VA had repossessed a house in the cul-de-sac. The house was an eyesore on the outside and wasted on the inside, and it detracted from the neighborhood. One other home, occupied by uncaring tenants, looked just as bad. So the rest of the owners on Martinvale Court had a feeling that their property values were going down.

When another house on Martinvale Court came up for auction, I stepped in and was the high bidder. Was I crazy? No. I knew the other two problems would soon be cured. The VA had told me its house would be on the market in sixty days. When I contacted the owner of the house with the destructive tenants, I was told that eviction proceedings had already started. The owner's daughter was moving in and would change this property from an eyesore to a pretty picture.

When I saw yet another homeowner on Martinvale Court had been served with a notice of default, I put that property on my suspect list. I contacted the owners, did all the right things, and found that the owners' parents were giving them enough money to get caught up. This time there was no deal for me. Sometimes borrowers find a way out of problems by themselves.

document loans secured by real estate, but they differ in several important respects.

Two parties are involved in a mortgage: (1) the mortgagor, also known as the debtor or borrower; and (2) the mortgagee, the creditor or lender who has the lien on the property.

Three parties are involved in a trust deed: (1) the trustor, or the debtor or borrower; (2) the trustee, the party who holds "naked" legal title to the property and has the power to sell it in case of default; and (3) the beneficiary, the creditor or lender for whose benefit the trustee holds legal title.

In the older form of land contract, used until about 1974, there were two parties: the vendor (seller) and the vendee (buyer). The newer form of land contract adds a trustee and therefore more closely resembles a trust deed.

Legal Title

In most states, a mortgage gives the borrower legal title to the property. The lender has a lien against the property.

With a trust deed, technically the trustee has legal title. However, as a practical matter and as stated by the courts, the borrower holds actual title and the trust deed is only a lien or encumbrance in favor of the lender (beneficiary).

In a land contract, the seller keeps legal title. But the buyer has equitable title and for most purposes is treated as the owner.

Remedies in Case of Default

With all mortgages, the lender may use judicial foreclosure to collect the debt if the borrower doesn't make payments. If the mortgage contains a power-of-sale clause, the lender may sell the property without judicial foreclosure and apply the sale proceeds to the debt.

With a trust deed, the lender (beneficiary) has two remedies: (1) judicial foreclosure through the court and (2) a trustee sale, in which the trustee sells the property and applies the proceeds to the debt. The latter is the usual remedy because it is much quicker than the other.

Under the old form of land contract, sellers could file a lawsuit called a "quiet title" action to have the court declare that the contract was breached and that they were entitled to possession. Some legal authorities have questioned whether the courts will continue to allow "quiet title" action or instead require judicial foreclosure. Under most newer forms of land contract, the seller can have the trustee sell the property using the same method as with a trust deed.

Foreclosure Procedures

Although both the trust deed and the mortgage contract are instruments for securing the payment of a promissory note, they have distinctly different foreclosure proceedings.

The more common instrument in most states is the mortgage contract. Here we have two parties—the mortgagor (the borrower, who retains title) and the mortgagee (the lender, who holds both the note and the mortgage contract). When default occurs, the lender usually forecloses through the courts.

In this type of *judicial foreclosure*, the mortgagee brings the court action, and the court can order the property sold if a cure isn't forthcoming. If the property is to be sold, an appointed official of the court advertises a Notice of Sale once a week for three or four weeks in a newspaper recognized as the community information center. In most states, some notice is posted on the property.

After a reasonable period, a court sale is made, and a certificate of sale is issued to the buyer. In most states, the mortgagor has a statutory right to redeem (buy back) the property for twelve months after the sale. The mortgagor also may remain in possession of the property, paying only a reasonable rent. If no redemption occurs during this period, a sheriff's deed is issued at the expiration point.

In contrast to this procedure, a *trust deed foreclosure* is quicker. The trustor (the borrower, who conveys title to the trustee) remains the equitable owner of the property. The beneficiary (the lender, who holds the note and trust deed) selects the trustee, who acts on the lender's behalf. The trustee, the person who acts, is the receiver of naked legal title and has the authorization to sell in the event of a default. The trustee will reconvey the title when the debt is paid off and, if necessary, will foreclose.

When default on a trust deed occurs, the beneficiary (lender) notifies the trustee. The trustee then files a notice of default and notifies the trustor and all others who have requested notice. The trustee carefully follows all regulations regarding disclosure so as to have a correct proceeding. In many states, the trustee waits three months or more, giving the trustor (borrower) time to reinstate the loan.

After this period, the trustee advertises a Notice of Sale in a general-circulation newspaper once a week for three or four weeks. Often a notice is also posted on the property. At the end of this time, the trustee conducts a sale (an auction) and issues a trust deed to the highest bidder. Until the time of the sale, the trustor still owns the property and can sell it. There is no period of time after the sale in which to redeem the property or buy it back. The action is final unless fraud can be proven.

After the Default Notice Is Filed

Most lenders prefer not to file default notices. They would rather be paid on time as agreed. But more and more lenders are learning that missed payments during hard economic times usually mean real trouble. So less time elapses now between the first delinquency notice and an actual default filing.

Within three to six days after the lender files the notice of default with the county recorder, the borrower receives some form of certified notification. The words are similar to these: "If your property is in foreclosure because you are behind in your payments, it may be sold without any court action. You may lose legal rights if you do not take prompt action." Recent California laws require that many of these notices be in large, boldface type.

At the very beginning of this process, the borrower can put off foreclosure by bringing the payments up to date. But as time goes on, the borrower faces the added legal expense of removing the default notice—in other words, having the action withdrawn and the status quo restored. These expenses can run from $150 to $500.

If the default notice is filed by a second or third lender, the primary lender can then demand and get the entire amount owed to it. Expenses and penalties may further increase the cash needed to correct a default action of this type.

As explained earlier, a nonjudicial foreclosure can move very rapidly. California law, for instance, allows only three months for the borrower to cure the default. This is a distressingly short period for borrowers who are indeed very short on cash and credit. Raising money under pressure like this can make borrowers do foolish things. Some rush into second or third loan refinancings guaranteed to cause further problems only a short time later.

Often the owners quickly recognize that the best course of action during this very short grace period is to seek out a serious investor or buyer. They correctly decide that they will never solve their problems by additional borrowing.

If the deadline for reinstatement passes without reinstatement occurring, then a notice of trustee sale is posted and advertised for a much shorter time (usually twenty-one days in many states that allow nonjudicial proceedings). During this final period, the loan cannot be reinstated, but the homeowners can save the home from actual foreclosure by paying the entire amount due.

When the Legal Clock Starts Ticking

In Stage II of the distress property cycle, you have to pay close attention to deadlines and legalities. This stage begins with the official default notice. You may see it in a local newspaper. Or you may see it when you stop by the recording office to read the postings. You may even get it in the mail if you subscribe to a local service that sends out foreclosure information on a daily or weekly basis.

However you receive the information, it is the starting point.

Then you must have a system to handle it. Specialists in distress properties have different ways to use the information they receive about default notices. Here are a few:

• *Complete mailing coverage.* Many specialists send letters to every defaulting owner in their territory. They offer to loan money, buy the property outright, or provide foreclosure consulting. Rigid state and local laws govern this behavior, however, so before you write any such letters, check out the legalities. (Portions of the California Civil Code covering foreclosure consulting appear in the appendix at the end of this book.)

• *Complete telephone canvassing.* Instead of mailing letters, many specialists try for direct telephone contact. Some reporting services include the telephone numbers of the troubled owners. Usually direct calling is faster, and it is more likely to lead to immediate meetings with the owners.

• *Combination of mail and telephone.* You can do both, alternately, to suit your purpose. There's a lot of room for creativity here. There is also room for a lot of wasted time. Most troubled owners who have received default notices get many letters and phone calls. I don't know a technique that will get you there first, but I do know that a good idea or two usually pops out if you know your territory and do your homework.

• *Very selective contact.* This is what I do. I only contact the people mentioned in the notices if I have had direct contact with them before or if I know something special about their property that might give me an edge. (See Case Study 8.2.)

Most unresolved notices of default lead to the auction sale. This phase of the cycle is the most risky. It involves lots of money in a put-up-or-shut-up manner. There is no negotiating. Unless you've seen the inside of the property at an earlier stage of the cycle, you're bidding sight unseen. But all the pitfalls are covered thoroughly in later chapters. On the plus side, I've made my biggest profits buying at property auctions.

Writing Letters to Delinquents

If you decide to write letters, you might find these suggestions useful:

• Never use your home address. Use either a PO box or a mail-service address. It's important to keep your business separate from

Case Study 8.2

Early one year I noticed that a foreclosure action had been started against a Mrs. Gray, who lived in an old house near one of my favorite condominium tracts. I called to see if there was any chance to be of help and discovered that Mrs. Gray had been ill and was now living with her son. I spoke to her son, who lived out of state. He told me that the family had refinanced Mrs. Gray's home to the maximum a few months earlier to help Mrs. Gray with her bills. They used most of the proceeds to care for her, and as far as they were concerned, the bank could take the property.

I asked the son if he would mind if I analyzed this situation with an eye toward recouping any equity that might still be available. He said I could do anything that would add to Mrs. Gray's estate but nothing that would cost it any money.

It didn't take me long to check comparables and realize that there was enough equity available to make a fair deal for everyone.

The comparable fair market value was between $75,000 and $80,000. The first loan was $45,000 (75 percent of the 1980 appraisal of only $60,000). It was at 10.25 percent for thirty years, with principal and interest payments of $403.25 per month. With taxes and insurance, the total monthly cost was only $507.50. The home was large and in excellent shape. It could easily rent for $750 to $850. The total delinquencies and expenses were a little over $7,200.

I agreed to buy the home subject to the first loan being brought current and to give the family a $20,000 straight note secured by a second trust deed. On my note I would pay 10.75 percent simple interest, all due and payable in five years. Mrs. Gray's son (her only heir) looked upon the note as found money that would help pay for his children's college education. The five-year period worked out well in his financial planning.

So for a cash outlay of between $1,200 and $1,400, I had a choice property that threw off $200 to $250 per month cash immediately and would pay off the second note out of the proceeds of its sale in five years. If it appreciated at 6 percent per year, the house would be worth over $100,000 by then. The balance owed on my note to the family would be about $33,323. My cash from the sale (after the first loan and expenses) would be about $55,000. So I would

continued on next page

Case Study 8.2 Continued

realize about $21,700 in cash plus the monthly payments as I went along. If the house appreciated at 10 percent a year, I'd realize an additional $20,000. On an initial investment of $1,400, even the lower amount would represent quite a profit.

The point of this story is to encourage you to check every lead and completely follow through on each possible deal. What may look like a dead end could turn into an opportunity to improvise. If there is equity, there is opportunity.

your home life, especially when you're dealing with people in trouble.

• Always include a return address and mail first class so the letters will be returned to you if the owners have vacated.

• Be very careful what you say. Never make an offer with your first letter. Be honest and simply ask the people to contact you so you might see if there's any room for a deal.

• Always include your phone number(s) and the best hours to reach you.

• If you are a licensed real estate person, most states require that you disclose this information up front. I definitely would put it in the letter. It's really a plus, because it adds to your credibility. It tells troubled owners that you have the right kind of knowledge.

If and when you receive a call from troubled owners, be very clear about what you can and can't do. You might offer to lend money to cure the default. You might offer to buy the house under a variety of conditions. You might offer to lease the house with an option to buy it later. The key here is to assure the troubled owners that you are a professional. If there is a way out of their problems, you can probably work with them. Even if there is no way you can work a deal, you may be able to help with an idea or two.

Making Loans to Troubled Owners

Sometimes the easiest way to make deals in this business is to offer to lend money to the owners. I don't mean as a door opener, but for real. Many lenders concentrate on lending in conjunction with foreclosure specialists. A good loan broker might also be interested in working this type of business with you. If you make loans at all or have access to funds, you may find this route doubly rewarding.

Before you make a loan, do all the regular homework on the property. With the troubled owners' cooperation, this is much easier, and you could get above-average returns.

During the course of your discussion, you and the owners may agree that a sale would be much better than a loan. Again, you would be on the inside first, and you could probably make a better deal.

If you make a loan and the troubles continue, there are several ways you can acquire the property at a bargain price. A deed in lieu of foreclosure or some kind of option to buy might be workable. On the other hand, if the owners make their payments or even refinance and repay your loan, you would have above-average returns.

Bad Apples in the Distress Property Business

Foreclosure consultant laws like California's are a great protection for troubled owners. As far as I'm concerned, they should be even tougher. Too many crooks in this business promise the moon, deliver nothing, and find some way to rip off troubled owners in the process.

In my area, several operators rush into action by giving the owners from $5,000 to $15,000 cash. They agree to pay all loans and possibly pay the owners more when the property is sold. In exchange, they take title and the owners move out immediately. Some owners jump at this offer because they feel their credit will be saved and they'll have some money to get replanted somewhere else.

Then these crooked operators rent the property to families with a large number of relatives and boarders (for higher rents). At the same time, they get as many small loans on the property as they can find from money-hungry loan brokers. But these operators never make any loan payments. They stall everyone for as long as possible and sometimes may even make a quick sale to a not-so-bright buyer, out of escrow and without a real estate broker. I am amazed that these deals still happen so often.

If you know of any such shady operators in your area, be sure to use this information when you're negotiating. By being honest and helpful, you will always make more deals.

CHAPTER 9
Negotiating with Troubled Owners

Ideas, like love, grow only when shared.

—*Max Hollis*

Remember that time is on your side when you are dealing with the owners of a distress property. The pressure is on them to do something, and the closer your contact with the owners, the better your chance of success.

Remind the owners that you are interested in helping them as well as in making a profitable business deal. You are in a unique position. You can act quickly to help the owners get out with some cash and a credit rating, so their life won't be unbearable in the near future.

If you can cure the owners' defaults, their credit won't be permanently damaged. Lenders are used to delinquent accounts and respect people who make a past-due bill current. Such people always get more credit. But borrowers who go into foreclosure may wipe out the hard-earned equity of many creditors, and they may have a serious problem regaining a good credit rating.

If the homeowners are able to bring the delinquent payments up to date by borrowing some more, fine. Be happy for them, but also keep in close touch, because now there is an additional problem. The owners must now keep up not only the regular payments but also extra payments on the newly borrowed money. The odds are that if you keep in touch, you will have another chance to make a deal on the property in the near future.

Some homeowners may tell you things that are not totally accurate because of the pressure they are under. You must check out everything homeowners say. Continue asking questions about every single detail. Keep the dialogue going to find out as much as possible about the owners, their financial condition, the neighborhood, and the house. Discuss these things aloud. When you talk with the owners, let them know exactly how you feel. The owners will either add more information or try to dispute some of the facts, allowing you to get the truth out in the open. You must make it plain that game playing is out. If the owners aren't willing to help you help them, then your time is better spent on another deal.

Remind the owners continually that if the home goes into foreclosure, their credit rating will be ruined for a long time. Explain the many disadvantages of foreclosure. Remind them also that quick action is the only thing that will get them out of their present problems. Emphasize the point that the more time they take making a decision, the deeper their debt becomes and the more difficult it will be for anyone to help. Accumulating late charges, expenses, liens, property taxes, and other charges will increase the debt on the property to the point where foreclosure is the only option left. Thus, the faster the owners agree to a deal, the less risk they run of disaster.

That First Call

Never be afraid of that first call on troubled owners. Remember that you are there to help them out of a major difficulty. Being completely realistic and assuming that things will work out is a good frame of mind to be in.

It's easy to break the ice when approaching troubled owners for the first time. Open the conversation in a relaxed manner. Begin with a simple introduction, with information about whether you are independent or working for someone else, and with the suggestion of mutual help. To get the owners' attention when you first approach, you may choose to include any or all of the following opening lines in your conversation:

"I want to see if I can help you and help myself at the same time."

"I like the neighborhood, and I might want to live here myself."

"I can move faster than any agent. Let me outline the procedure I would follow for you."

"You would have a quick and sure sale dealing with me. If we make a deal, there will be no delays waiting for bank approvals of your credit, escrow, or special inspections and certifications."

"After I make a financial analysis—and I could do that beginning today—within twenty-four hours I'll come back with a firm offer for you."

"We'll go over all the numbers together and analyze what all your real alternatives are."

"I'm not the one who put you into this bind. I understand how you feel. This is a way you can be sure the lender and other professionals won't profit by your bad luck."

"I'm here to help you save your credit."

"I'm here to try to get you some cash so you can drive away with your self-respect and start all over again."

"Let me see your papers on this home. Let's see the grant deed, the title policy, the insurance policy, and your payment cards."

"For your own sake, don't tell people you and I are talking about a deal. If your other creditors knew I was going to give you some cash, they would try to get their hands on it, and that could make the deal impossible."

"One or two more liens on the property would be bad."

"Your creditors may send people around pretending to be buyers to test and see if anything is happening. Be extra careful during our transactions."

"Once you sign the deed over to me and I record it, your creditors have no right to this property."

You can also mention that you discovered from the listing service (or from other information) that the property might be for sale. If the owners are definitely going to sell, you can mention the need to talk about a possible transaction. Once the discussion has begun, ask them how many payments they are behind to point up the urgency of the timetable.

About Refinancing

If the troubled owners keep mentioning that they intend to refinance or to get the money somehow, encourage them. Say, "Fine, if you can do it. If you can't, then please call me back." The thing to remember when a house is in foreclosure is that the owners probably can't get refinancing. No legitimate lender would write a second mortgage or trust deed, because the owners are obviously in trouble. Owners who cannot pay a first loan probably cannot pay a second. Additionally, if the owners succeed in getting another loan from someone, they will have increased the payments they have to make. They may put off the agony for a while by refinancing, but they won't completely avoid it.

Since you may well hear back from these owners in two, three, or six months, leave a positive image now. Show the owners that you're there to help, if need be. Reemphasize that your plan would allow them to maintain a credit rating and get away from the deal with money in hand.

In discussing refinancing, one of the first questions you should ask the owners is whether the primary lender still owns the loan. Or has it been sold? If the loan has been sold to Fannie Mae, you might have a great advantage, for then it might be refinanced easily for more dollars at below-market rates. Fannie Mae is a nickname for the Federal National Mortgage Association (FNMA), the nation's largest single investor in residential mortgages. It is federally chartered, but owned by shareholders and privately managed. Fannie Mae purchases loans from local lenders, thus replenishing those institutions with new supplies of mortgage money. Since Fannie Mae owns a large number of older loans at low interest rates, it has a policy of allowing the principal of those loans to be increased. The new amount added to the loan could be at (or slightly above) the prevailing thirty-year fixed interest rate, but the average of new and old could be less than the current rate. If the owners' loan has been sold to Fannie Mae, they could get maximum refinancing at a lower interest rate. (See Case Study 9.1.)

The Best Deal Around

You must always tell the owners the truth. They need to know where they stand and what can be done for them. If they have a better alternative, they should be encouraged to take it. The only reason to deal with you is because you will be more helpful than anyone else. That is a fact. There is no magic involved.

Tell the owners that you can help them save their credit rating and walk away from their debt with some cash in their pockets. Tell them that they must act quickly to avoid foreclosure and the extra expenses incurred in the default process. The owners need to know that yours is the best deal around.

You Can Make It Happen Faster

You can get more money to the owners faster than any other person—for several reasons. First of all, another person probably will not be able to close a deal on time. Most people dealing in foreclosure property try for new financing, which takes a new appraisal, new credit applications, and new submissions to lenders and government agencies. Ninety-nine times out of a hundred, the deadline will pass before the deal closes. What's more, the lenders usually come back with special requirements to be met.

Case Study 9.1

People usually don't like to talk about the deals that got away. I feel that way too, but it's important for me to tell you about George the hair stylist and how I forgot one of the cardinal rules of deal making.

Before he moved out of our area, George cut my hair about once a month. For about three visits in a row, George was complaining about the difficulties he was having making a move from his present condo (in my area) into a home in a nearby town. The sale he thought he was about to close had fallen through. He still went ahead with his move and was now paying for two residences. His trouble was cash flow. Even though he did not need the equity from this first home to close his second, he was not able to make the payments on both. He became delinquent on his payments, and he foresaw trouble ahead.

Fair market value	$105,000
First loan ($47,500 at 8.75 percent, principal and interest)	$373.68
Second loan ($25,000 at 19 percent, interest only)	395.83
Third loan ($10,000 at 23 percent, interest only)	191.67
Total Payments	$961.18

Adding taxes, insurance, and association fees, the total monthly outgo was over $1,125 per month. I could easily rent his condo for $800 to $850 per month, but I'd still have a negative cash flow of about $300 per month.

I asked George for the name of his lender and the number of his first loan. After one call I learned that it had been sold to Fannie Mae. Thus it could be rewritten for a higher amount at an interest rate somewhere between the low existing rate and the present market rate. It turned out that his loan could be rewritten for $97,500 at 13 percent interest, which would mean payments of $1,078 for principal and interest. The total payments would be about $1,240, and the initial negatives would be about $400 per month. But after paying off the other loans, I would have about $14,000 extra cash with which to fund the negatives. Simply by raising the rent 10 percent per year and keeping this $14,000 invested at 10 percent or more, I would have a sinking fund that would last me more than five years. That would be enough time to sell this unit at a substantial profit.

When I asked George for an option, I explained that, as a condition of my deal, I would refinance his Fannie Mae loan. George asked me for the complete strategy. I explained in detail every aspect of my plan and agreed to pay him $105,000 less 6 percent, less the debts, or about $15,000 on a five-year straight note at 10 percent, one payment only.

George seemed to go for the deal but asked for time to talk to his wife and her father, who was also a real estate broker. That's when I realized I had not done all my homework. Usually I ask if any member of the family or close friends are in the real estate business. If there are any, I suggest that they make the first analysis and offering so I can deal with their best shot first. If I give my ideas first, nine times out of ten they like the strategy so well they end up with the deal.

That's what happened here. George's father-in-law thought it was a super idea. But they figured they didn't need any outside help. So I gave them the course of action, which they followed to the letter.

The deal worked perfectly for them, and I received a warm thank-you from my friend George, the departing hair stylist.

For example, they might require repairs to the house. But if the owners can't find enough money to make payments, they won't have enough money to make repairs.

A quick sale by a real estate broker is equally difficult. There's usually not enough time. Sometimes the broker strings the owners along by walking relatives through the house, pretending to have somebody interested. At the last minute the broker may pounce on the sellers and try to get a deal that is not as good as the one you were offering.

It is more advantageous for the owners to consider a sensible business proposition that will get things done within the required time. This is the point you have to make.

Everything on the Table

The owners should know the exact procedure you will use to buy their home and know what to expect. That's the purpose of the Financial Analysis form presented in Chapter 5 (see Figure 5.3). When you discuss the Financial Analysis with the owners, they can get a feel for the direction the deal is taking and get a better idea of what to expect. Do not leave the form with them, however, because the owners, who are under a great deal of stress, might use some small part of it that has changed as the basis for an argument later on. I have found it more beneficial to leave the owners with the spirit of the deal rather than the written outline of it. That way you can both view it clearly when the time comes to conclude a proper contract. Besides, your form could fall into the hands of someone else in the same business to be used against you. Why improve your competitor's technique?

It is important that you take all the papers (checklists, comparables, etc.) with you when the first meeting is over so you can re-examine them at home. It is also very important that you get the loan cards from the owners so you know the exact amount of the loan balance. The owners can misinform you, either through mistake or misrepresentation. With the loan cards on hand, you can make an accurate financial analysis. More importantly, if you take the cards, you essentially lock up the property. Then you need not worry about spending time on a piece of property that someone else might also be working on.

Stay with a Stall

Many times you will notice that a troubled owner who had been going along with everything you are saying suddenly begins to stall. The stall is simply the owner's way of saying that he or she would like to have more time to consider this decision. Often the owner would like to discuss your proposal with his or her spouse or would like to consult with somebody else. In any case, an owner who's stalling isn't ready to make a move. Although this troubled owner may understand the benefits of your deal and believe it will work, at that moment he or she lacks the confidence to take immediate action.

The key to overcoming this kind of behavior is to totally reassure the troubled owner. You can do this in the following manner:

• Be willing to listen to all his or her comments. Let the owner get it all out so you can understand what he or she is thinking about.

• Before reacting to the stall, make some kind of agreeing statement. Tell the owner that you probably would be thinking the same way if you were in his or her shoes.

• Remind the troubled owner that time is of the essence in this particular case.

• Repeat your whole presentation. Go back to the very beginning with your comments about the possibility of doing some good for the owners and good for yourself.

• Reassure the owner strongly that you know what you are doing. Going along with you will win the owner the benefits you promised.

• Ask the owner if he or she believes that you will do what you say you can do. If the owner says yes, then say again that time is of the essence and that you want to go ahead with this deal as quickly as possible. Tell the owner you'd like to get right down to the closing details. If he or she says no, ask for specific reasons why not, and then tackle those reasons.

You should be able to handle all kinds of objections and all kinds of strategies that troubled owners may be using if you are interested in their property. The truth is that you are not going to make any money for yourself unless you help the owners. So the sooner you deal with any reservations the owners may have, the better off both of you will be.

The Basic Psychology of Negotiating with Troubled Owners

At this stage, you're really going to spend a lot of time negotiating with the owners. You'll have to prove your case for offering a price that may at first seem too low to them. But the time you spend negotiating will pay off handsomely in the following ways:

• The owners will be satisfied. When the negotiations are tough, the owners feel they are getting the best deal no matter what the final price is. If an agreement comes too quickly, they often wonder whether they have made the best possible deal. They could be doubtful enough to back down or find ways to sabotage the deal just when it seems set. If you bargain hard, the owners will feel good about finally making the deal. It will be in their best interests to see the deal nailed down as soon as possible.

• By paying the lowest price possible, you reduce the cash requirements and increase your profit potential.

• You improve your ability to sell the property at a higher price. In effect, you've rehearsed with the owners in what might be considered a "dry run" for the upcoming sale.

Some people think it's very difficult to confront troubled owners face to face and offer them less (sometimes considerably less) than they think their property is worth. However, that is not always the case. Troubled owners need personal attention. You must remember that they usually have great emotional problems as well as financial problems. They do not want to be treated indifferently. They want and need a one-to-one relationship. By talking directly to the troubled owners, you increase your chances of success.

Many people are tempted to have a middleman in this kind of transaction. They feel that a real estate broker can act as a neutral party and not become emotionally involved. But the owners usually think a realtor is cold and indifferent. The owners know that the realtor's income is based exclusively on a commission taken out of the sales price.

The owners will be much more amenable to a direct approach. Bringing in personal experiences, such as your own financial reverses, can help in your discussions. You can show understanding of the strains they are undergoing. You have the opportunity to offer real sympathy for their problems.

At any rate, time is important. The cards must be put on the table. As quickly as possible, the owners must realize that their time is running out. There is only one route they can take to save their credit rating and salvage some kind of money from their property. It is up to you to convince them that route is to deal directly with you, as rapidly as possible.

Some troubled owners try to play the game of offer and counteroffer. Remind them that time is working against them. Now is the time to sit down and determine once and for all if something can be worked out. By retracing the steps outlined in the beginning of this book, you can show the owners that the deal can be made faster. It is very important at all times that they should know what is going on, even though you will analyze the profit potential privately. They should see the other forms you use. They need to be reassured that everything is on the up and up.

One further point: If you get to the bottom line and only a few hundred dollars separate the two sides, I suggest that you split the difference in half. Tell the owners, "Look, you think it is worth this, and I think it is worth that. We are separated only by so many hundred dollars. Let's split it down the middle and have a deal." Nine times out of ten this works, providing the previous negotiations were carried out in good faith. Remind the owners that the offer is contingent on examination of the other facts and on everything being as represented. But keep in mind that a few hundred dollars could be the difference between making a deal and not making a deal. You have only so much time to work on deals, and therefore it is in the best interests of both sides that you reach an acceptable price.

There is no sample script you can follow that will guide you through a negotiating session with troubled owners. Each situation is different in too many ways. But I've settled on a technique that I use every time I meet a new suspect. It works for me, and it may help you. I call it my Four F's routine:

1. *Friendliness.* Everything I do and say in the first minute of my meeting is to establish rapport with the owners. I want to be perceived as a friend. Since I honestly want to help the troubled owners, this is a natural first step.

2. *Facts.* I must get all the correct facts in order to make intelligent suggestions. If I have "garbage in," I'll get "garbage out." I must know as much as the owners do about the situation.

3. *Feelings.* How are the owners feeling about their plight? What do they really want to do? How can I fit into their vision of a solution? What do their hearts say?

4. *Foundations.* Before I leave, I must have begun to lay the foundation for a reasonable deal. I must have mentioned an alternative that appeals to the owners. It must make sense for both parties. We can build on that basic idea to solve the problem.

When I meet with suspects for the first time, I concentrate on being sincere and sensitive to the problems at hand. I stay relaxed and calm. I project a self-confident attitude, because I want the troubled owners to feel assured that together we'll find a way out of their financial problems. This is an approach that works almost every time.

Regarding Personal Appearance

Another important rule to follow is to look successful. You should convey the impression that any deal you propose can be consummated. Your clothes should be neat and clean, shoes clean, and attitude positive. You should treat the people you're meeting with understanding and consideration. Although you're a stranger in their household, you should give the sincere impression that you are concerned for them. If you don't really feel that concern, then it's advisable to forgo the meeting.

Because this is such a delicate transaction, avoid anything that might offend the people in the house. Nothing should distract them from the discussion of what kind of deal you can structure to help them. Your personal appearance is a positive factor when it is acceptable to the people in the house. If it is somehow conspicuous and causes them to think about you instead of the all-important deal, it could be a negative factor.

How to Deal with Emotional Problems

Although the troubled owners surely are facing some strong emotions about their situation, you shouldn't assume that they want to stay in the house. Remember that their problems probably did not spring up overnight but have been building for some time. These problems are deep and personal, and they probably hurt. In all cases, the problems are associated with living in that house. The chances are great that everyone really wants to get out.

Other people in the neighborhood know the owners have financial problems. The children at school, people in church, people in the stores—probably they all know what is happening to the troubled family. The family most likely wants a fresh start somewhere else.

Under those circumstances, only very rarely is a family so attached to the house that they would do anything to stay. In that special case, tell the people that they would be better off not to stay, because they would be reminded forever of their problems. Usually, as the saying goes, "A long illness is a sure death." Chances are, the very same factors that caused them the present problems would recur if they stayed. The family would be much better off restructuring their financial situation, getting into less expensive shelter in another area, and working to avoid future entanglements. These major changes are accomplished more easily in a new neighborhood. Realistically, these people are better off getting out of the old, troubled environment and into a new, hopeful situation.

How to Use Empathy

In talking with a troubled family, make a point never to disagree with how they feel about their circumstances. No one else can really know how they feel. In fact, when they use an emotional expression, take the opportunity to move the transaction along faster. Whenever they say something emotional, expand on it with the owners, showing understanding of how they feel.

You can always find an opening by agreeing with them and bringing the conversation around to the process of making a deal. Keep the Financial Analysis form in the forefront. The step-by-step procedure you are proposing will either help the family or it will not.

There's no reason to shy away from emotional outbursts. By agreeing with the owners, you will help them release their tensions and thereby help them conclude a deal more quickly.

When the Owner Wants to Use Real Estate Professionals

Sometimes troubled owners will insist that they are better off using a real estate broker to get rid of their property. They forget that they would be just one of many listings the broker might have. The broker might be thinking, "Since time is running out, why make an effort on this transaction when others would be easier and cleaner to arrange?"

Specifically, a broker would have to get a deposit, qualify the new buyer, go into escrow, and go through all the usual time-consuming activities that most real estate transactions require. In addition, the broker would have to be paid a large commission. The seller would have to pay the usual lender fees, closing costs, escrow charges, and attorney's fees. Under such circumstances, the chances of this deal going through within the time limits imposed on troubled owners are not very good.

You can remind the owners that they have nothing to lose by

going through your procedure. When your analysis is complete, they can make an honest comparison of what they might get selling to you, a private party, versus what they might get selling through a real estate agent. In most cases your alternative will make more sense than the possibility of selling through a broker.

The Professional Appraisal Trap

Many troubled owners are sophisticated enough to attempt to tie any transaction into an appraisal made by a commercial appraiser. Avoid getting an appraisal at all costs. Many appraisals are not impartial but are "made as instructed." You've been studying this particular territory and tracking the sales for a good period of time, so you are well aware of the worth of the property. No deal should be made contingent on an outsider's opinion of what is happening in your territory. The whole basis of being in this business is to become the one person most knowledgeable about property in the area.

How to Use Neighbors to Help

The problems of troubled property owners did not develop overnight. They probably built up over a period of months or even years. Thus, the neighbors are usually well aware of what is happening. The neighbors have a substantial investment in their own property. They are probably very concerned that the troubled property owners are in effect jeopardizing their investment because the property is in bad shape and detracting from the values in the neighborhood.

For this reason, you can logically expect help from the neighbors in correcting a bad situation. It's advisable to go to them and explain their personal interest in the property. If a deal is made, the property will be fixed up, made presentable, and become something of pride in the neighborhood. You can usually expect complete cooperation and gratitude from the neighbors. You always should assume that you are going to be living next to these people and that you need their cooperation to make a good deal. Ask more than one neighbor for advice and information. They may hide important facts because they may be afraid that the deal will not be consummated if you find out something particularly bad about the area. This situation may be avoided by asking two, three, or four neighbors for information. The truth eventually surfaces.

Neighbors can be of great help in offering clues as to the important factors involved in the final negotiation with the troubled owners.

Exclusive Right-to-Sell Agreements

Warn troubled owners that it is in their best interests not to sign an exclusive right-to-sell agreement with anybody, including you. It is especially detrimental to give this exclusive right to a broker because it will jeopardize the owners' ability to deal freely with whomever they wish.

The freedom to act independently is extremely important to the owners, because the foreclosure deadline relentlessly moves on. The owners need time on their side. They do not need to be boxed into a corner. Any kind of exclusive right works to their detriment, as it removes 99 percent of the possible buyers for the property.

Highball Offers and Common Sense

Give troubled owners credit for being reasonably intelligent, even though they have problems. You will lose credibility with the owners if you bring in a highball number as a tentative offer and then have to lower the offer sharply later on. Some people believe that once the highball offer gets them in the door they can work things out. But time is your enemy, and this sort of tactic only slows you down.

It's better if you explain to the owners that you could give them a highball number, as others might do, but that it's to everyone's advantage in this situation to be realistic. There is too much risk of having time run out. They are the ones who will be hurt, not you. You are doing them a friendly favor by not subjecting them to the strain, tension, and false hopes of unrealistically high numbers. Present this case rationally and truthfully. You will improve your credibility, and you will also have a better chance of making a deal with them if some other possible buyer entices them with unrealistic numbers. The one who comes up with the correct information most quickly is the one with the lead in negotiations and the best chance of closing the deal.

However, if someone else throws the owners a high number and they believe it, keep in touch with them and stay friendly. After all, your knowledge of the neighborhood makes you certain the offer will have to be reduced. You can suggest to the owners that they quickly nail down the high number so the highball offer doesn't become a lowball offer over a period of two or three very valuable weeks. Advise the owners to demand a firm contract at the high price within twenty-four hours. If they ask for this contract, they will either find someone foolish enough to pay that kind of money (and thus make a beneficial deal) or they will find that you were right. In most cases, they will come running back to you with the understanding that they do not have the luxury of enough time to keep trying all the highball offers that come down the road.

Exposing a highball scheme can be such an advantage to you that this procedure bears repeating:

1. Warn the troubled owners about the possibility of highball offers, and tell them about the strategy behind the whole concept.

2. Suggest that the owners insist on any highball offer being translated into a firm contract within twenty-four hours so they don't waste precious time.

3. Be prepared for the owners to come running back to you with renewed confidence in your expertise, ready to make a deal.

Time Is on Your Side

Until now your discussion with the troubled owners has centered around their time problem. Now mention your own time problem. You are arranging other deals, and your capital is limited. The owners will have to make up their mind about the deal within twenty-four hours. Remain friendly, firm, and truthful. If you have followed all the steps of this procedure up to now, the owners will believe you. They must be keenly aware that time is as important to you as it is to them.

The reason you require an answer within twenty-four hours is that unknown factors could adversely affect the value of the property. Through experience, you know that an offer cannot stand for more than twenty-four hours under all the same conditions.

You should remind the owners that you are only one person and that you can only concentrate on one deal at a time. You would like to make this particular deal, but you have to make a deal to keep on operating. Tell the owners that if you make some other deal, you won't be able to make this one. Two deals are too much for you to handle, and therefore it is important that the owners reach a decision. Leave the troubled owners with an understanding that the figures you've just discussed would not apply if the conversation is resumed at a later date. If the owners can't say yes within twenty-four hours to the deal you've offered, you'll have to renegotiate later from square one.

Negotiating Points to Remember

Although you are negotiating with the troubled owners, you are also working with them to find a solution to their problem. You are not haggling in the truest sense of the word. One antagonist is not pitted against another, and no information is withheld. Your knowledge of the territory is a great advantage, in that you know as much as you need to know to make a good deal. But basically, time is pushing both sides into a deal. You must be in step with the owners, and this will become second nature for you.

To help the owners and close the deal faster, remember a few basic facts about these situations:

• Your first discussion of price is most important. Your idea of what the property is worth will undoubtedly be different from what the owners think the property is worth. The greatest concessions are made by both parties at this first meeting. The owners will drop their price more in this first session than they will later. The longer the talk continues, the more the owners will stick to their position and the less they will reduce the price.

• You should be as prepared to increase your price at the first session as the owners are prepared to drop theirs. In other words, bring a price into the first session that is lower than what you are willing to accept. But after you've increased your price once, it should stand.

• It's important that you learn as much as possible about the troubled owners' situation, but they should know as little as possible about yours. Stressing the experiences you've had that are similar to the owners' helps build rapport, but don't tell them too much about your financial situation or the deals you've worked on. You can be sidetracked into wasting time.

• Always stress that you are considering other deals. Let the owners know that you have limited time and limited funds available, and put a little pressure on them to move so you can make a deal with somebody.

• Continue the discussion regardless of the emotions encountered, and do not worry about them. Bad feelings can be turned into good feelings, and when that happens, your chance of making a deal is better. You cannot afford the luxury of postponing discussions and coming back at a later time.

• When you are walking through the house, point out the problems that will arise when the house is to be resold. Don't be offensive about this critique. The owners must know that the house is not perfect. The people who have lived in a house know all its defects. They have been upset many times by the squeaky floor, the drippy roof, and other flaws, so your remarks will not come as a surprise. The problems should be reflected in the price being discussed. The owners may well be thinking, "Yes, that's right, that's right. I'd better get rid of this turkey as quickly as possible."

Reverse Tactics of Troubled Owners

Many times the owners will say they have an offer better than the one you are suggesting and that they can make a deal that will go faster. In every case it's best to say, "Great, please do yourself a favor and take the deal. If I can help you in any way to speed it up, I will." Remind them how important time is, and if they can make a deal like that, so much the better. Always call the owners' bluff.

In some cases the troubled owners will have a bona fide offer, in which case you probably would not have made a deal anyway. When they do not actually have a bona fide offer, your position will be strengthened. The owners will know that you will call their bluff at all times. They will also know that you are working with firm figures and that there is only one figure you will agree to.

Divorced Owners

When dealing with divorced couples, you are on very shaky ground (see Case Study 9.2). Remember these very essential requirements:

• Always get both signatures on all documents if the property is in both names.

• Never give all the money to either one in trust for the other. Always write two checks, half to each, or one check in both names.

• Make sure that both signatures are notarized, and make sure there is no risk of either party forging the other party's signature.

• Expect to have disagreements with both parties. Rarely is a divorce friendly. There are all kinds of opportunities for one party to foul up the transaction in order to hurt the other party or to benefit himself or herself.

Case Study 9.2

Early in my career as an investor, I contacted Lou and Ruth Harmon, who were trying to sell their home quickly. They wanted no agents involved. The moment I walked into their living room, I knew how unfriendly the situation was. They sat at opposite ends of the room. If Lou said they wanted $90,000, Ruth would contradict and ask for $92,500. If Ruth said they wanted $10,000 cash, Lou would disagree and ask for more.

They only things they agreed on were their dislike of each other, their pending divorce, and their desire for a deal as quickly as possible.

I spent more than three hours at my first meeting trying to get ready for an offer. Two more visits produced no further results. Whatever I said was twisted and distorted, first by one, then by the other.

Finally I decided to give the deal one last try. I wrote up an offer and mailed them a note stating that they could both accept and sign the offer WITHOUT ONE CHANGE ALLOWED or they could destroy the papers and count me out as a possible purchaser.

This cold-turkey ultimatum worked. It also taught me a lesson in dealing with couples who are separating. It's tactful to let the parties talk and then make a firm offer, but you should not get involved in the details and the hair-splitting on a personal basis.

Legal Protection for Sellers

Most states have laws designed to protect troubled owners against unscrupulous people who might cheat them. And rightly so, because people in foreclosure are vulnerable to fraud and unfair dealings.

Each state has different rules concerning the proper wording in your contracts and regarding the sellers' right to repurchase. They usually cover all stages in the distress property cycle, starting with the first notice of default.

The best way to ensure that you're doing everything correctly is to use either an attorney or an escrow company to close the sale. Ask one of these experts to review your documents for any problems. Tell them that you want them to make sure you have made no legal or moral errors that could cause problems later.

As an added safety factor, if you still feel one is needed, you might ask the sellers to take your agreements to an attorney of their choosing.

You have absolutely no reason to fear the laws designed to protect sellers. They are good laws, and I'm sure you favor them. What you have to fear is unknowingly breaking the laws. That's why you must know all local rules and procedures. The appendix includes portions of California laws designed to protect the sellers of property in foreclosure. Many states model their laws after the California codes. I suggest that you spend a few minutes reading these laws so you know in general what factors you have to be careful of. Knowing the areas that need special care (like full disclosures and fraudulent conveyances) could save you time just when that's what you need to save the most.

CHAPTER 10
Negotiating with Lenders

Lenders respect property. They merely want the property to be theirs so they can respect it more.

—*Ex-Builder*

There are three times during the process of acquiring troubled properties when you may have an opportunity to discuss the sellers' situation with one of the lenders: before a default action is started, after legal action is initiated, and before a trustee sale.

Quite often you learn of a troubled property before a notice of default is filed. A friend in the neighborhood may have heard that the Joneses are behind on their house payments. Others may tell you that it looks as if the Joneses are headed for trouble.

After you meet with Mr. and Mrs. Jones and get to know their situation, you may feel it would be a good idea to visit their lender (or lenders) to let them know you are becoming involved with the borrowers. Never approach a lender unless the owners give you authority to discuss their situation. Any reputable lender will want the borrowers' okay before talking to a third party about them. Most owners welcome help in this matter. Explain to the owners that your inquiry can only help. It will show the lender that they are diligently trying to solve the problem.

Visiting the lender can be helpful in various ways. On the one hand, it may relieve any pressure building up on the lender to file a notice of default. Avoiding this step can save you hundreds of dollars in expenses and give you more time to negotiate a better deal. On the other hand, it may increase the pressure on the troubled borrowers to make some kind of a deal because now the lender is more aware that they cannot solve their financial problems alone. In addition, you may find a lender willing to help you

99

restructure the loan package. The lender's security would be increased by your own credit and effort.

Generally speaking, lenders will do everything they can to further ensure the return of their principal and the continuing return of interest. If you can solicit their help before legal action is started, you make everyone's job easier.

After a notice of default is filed, lenders are usually more difficult to deal with. The borrowers' "file" has by this time been discussed by many people in the lending organization. They've spent money on legal services and other fees. They've developed a set of best-case/worst-case scenarios and have probably set conditions regarding releases before anyone can move forward. You'll have less flexibility at this point.

However, it's still important that you see the lender with your ideas and suggestions. If nothing else, the lender will be favorably impressed with the fact that the borrowers are trying to save the deal. If the borrowers were simply resigned to losing the property, the lender might be faced with additional expenses and problems, such as:

• Damages to the property that is collateral for the loan

• Delays in procedures due to the borrowers' legal maneuvering

• Bad publicity due to the borrowers' allegations or other antagonistic actions

• Negative neighborhood reaction that could harm property values and also hurt the lender's business reputation

Most lenders will therefore be happy to meet with you and discuss ways of avoiding these consequences. Your ideas and the lender's experience could be complementary. If your previous dealings with the lender have been satisfactory or if the lender knows other people you have worked with, so much the better.

One of the extra benefits of meeting with a lender under these circumstances is that he or she very quickly sees you as a person of positive action who may help on other, similar deals. Nothing succeeds like success. If you can save a deal with this lender, the chances are good that your next deal may even originate with the lender and be easier to restructure.

Probably the hardest time to see a lender for help in saving a threatened property is when the only way to keep the property is to pay off the loan in full. In the case of trust deeds, that usually happens three months after the filing of a notice of default. In California, you then have only about twenty-one days to pay back the loan in full. In the case of a mortgage contract and a judicial fore-closure, redemption could be after the court sale. You may have up to one year to redeem (or pay back the loan in full) while the former owners live in the property paying rent.

Even when this point has been reached, you should seek out the lenders and talk with them. Lenders are aware that troubled borrowers are a source of possible harm and embarrassment. If you, a serious investor with credibility, approach the lenders with a plan, even at this stage, they will usually give you their full attention.

How to Make a Presentation

Most states have many types of primary lenders. They include state savings banks, federally chartered savings banks, commercial banks, and institutional lenders. It makes little difference to you who the primary lender is. Your job is simply to make sure that you reach a responsible representative of the lender. The person you are speaking to must, in fact, have some authority. He or she must be able to get a yes or no answer for you. You can find out whether you're talking to the right person simply by asking. Mention that you can act as the principal for your part of the transaction and that you want to be sure the person you're dealing with can act with equal authority as a representative of the lender.

Fortunately, in most cases you will be dealing with a relatively small single loan. These are much easier to deal with than a larger loan for a multi-unit structure or for a commercial property. Not only is the amount smaller, but the lender recognizes that the single-dwelling borrower is in a better bargaining position. Your very presence in the lender's office, as a potential saver of the troubled owners' property, gives the lender a reason to work out the deal with you.

It's better if you bring the lender more than words. You should prepare a financial summary showing the borrowers' present obligations. Use the Financial Analysis, which is in Chapter 5 (see Figure 5.3), to dramatize your seriousness. Then extend over time each element in the worst way possible. For example, suppose the borrowers are two months behind in the payments on their first loan. They may also be behind in their second loan. They may be in arrears on several debts not related to real estate. Now paint a worsening picture. Explain to the lender that the borrowers' income is uncertain and could become worse. Mention that the other lenders are also concerned about the safety of their loans. You probably won't be telling the lender anything he or she doesn't already know or guess. But you will impress the lender with your thoroughness. What you are doing at this point is defining the problem, which happens to be half the solution.

On another sheet, present your proposal for helping the borrowers and the lender. List the items that will require the lender's cooperation. The simpler your proposal is, the better it will be received. The lender will see that a final solution for this troubled property lies in everyone's cooperating. In the end, all parties will be stronger if they cooperate, and much expense and aggravation will be avoided.

Ask the lender for advice. He or she may have a better way of working out the debt. In many cases the lender will suggest an idea or two that can make the entire package a better deal for you. Also ask the lender when you will receive an official response. (See Case Study 10.1.)

The most important part of your presentation is to leave the lender copies of your proposal. Your name, address, and telephone number should be on each sheet. Lenders live for details on paper, and without a record of the gist of your conversation, the deal will not proceed.

You may find two or three visits necessary. They are almost never a waste of time. In most instances, you can eventually work out a deal. And in more than a few instances, the lender (liking your style and presentation) will bring to your attention yet another troubled owner. In a new situation presented in this manner, about half the hard work has already been done for you. The lender has already done a lot of analysis and probably has several good ideas on how you can profit from this deal.

Waivers and Special Concessions

Some loans are written with stiff prepayment penalties. Others have due-on-sale or alienation provisions. In a few cases a balloon payment may be included in the original contract. During the course of your conversation with the lender, you may refer to these clauses as bargaining points. Your position should be that you recognize them, but the bottom line is that all parties concerned want to save the deal. If the borrowers can't make their monthly payment, they certainly can't make a balloon payment. By acknowledging and accepting these provisions as valid, you show that you won't argue about them (at this point).

At the end of your negotiations, when all parties appear in agreement on all points, you may want to remove one or more of the objectionable clauses from the new agreement. At this point, with so much time and energy invested, the average lender would be glad to accommodate you to close the deal.

Case Study 10.1

This condominium deal involved four brokers living thousands of miles apart and took over a year to finalize. But the day title closed, I had $4,000 in cash invested in a $110,000 property that I had purchased for $84,000 and a positive cash flow equal to 60 percent on my investment.

Three brokers owned the unit as tenants-in-common. They were two brothers and a sister all planning on moving to different parts of the country. Although the moves were for business reasons, friction developed among them, and when they moved out they weren't speaking to one another. The last thing they agreed on was to put the sale of this unit into the hands of their cousin, Gus, who was also a real estate broker.

The fair market value of this condo was hard to determine. It was the only 4 bedroom, 3 bath unit with built-out patios and many upgrades. The owners had continually upgraded it. But since the highest sales price in the tract hovered in the high eighties, we agreed on a market value, less the 6 percent they would have normally paid in commissions, of $86,000.

> First loan ($38,500 at 9.25 percent, principal and interest) = $329.07 a month
> No other indebtedness
> Taxes about 1 percent per year
> Association fee about $50 per month
> Total monthly outgo about $450.00

This was not really a troubled property, but it still qualified as having troubled owners. Their personal disharmony prevented any kind of deal with terms to be met. I offered three separate deals, all with reasonable, creative financing. Everyone discussed them, but no consensus was arrived at.

Finally I offered the sellers $80,000 gross, payable in ninety days from the date of opening escrow. Gus, the broker cousin, got verbal agreement over the phone within four days of my offer. The escrow didn't open until forty-five days later, so I had plenty of time to arrange my financing. My risk was a $100 down payment to open escrow and the time I was spending.

During the course of my investigation, I learned that the first loan was held by a private party located in a nearby town. This lender was a successful importer with excess cash flow who was known for his fast action and competitive rates. I called the lender and told him I would like to buy the condo if I could refinance it with him. We discussed various possible financing arrangements, and he agreed to the following:

• A new appraisal by a certified appraiser whom he would select

• 85 percent loan-to-value new funding (in the form of a second loan)

• A new loan at 18 percent interest, written for five years, with no interest payments for three years (and then only if demanded by the lender), all due and payable at the end of five years

Much to my surprise, the lender's appraiser put a $110,000 value on the unit. This meant a $93,500 loan was possible, but I decided to ask for only the $80,000 I needed. After taking into account the first loan, I had $41,500 of new money at 18 percent, with an accruing monthly debt of $662.50.

Renting out the unit at $650 a month would net me over $200 in positive cash flow after making the original payments. Over the three years I had before starting to pay on the new loan, I could increase the rent by $50 every six months. In those three years, my total positive

continued on next page

Case Study 10.1 Continued

cash flow would be $11,700. My negative accrual on the second loan would be $22,410. The difference would be a negative $10,710.

If the fair market value of the condo were only $80,000 to begin with, a 6 percent annual rate of appreciation would mean a net gain on the deal of only $15,000, but that would be more than enough to pay off the lender. If the appraisal was correct and the present fair market value was $110,000, a 6 percent annual appreciation rate meant a huge profit for me. And, of course, if the appreciation rate exceeded 6 percent, the deal would be much more profitable. Factoring in the tax advantages and the amortization on the first loan made this a first-class deal.

Everything went smoothly until the closing. Then I realized I had forgotten to include the broker's fee. I could have done so, as I had plenty of room to increase the second loan, but I did not want to destroy the deal's momentum and risk losing it. So I negotiated a $4,000 fee with Gus and closed the deal.

Bankruptcy Threat

A surefire way to get a lender's complete attention when you are trying to save a deal is to say the borrowers are considering filing for bankruptcy. Should they do so, if a notice of default were filed and a foreclosure sale started, it all would be set aside by the bankruptcy court.

Bankruptcy is a court proceeding whereby the assets of a debtor unable to pay debts are allocated by the court to satisfy the claims of creditors. The bankruptcy laws are exclusively federal laws. Any state laws that contradict or frustrate federal bankruptcy laws are invalid.

The bankruptcy court appoints an administrator or trustee of the debtor's estate. When someone files a petition for bankruptcy, his or her property automatically vests in the trustee. Title stays with the trustee until the bankruptcy court orders differently. It is the trustee's duty to maintain all property until an orderly process is devised to distribute the assets to certified creditors in an equitable manner.

Bankruptcy proceedings may be involuntary (initiated by creditors) or voluntary (initiated by debtors). But once a bankruptcy petition is filed, no creditor may take an action against the debtor outside bankruptcy court. All actions, such as foreclosure, are automatically halted while the bankruptcy is pending.

By filing for bankruptcy before the foreclosure sale, the owners can stop the sale. Even if they allow the sale to occur, they can have the sale voided up to one year later if the sales price was not sufficient and the owners are insolvent. The foreclosure proceeds are usually so low that they cause a loss of equity, which in turn usually causes insolvency to the homeowners. When this is the case, the court could require the lender to turn over all proceeds to the bankruptcy trustee.

Lenders do not want their assets or actions held in abeyance through the bankruptcy courts. Thus they will be doubly willing to help you structure a deal that can help save the property and avoid the bankruptcy. (See Chapter 19 for more details.)

"Homestead" Protection

California homeowners have a special legal device—the homestead declaration—by which unsecured creditors may be prevented from turning debtors out of their homes. Many other states have similar devices under different names. The principles are the same in all states.

A homestead declaration provides that, as head of the family, the homeowner is entitled to a specified dollar exemption from the net equity's cash value over and above all liens and encumbrances. Thus the homeowner's property must be valued in excess of the trust deeds plus the exemption before any creditor could begin to look to the properties to satisfy a judgment.

For example, suppose that a homeowner in California who has recorded a declaration of homestead is sued and judgment is entered against him for $30,000. Let's assume that the real estate involved is worth $150,000 and subject to trust deeds in the amount of $90,000. The homeowner is entitled to a $100,000 exemption over and above all liens. So the property would have to be valued at over $190,000 ($90,000 trust deeds plus $100,000 exemption) before the creditor could even begin to look to the property to satisfy the judgment. Thus the creditor would be unable to force the sale of the property.

Many states have similar exemptions, some of which are automatic and statutory. This means that whether or not the homeowner chooses to declare a formal homestead exemption or claim the automatic exemption, by statute he may be assured of maintaining a residence for himself and his family.

The homestead exemption need not affect your dealings in pending foreclosures unless there are also liens against the property. If there are, you will need to factor this information into your analyses.

Trouble with Junior Lenders

Sometimes the second or third loan holder thinks he or she may make some extra profit by forcing the borrowers into foreclosure. Then the entire amount is usually due. (See Case Study 10.2.) Occasionally such a lender may take over the equity through direct ownership by bidding the most at an auction. You can turn this lender into an ally by making some simple observations about his possible gain. At this stage you (and others) realize there is equity above the loans. All the lender will get through foreclosure is his or her principal and agreed interest. There will be no premiums added. In fact, there may even be a few delays. However, if the lender cooperates with you, you would not only increase the interest rate on the loan but may even increase the loan amount.

Other negotiating maneuvers are possible with junior lenders, depending on the equity left in the deal. You might even share some of the profit with a lender who can help you solve some other problems in the deal.

The Image You Project

Through all your contacts and meetings, you must project the image of a person with the power to solve everyone's problems. If you have done your homework properly, you will have all the information you need for a correct analysis. You will have more information than everybody except the borrowers. But as soon as you make your first contact with a lender, you will know more than the borrowers. Very quickly all parties concerned will look to you as the quarterback. You become the middleman between the borrower and the lenders.

Be sure to spend lots of time with each person in the negotiat-

Case Study 10.2

Sometimes good deals fall right into your lap if you are alert to their signals. One Sunday morning I saw a reconditioned Porsche 914 with a For Sale sign on it. Out of an interest in Porsches, I called the owner for information. His first asking price was too high. I asked him why he wanted to sell the car. He said he was moving because he would be losing his home to the bank. I immediately switched the subject from the Porsche to his home and found out that his problem wasn't really the bank but a private lender who had a large second loan on the unit.

As it turned out, the seller was a pilot for the now defunct Western Airlines. He had recently been laid off because of problems in the airline industry. He was also more interested in talking about his home than about his car. He may have been an excellent pilot, but he was a poor manager of his personal funds. A quick analysis of his situation showed it to be unsolvable:

Market value of home	$80,000
First loan (9 percent, thirty years)	$36,000
Second loan (plus arrears, 10 percent all due)	29,500
Automotive company lien against property	15,500
Total indebtedness	$81,000

I'd learned from experience not to give up on any prospect unless I knew all the details. So I called the second lender and learned that he was a very successful doctor who had owned the home as an investment and sold it to another party who sold it to the pilot. As it turned out, the last thing the doctor wanted was to receive any money this year because of his high tax bracket. He simply wanted to protect his investment, so he sent the pilot notice that he would foreclose if he wasn't paid. I asked the doctor if he would work with me as the borrower, on a straight note basis, all due and payable in five years. This seemed to fit right into the doctor's plans, but he had lost faith in the pilot's financial integrity and wanted the pilot out of the deal.

continued on next page

Case Study 10.2 Continued

Before I spent more time on this home, I obtained an option from the pilot to buy his home under these simple conditions: I would assume his first and second loans and would help him resolve his dispute with the automotive company that had the $15,500 lien against his property. If successful, I would pay the pilot a $10,000 bonus within five years or when I sold his home (whichever occurred first). This $10,000 bonus would be in the form of a promissory note secured by a third lien on the property. My reasoning to the pilot was this: With no third lien, the property would have equity of about $14,000. If he sold the home through a broker, he would have expenses of over $5,000 and be left with about $9,000. I promised him more. I also agreed to do most of the work. The pilot gladly agreed, as the whole problem was becoming depressing to him.

Next I checked the $15,500 automotive lien on the property. As often happens, the total debt claimed was less than the lien, and the final settlement figure was less than the debt. This bill was directly connected with work done on the Porsche. I had the lien removed by helping the automotive company buy the Porsche 914 from the pilot in a manner satisfactory to both parties.

So within thirty days after inquiring about a Porsche 914, I was the owner of an $80,000 home with $76,000 worth of debt but with a positive cash flow from rental income. If appreciation were only 6 percent a year, I could sell the home for about $108,000 in five years and have a clear profit of over $20,000 with no cash investment.

ing sequence. Ask each person for information that will require some extra work. Leave everyone with copies of your written proposals, and invite all the parties to review your work with an eye toward giving you new ideas and input. Very quickly you will have a group of people committed to making a deal with you to solve the troubled borrowers' problems. The more time you spend on seeking cooperation, the more committed everyone will become.

Turn time into your ally by setting deadlines for answers to your proposals. Always mention that you are working on another deal and that you can't swing both of them.

Toward the end of these negotiations, you will be able to extract concessions and benefits that will more than compensate for the time you spend on this phase of your work.

CHAPTER 11

Inspecting the Property

A pig in a poke is a very bad joke.

—Anonymous

The cornerstone of every real estate deal is the property itself. You can throw all the numbers on paper and all the legal documents out the window if the property itself has too many problems. In the beginning your interest is aroused because you know quite a bit about the neighborhood in which the property is located. But after your preliminary investigations and detail gathering, you have to inspect the property. Now you get down to the realities of value. Your profit or loss in a transaction will be affected by how well you inspect and evaluate the property.

How to Inspect

It's easy to forget the details about a property, especially if you're considering several at the same time. An active investor may have ten or more potential acquisitions in the works at once. But the details affecting value are too important to leave to your memory.

The Detailed Property Checklist in Figure 11.1 will help you inspect the property thoroughly and remember what you saw. Photocopy the checklist, and use one copy for each property. Keep it in a separate manila folder.

As you go through the house, consider each point on the checklist separately and in detail. Tactfully state your negative comments or observations out loud in the presence of the owners. Then note these items on the checklist. Positive items should also be listed on the checklist but need not be orally noted. Remember that you are negotiating as well as inspecting.

Bring in experts if you are uncertain of any aspect—the condition of the roof or the plumbing, for example. This research

DETAILED PROPERTY CHECKLIST (Page 1 of 4)

AREA

1. Neighborhood—What is the general apearance? _____

2. Other homes—Are they of like value? _____

3. Streets—Are they paved? _____

4. Amenities—Street lights, parks, landscaping? _____

GROUNDS

1. Easements—Be specific about all encumbrances. _____

2. Landscaping—General appearance will help or hurt sales. _____

3. Driveway—Will it need repair or replacement? _____

4. Walks—Are they usable or dangerous? _____

5. Runoff drainage—Any evidence of problems here? _____

6. Seepage signs—If house has a septic system, be cautious! _____

7. Outside lighting—Enough to make a sale? _____

OUTSIDE OF BUILDING

1. Foundation—Any cracks or signs of settling? _____

2. Siding—Clean and continuous or chipped and rotting? _____

3. Water connections—Enough to keep up grounds? _____

4. Electrical connections—Enough for outside needs? _____

5. Gutters—Solidly attached and functioning? _____

6. Roof—Do shingles lie flat in even rows? _____

7. Chimney—Check flashing and caps. _____

8. Telltale signs—Note problem areas and ask about them. _____

GENERAL IMPRESSIONS INSIDE

1. Decorations—Will any rooms need redoing? _____

2. Size of rooms—Any room noticeably over- or undersized? _____

Figure 11.1 Detailed Property Checklist for Inspecting a Distress Property

DETAILED PROPERTY CHECKLIST (Page 2 of 4)

3. Traffic flow—Does the walking pattern work?

4. Personality—How does the house feel?

LIVING ROOM/ENTRY

1. Foyer—Can guests stop before entering?

2. Coat closet—Any place to hang coats?

3. Size of room—Does it separate itself as a special room?

4. Electrical outlets—Enough for normal uses?

5. Fireplace—Does it really work?

DINING ROOM

1. Size of room—Will eight people be comfortable here?

2. Circulation—Can people move about?

3. Separation—Will diners feel apart while eating?

4. Convenience—Is the kitchen too far to be practical?

KITCHEN

1. Size of room—Most important room in the house.

2. Location—Needs to be near dining facilities and garage.

3. Appliances—Normally included with each purchase.

4. Cabinets—Enough for comfortable living? Storage?

5. Ventilation—What happens when something burns while cooking?

6. Personality—How does it feel to you?

BEDROOMS

1. Number—Never fewer than three.

2. Location—Must have privacy.

3. Bathroom—Must be close.

4. Windows—Ventilation and openness needed.

5. Special features—List closets, cabinets, etc.

Figure 11.1   *Continued*

DETAILED PROPERTY CHECKLIST (Page 3 of 4)

6. Electrical outlets—Enough to move appliances around.

BATHROOMS
1. Number—Minimum of two.
2. Size—Room to move around.
3. Locations—One for guests, one or more for family.
4. Windows—Ventilation and view?
5. Water conditions—Any leaks? Enough pressure?
6. Door locks—Most important. Check if operational.
7. General conditions—Shower heads, grout, leaks, etc.

BASEMENT
1. Water problems—Check the covered sections.
2. Storage—Enough to be a sales feature?
3. Floor joists—Any sagging, rotting, or problems?
4. Outside access—Always a big plus.

LAUNDRY
1. Location—Must be close to kitchen.
2. Cabinet space—Enough to be convenient?
3. Electrical—Wired for 220 V?
4. Water—Check volume, pressure, and drainage.
5. Ventilation—Adequate for clothes dryer?

GARAGE
1. Size—Minimum two-car.
2. Convenience—Easy in and out a must.
3. Storage—If no attic or basement, need storage space.

ATTIC
1. Entry—Easy to get in and out?
2. Storage—Enough for a sales feature?
3. Ventilation—Most important.

Figure 11.1 Detailed Property Checklist for Inspecting a Distress Property *Continued*

DETAILED PROPERTY CHECKLIST (Page 4 of 4)

4. Insulation—Save money on heating and cooling.

5. Problems—Check corners and ask questions.

PLUMBING

1. Water supply—Stay away from private wells.

2. Sewage disposal—Septic systems must have service contract.

3. Quality of pipes—Plastic pipes are suspect.

4. General condition—How does the system look?

5. Noises or warning signs—Ask about all of them.

6. Hot water system—Is it adequate for large families?

HEATING

1. General conditions—How does it all look?

2. Turn it on—Pretend you're living here in winter.

3. Noises or warning signs—Ask about each one.

4. Service arrangements—Check with service people on questions.

AIR CONDITIONING

1. General condition—Enough ducts in each room?

2. Turn it on—Pretend it's midsummer.

3. Noises or warning signs—Ask about all of them.

4. Service arrangements—Check for specific information.

ELECTRICAL SYSTEM

1. Capacity—Must be 100 amps, 200 volt minimum.

2. Add-ons—Must have at least two spare circuits.

3. Age—If house is old, new system may be needed.

Figure 11.1   *Continued*

doesn't take much time. It just requires a determination to go from top to bottom, foundation to roof, to see what shape everything is in.

Your next step is to evaluate what you've seen. Using the Inspection Evaluation form in Figure 11.2, assign numerical weights to each item of your inspection on a scale from 1 to 5—1 being unfavorable, 3 being moderately favorable, and 5 being very favorable. To compare the total number of favorable and unfavorable elements of the property, count the number of entries in each column.

Most investors using this system look for at least a three-to-one favorable ratio before proceeding further. But this is a personal decision and very subjective. I usually compare the totals and let my overall feelings make the decision rather than letting the totals automatically decide for me.

No one should see your totals and analysis except you. This information is the basis for your future negotiations with the owners. It will also aid you in deciding whether to rent or sell after you acquire the property. Thus your inspection is not a waste of time.

After all the numbers are together, you may find that they simply do not work. A few substantial defects could cost you a lot of money in the future. If the total costs of buying and repairing the house are more than the resale value or not worth what you could get by renting it out, you may just want to walk away from the deal. Or you could go back to the troubled owners and see if there's another way of negotiating the deal. You should point out that you need to make a profit, explain the figures, and seek a better arrangement. If you are unable to reach an agreement, bow out gracefully. The odds are 50-50 that negotiations will take place again with the same people in thirty, sixty, or ninety days, so always keep information you've gotten. If you've carefully chosen the right neighborhood, no information about properties within that neighborhood is ever useless.

Uncooperative Owners

Occasionally you will run into owners who balk at showing you the property. They may come up with any number of excuses, but they all mean the same thing: trouble. Under no circumstances should you proceed with a deal unless they allow you to inspect the property. (See Case Study 11.1.)

If you encounter this situation, start by overcoming the owners' doubts. Explain that you are a seasoned investor and that you have seen all kinds of properties. Tell the owners to relax and not to worry. Assure them that you probably can understand and correct any deficiencies. Mention that anyone else who would con-

INSPECTION EVALUATION

Date _____

Name _____

Location _____

	Unfavorable			Favorable		Comments
A. AREA						
1. Neighborhood	1	2	3	4	5	_____
2. Other Homes	1	2	3	4	5	_____
3. Streets	1	2	3	4	5	_____
4. Amenities	1	2	3	4	5	_____
5. Other	1	2	3	4	5	_____
B. GROUNDS						
1. Easements	1	2	3	4	5	_____
2. Landscaping	1	2	3	4	5	_____
3. Driveway	1	2	3	4	5	_____
4. Walks	1	2	3	4	5	_____
5. Runoff drainage	1	2	3	4	5	_____
6. Seepage signs	1	2	3	4	5	_____
7. Outside lighting	1	2	3	4	5	_____
8. Other	1	2	3	4	5	_____
C. OUTSIDE OF BUILDING						
1. Foundation	1	2	3	4	5	_____
2. Siding	1	2	3	4	5	_____
3. Water connections	1	2	3	4	5	_____
4. Electrical connections	1	2	3	4	5	_____
5. Gutters	1	2	3	4	5	_____
6. Roof	1	2	3	4	5	_____
7. Chimney	1	2	3	4	5	_____
8. Telltale signs	1	2	3	4	5	_____
9. Other	1	2	3	4	5	_____
D. GENERAL IMPRESSIONS INSIDE						
1. Decorations	1	2	3	4	5	_____

Figure 11.2   Inspection Evaluation Form for Determining Distress Property

2. Size of rooms	1	2	3	4	5	_____
3. Traffic flow	1	2	3	4	5	_____
4. Personality	1	2	3	4	5	_____
5. Other	1	2	3	4	5	_____

E. LIVING ROOM/ENTRY

1. Foyer	1	2	3	4	5	_____
2. Coat closet	1	2	3	4	5	_____
3. Size of room	1	2	3	4	5	_____
4. Electrical outlets	1	2	3	4	5	_____
5. Fireplace	1	2	3	4	5	_____
6. Other	1	2	3	4	5	_____

F. DINING ROOM

1. Size of room	1	2	3	4	5	_____
2. Circulation	1	2	3	4	5	_____
3. Separation	1	2	3	4	5	_____
4. Convenience	1	2	3	4	5	_____
5. Other	1	2	3	4	5	_____

G. KITCHEN

1. Size of room	1	2	3	4	5	_____
2. Location	1	2	3	4	5	_____
3. Appliances	1	2	3	4	5	_____
4. Cabinets	1	2	3	4	5	_____
5. Ventilation	1	2	3	4	5	_____
6. Personality	1	2	3	4	5	_____
7. Other	1	2	3	4	5	_____

H. BEDROOMS

1. Number	1	2	3	4	5	_____
2. Location	1	2	3	4	5	_____
3. Bathroom	1	2	3	4	5	_____
4. Windows	1	2	3	4	5	_____
5. Special features	1	2	3	4	5	_____
6. Electrical outlets	1	2	3	4	5	_____
7. Closets	1	2	3	4	5	_____

Figure 11.2   Inspection Evaluation Form for Determining Distress Property   *Continued*

8. Other   1   2   3   4   5   _____

I. BATHROOMS
    1. Number   1   2   3   4   5   _____
    2. Size   1   2   3   4   5   _____
    3. Locations   1   2   3   4   5   _____
    4. Windows   1   2   3   4   5   _____
    5. Water conditions   1   2   3   4   5   _____
    6. Door locks   1   2   3   4   5   _____
    7. General conditions   1   2   3   4   5   _____
    8. Other   1   2   3   4   5   _____

J. BASEMENT
    1. Water problems   1   2   3   4   5   _____
    2. Storage   1   2   3   4   5   _____
    3. Floor joists   1   2   3   4   5   _____
    4. Outside access   1   2   3   4   5   _____
    5. Other   1   2   3   4   5   _____

K. LAUNDRY
    1. Location   1   2   3   4   5   _____
    2. Cabinet space   1   2   3   4   5   _____
    3. Electrical   1   2   3   4   5   _____
    4. Water   1   2   3   4   5   _____
    5. Ventilation   1   2   3   4   5   _____
    6. Other   1   2   3   4   5   _____

L. GARAGE
    1. Size   1   2   3   4   5   _____
    2. Convenience   1   2   3   4   5   _____
    3. Storage   1   2   3   4   5   _____
    4. Other   1   2   3   4   5   _____

M. ATTIC
    1. Entry   1   2   3   4   5   _____
    2. Storage   1   2   3   4   5   _____
    3. Ventilation   1   2   3   4   5   _____

Figure 11.2   *Continued*

4. Insulation	1	2	3	4	5	_____
5. Problems	1	2	3	4	5	_____
6. Other	1	2	3	4	5	_____

N. PLUMBING

1. Water supply	1	2	3	4	5	_____
2. Sewage disposal	1	2	3	4	5	_____
3. Quality of pipes	1	2	3	4	5	_____
4. General condition	1	2	3	4	5	_____
5. Noises or warning signs	1	2	3	4	5	_____
6. Hot water system	1	2	3	4	5	_____
7. Other	1	2	3	4	5	_____

O. HEATING

1. General conditions	1	2	3	4	5	_____
2. Turn it on	1	2	3	4	5	_____
3. Noises or warning signs	1	2	3	4	5	_____
4. Service arrangements	1	2	3	4	5	_____
5. Other	1	2	3	4	5	_____

P. AIR CONDITIONING

1. General condition	1	2	3	4	5	_____
2. Turn it on	1	2	3	4	5	_____
3. Noises or warning signs	1	2	3	4	5	_____
4. Service arrangements	1	2	3	4	5	_____
5. Other	1	2	3	4	5	_____

Q. ELECTRICAL SYSTEM

1. Capacity	1	2	3	4	5	_____
2. Add-ons	1	2	3	4	5	_____
3. Age	1	2	3	4	5	_____
4. Other	1	2	3	4	5	_____

TOTAL _____

Figure 11.2 Inspection Evaluation Form for Determining Distress Property *Continued*

Case Study 11.1

Once I noticed an ad in our local newspaper that interested me very much:

> **Investor's Special**
> Getting divorced, transferred, need quick sale. 3
> bedroom, 2 bath, many extras. Terms. No agents.
> Call Phil 855-7111 days, 877-3509 evenings.

I called Phil at work that day and arranged to see him during his lunch break the next day. His property was a condo in an area with which I was very familiar. It seemed too good to be true. His asking price was $110,000 (which was $10,000 to $12,000 below comparable properties). His financing consisted of a first loan of $62,500 at 11.5 percent and an interest-only second loan of $28,500 at 15 percent. He wanted $5,000 to $10,000 cash down and would take a three-to-five-year straight note for the balance.

I felt I should act fast. I asked to see the place. He gave me the address and suggested I drive by to see if I liked the area. I drove by, and I did like the area. For several days thereafter I asked to see the inside of the property.

"First, let's make the deal," he said. After we penciled out and agreed on most aspects, I tried again to see this inside. He always had excuses:

"My wife is upset about our divorce, give me time."

"Why worry—you know what the model looks like."

"You've seen one, you've seen them all."

"At the price I'm selling it to you for, you don't have to see it."

I was days from closing the deal without seeing the property when I decided to fake my way into the unit. One of the few times I went by I noticed an Arrowhead truck making a delivery in the neighborhood. I bought a five-gallon bottle of Sparkletts water and knocked on the door. When Phil's wife answered, I offered her a free bottle of water as a promotional gimmick. Although she seemed spaced out, she quickly accepted the freebie and told me to take it to the end of the hall, into a bedroom that was her study.

What I saw and smelled as I walked through the home ruined my day. Two dogs and four cats were roaming through their six-room litter box, leaving their marks everywhere. Crude, hateful remarks about her soon-to-be ex-husband Phil were written with a ballpoint pen on each wall, and defaced pictures of him were taped beside them. Plaster was cracked, and the carpeting was gone. In short, the place was a disaster.

Usually, after seeing something like this, I would simply reduce my offering price by the dollar amount I deemed sufficient to cover all the extra expenses. But this time I decided to pass on the opportunity entirely. Why? Because I sensed an even greater problem with Phil's wife. She looked on the verge of irrationality, and no deal is worth getting involved in a situation like that.

No matter how you do it, either see the property or go on to the next one. Never buy into unknown problems. It's a surefire way to lose.

sider helping them would first have to inspect the property just as you want to. Tell them that you have more experience than most and are prepared for all types of surprises.

If nothing you say changes their mind, put the deal on hold. Tell the owners that valuable time is slipping away and that they are the ones who will be hurt most by any delay.

No smart investor buys a pig in a poke. The truth is that you must never take a chance on the condition of a property. Nor should you accept anyone's word about property details. It's your money at stake. Be firm, and hold fast.

CHAPTER 12
Closing the Deal with Troubled Owners

It's a good deal when both sides are winners.

—Ed Adelman

After one or two meetings with the troubled owners, most of the problems will be out in the open. The urgency of making a deal will be apparent. The owners will recognize the need for action. Reality will have set in.

But by positively stating your plans, you should have convinced the troubled owners that at least a possibility of help is at hand.

If you've done your job right, they will appreciate your personal interest in their problems. They will feel that they can talk openly and honestly with you, because you know the dimensions of their troubles. They gain comfort from not having to act out a part. Because they realize that you are a specialist in this business and know the good and bad aspects of the neighborhood, they will believe that the deal you've outlined is real and will work.

They will be ready to accept the cold facts of their situation. They will be convinced that time is the critical factor. They will know that you can do the job better and faster than anyone else. They will be ready to make a deal.

Appraising the Property before Making the Offer

There are many ways of putting a value on the property before you make a final offer. The true market value is what the buyer is willing to pay and the seller is willing to take. Thus it is always an objective value. It is the highest price that a property would sell for on the open market, where the seller is not obliged to sell and the buyer is not obliged to buy.

You should have a good idea of what the true market value is

121

before you make an offer. But this is the highest value of the property. The offer you make to the owners should be considerably less. The price you ask of potential buyers, after you've bought the property, should be considerably more. But in both cases, the market value is the key to all other prices.

The best way to determine the true market value of any property is to have a good working relationship with a title company. Your title company can give you a rundown of comparable market values in the chosen area. Title companies usually know what properties have been transferred, and they keep their information current. Usually they can tell you within a few hundred dollars what the sales prices have been over the past six months.

It's easy to get help from a title company. Just ask your real estate friends to name the best two title companies in your area. Call these companies and ask for the names of service representatives who might be able to help you. Then call the reps and tell them exactly what you are doing. Ask them for help, and agree to give them your business on deals that require title insurance.

You can add to the information you get from title companies by checking with people who have recently moved into the area. Ask the neighbors who the new people are. Once you've met the new buyers, you can ask what they paid for the property and what they've added to it. This is just another way to increase your knowledge of market values in a particular area.

Market values are easy to determine in a district where properties turn over rapidly, because there are always willing buyers and willing sellers. It is more difficult to get a good reading of market values in a district where there is very little activity.

Never confuse listing prices (which brokers use) with market value. The listing price for a property is usually set considerably higher than the market value. The listing price is usually the utility value that the property has in the eyes of the owners. But it rarely translates into market value.

The Financial Analysis form included in Chapter 5 (Figure 5.3) shows market value as your top value. You need to deduct from it all distress factors that reduce the price. Even though the property is not in a distress neighborhood, it is a distress property that requires some additional expense to make it marketable. The form lists most of the factors you must consider in adjusting the price to a level that makes the deal worthwhile for you.

The Longer It Takes, the Lower the Price

As in all other aspects of economics, time is money. The offer you make to the owners in the first thirty days of the foreclosure period will be considerably higher than your offer during the second thirty days. Unfortunately, in the last days of the foreclosure period, your offer will be the lowest it possibly can be. That's because the late charges have increased, another payment must be made, and the time pressures have complicated your negotiations with lenders.

You must let the troubled owners know immediately that the quicker they act, the better off they will be. They need to be reminded that the deal could always be killed by such unexpected "knockout drops" as another dramatic increase in oil prices, which could cause a recession. Gasoline rationing, war, or some other aspect of Murphy's Law would do more harm than good. Owners must understand the urgency of this transaction.

The Equity Purchase Agreement

Any deal involving defaults and liens has a great many variables. I use a special sales contract called an Equity Purchase Agreement (see Figure 12.1) to deal with these variables. This agreement documents the highlights of the deal with the owners. It stresses the net dollars to the sellers to alleviate any fear that they are being shortchanged. It also repeats the key financial information. If anything comes up that costs the buyer more money, the costs are deducted from the net amount owed to the sellers.

This agreement has some special protective highlights:

• *Vacate clause.* If the property is not vacated by a certain date, all daily expenses are deducted from the net amount owed to the sellers.

• *Impounds.* Any surplus in the impound account is credited to the buyer as reserves. Any shortage comes out of the sellers' net proceeds.

• *Title test.* A grant deed is executed and recorded. Then a preliminary title report is called for. If the report shows no new adverse facts, the deal closes on schedule. If the report reveals different information, the buyer may drop out.

• *Final safeguard.* The buyer agrees to pay the balance of all funds due to the sellers after checking the title, loans, and liens and after the property is vacated.

Special conditions come up now and then that are not covered in any sales contract. The Equity Purchase Agreement has space

Equity Purchase Agreement

❏ Copy Buyer
❏ Copy Seller
❏ Copy File

Date _____

Lot _____ Block _____ Tract _____   Lender _____
Address _____   _____
                                                          Loan No. _____

Buyer	Seller
_____	_____
_____	_____

In consideration of the sum _____ , receipt of which is hereby acknowledged by the Seller, the Seller agrees to sell, and the Buyer agrees to buy, the above described property for the sum of _____ NET to the Seller.

The Buyer agrees to take title subject only to the existing liens and encumbrances not in excess of _____

It is also agreed:

1. The monthly payments on the above loan, including principal, interest, taxes, and insurance are _____

2. The Buyer agrees to pay all escrow, title, loan transfer, and closing costs.

3. If the property is not vacated by the agreed date of _____ , all payments and further expenses incurred from that date forward shall be deducted from the net amount to Seller.

4. Impounds and/or reserves for taxes and insurance, if any, are to be assigned without charge to the Buyer.

5. Any unexpected shortage in the above-mentioned impounds and/or reserves will be deducted from the net due Seller at closing.

6. Seller agrees to immediately execute a GRANT DEED in favor of the Buyer. Seller authorizes Buyer to record said DEED.

7. After Buyer records said DEED, a TITLE report will be drawn in the name of the Buyer. If the title, loan, and liens are not as agreed to by both parties, the Buyer has the option to rescind this agreement and record another GRANT DEED in favor of the Seller herein without liability to the Buyer.

8. Seller agrees to leave property in clean and good condition.

9. Seller agrees not to remove any real property.

10. Seller agrees to give possession of property on or before 12 Noon on _____

11. Seller agrees to allow Buyer access to property for any reason prior to possession date.

12. Buyer agrees to pay balance of all funds due to Seller after checking title, loans, and liens and when property is vacated.

Other Parts of This Agreement _____

_____

Dated This Day _____ At _____ State _____

Buyer _____ Seller _____
                                                              (Husband)
_____   _____
                                                              (Wife)
                                                              (Witness)

Figure 12.1 Equity Purchase Agreement Form Used as Sales Contract

to include these additional items. For example, the owners may have started some home improvement work that must be completed before you complete the transaction. Or they may have made plans to pay off one of the junior liens by working off the debt. In one deal I made, I agreed to allow the owner's son (who was visiting his fiancee) to stay in the house for several days after the deal closed. He slept on the floor in his sleeping bag and was no problem.

In many states you cannot use an equity purchase agreement once a notice of default has been filed. After that point you must get a special agreement prepared, usually by an attorney who is familiar with these particular laws.

Get the Name on the Dotted Line

When it's time to finalize your deal with the sellers, review with them the summary figures on the Financial Analysis form (see Fig. 5.3) and repeat the reasoning behind your offer. Nine times out of ten, they will decide to take the deal.

The next step is to execute a grant deed. Make sure all the information is correct. The information on the deed transferring the property must be identical to the information on the deed the sellers received from the lending institution. If a seller's middle initial is really B as in Barbara but the deed shows a V, put down V. Too many titles have been messed up because people have copied the information from the bottom of the sheet supplied by the information service, from the newspaper, or from a seller. In no case should anything be used but the original information appearing on the deed.

As soon as the deed is signed over by the owners, you must take it immediately to the recording office. Record the deed, get a copy, and take it right to the title company. Make sure that your name is first in line of title. Then any liens that come in after you record the deed will be added after your name and will thus be invalid.

Choose the Right Transfer Instrument

Ownership transfers are carried out in many different ways. You will have to check state and county laws in your own area. But one easy way to obtain information is to check all the documents used by the present sellers to acquire title. Most sellers were first buyers and have copies of all the documents used in the original transfer of title.

In most areas, the three most common transfer instruments are these:

- *Joint tenancy grant deed* (see Figure 12.2). Both husband and wife are owners of the property. Everything is recorded and listed in both names. Any conveyance to you as the new buyer must have the signatures of both owners exactly as they appear on the original conveyance to them.

- *Individual grant deed.* Essentially the same as above, except only one name appears as the owner.

- *Quitclaim deed* (see Figure 12.3). This instrument is used when special circumstances, such as financing or legal problems, prevent a normal grant deed transfer. All it does is convey to the buyer whatever rights of ownership the owners have. Only seasoned investors with good legal advice should use this method of acquiring properties.

Save Money When Passing Title

You will be able to save some of the extra charges associated with real estate transfers by doing much of the work yourself. In some cases, the total costs for transferring property amount to well over a thousand dollars.

First get the equity purchase agreement signed, which gives you control of the property. Then ask the title company to check the property to make sure that it is in fact transferrable. Now you may personally execute the deed. It is prepared exactly as the previous deed was, then signed by the owners and notarized. As long as the papers are prepared essentially as before and as long as there are no local or state laws to the contrary, you will probably be able to save the legal preparation fees usually charged for this set of events. Verify that you can do this yourself by consulting the county clerk, the county recording office, or any good stationer who supplies grant deeds. Learning how to handle this part of the process is worth the effort because you probably will be doing the same thing over and over again.

Once the deed has been properly signed, it must be recorded. This may be the easiest part of the whole transaction. All you have to do is go to the county recorder's office, pay whatever fees are required, and record the deed.

A good relationship with a title company offers many opportunities to save money. Sit down with a title officer and discuss what each of you will do. Explain that you want to pay only one title policy cost and only one escrow fee, even though the property may be bought from one party and sold to another at the same time. You'll have to negotiate on this, but point out that you are going

RECORDING REQUESTED BY

AND WHEN RECORDED MAIL TO

NAME _____

ADDRESS _____

CITY/STATE/ZIP _____

SPACE ABOVE THIS LINE FOR RECORDER'S USE

DOCUMENTARY TRANSFER TAX $ _____

☐ COMPUTED ON FULL VALUE OF PROPERTY CONVEYED,

☐ OR COMPUTED ON FULL VALUE LESS LIENS AND

ENCUMBRANCES REMAINING AT TIME OF SALE.

ASSESSOR'S PARCEL

_____

Signature of Declarant or Agent determining tax. Firm Name

Joint Tenancy Grant Deed

FOR A VALUABLE CONSIDERATION, receipt of which is hereby acknowledged,

hereby GRANT(S) to

, AS JOINT TENANTS

the real property in the

County of the State of California, described as:

Dated:

STATE OF CALIFORNIA

COUNTY OF _____ }SS.

On _____ Before me, the undersigned, a Notary

Public in and for said County and State, personally appeared

_____

_____

_____

_____

_____ , known to me to be the

person _____ whose name _____ subscribed

to the within instrument and acknowledged that _____

executed the same.

(seal)

_____

_____

Name (Typed or Printed)

Notary Public in and for said County and State

MAIL TAX

STATEMENTS TO: _____

      Name   Address   Zip

FOR NOTARY SEAL OR STAMP

Figure 12.2   Joint Tenancy Grant Deed Commonly Used to Transfer Ownership

RECORDING REQUESTED BY

AND WHEN RECORDED MAIL TO

NAME

ADDRESS

CITY/STATE/ZIP

QUITCLAIM DEED

$\longleftrightarrow$

SPACE ABOVE THIS LINE FOR RECORDER'S USE
DOCUMENTARY TRANSFER TAX $
☐ COMPUTED ON FULL VALUE OF PROPERTY CONVEYED,
☐ OR COMPUTED ON FULL VALUE LESS LIENS AND
   ENCUMBRANCES REMAINING AT TIME OF SALE.

_____

Signature of Declarant or Agent determining tax. Firm Name

This Indenture, Made the _____ day of _____ ,20_____ ,
_____

Between _____
_____
_____ , the part _____ of the first part.
And _____
_____ , the part _____ of the second part,
Witnesseth: That the said part ____ of the first part, for and in consideration of the sum of

_____ Dollars,
lawful money of the United States of America, to _____ in hand paid
by _____
the said part ____ , of the second part, the receipt whereof is hereby acknowledged, ha __
remised, released and forever quitclaimed, and by these presents do __remise, release and
forever quitclaim unto the said part ____ of the second part, and to _____ heirs and
assigns, all th ____certain lot__ , piece __ or parcel__ of land, situate, lying and being in
the _____ County of _____ and
State of _____ , and bounded and particularly described as follows, to-wit:

DEED—QUITCLAIM

Figure 12.3   Quitclaim Deed Used in Special Circumstances

Together with all and singular the tenements, hereditaments and appurtenances thereunto belonging, or in anywise appertaining, and to the reversion and reversions, remainder and re-mainders, rents, issues and profits thereof; and also the estate, right, title, interest, _____ _____ property possession, claim and demand whatsoever, as well in law as in equity, of the said part ___ of the first part, of, in or to the said premises, and every part and parcel thereof with the appurtenances.

To Have and to Hold, all and singular the said premises, together with the appurtenances, unto the said part ___ of the second part, and to _____ heirs and assigns forever

In Witness Whereof, The said part _____ of the first part ha ___ hereunto set _____ hand _____ and seal _____ the day and year first above written.

Signed Sealed and Delivered in the Presence of

_____   }   _____ [SEAL]

_____   _____ [SEAL]

_____   _____ [SEAL]

State of California,

County of _____   }SS.

On _____ , 20 ___ before me, a Notary Public in and for said County and State, personally appeared _____

_____

_____ ,known to me to be the person _____whose name _____ subscribed to the within Instrument, and acknowledged to me that____ he ___ executed the same. Witness my hand and official seal.

_____

Notary Public in and for the County and State

Title Order No. _____   Escrow or Loan No. _____

Mail Tax Statements to

Name	Address	Zip

Figure 12.3   *Continued*

to find some title company to do this and, if this particular company is not agreeable, you will find another company that is. You should mention that you are not transferring the loan to yourself (if the lender is not federally chartered). You are buying the property subject to the existing loan. When you sell the property, the loan will be transferred from the current owners to the new buyer, bypassing you. Mention, however, that if you decide to keep and lease the property, the loan will be transferred to you and you will pay a transfer fee at that time.

Any information from the lender, such as a beneficiary statement, should be supplied by the troubled owners or by their representative. You should bear no expense in this matter. Some lenders will try to charge you extra for providing it, but they are usually required to supply this information to the people borrowing from them. Any information regarding the condition of the account, the amount of money owed, and other financial matters should be supplied by the lender without additional charge.

People have become so used to large closing costs that they have a lot of trouble thinking along different lines. To succeed as a specialist in distress property, you must do every legitimate thing possible to save on every expense.

Use of Installment Notes

A deed is usually the collateral for a debt, and the debt is evidenced by a note. So the deed and the note go together as a package.

Always check to see that you have copies of both the deed and the note when you are analyzing a transaction. Be sure all the facts on both documents conform to the facts as you have them. Also, when you order a preliminary title report, be sure the title report has the same information as you have on the deed and on the note.

On the sample Installment Note shown in Figure 12.4, notice the paragraph under the heading. Do not destroy the original note. It must be surrendered, together with the deed of trust securing the note, when the loan has been fully paid and title to the property is reconveyed.

Removing Liens and Judgments

Except for the first mortgage loan, you can possibly remove any other loans and liens on the property without paying dollar for dollar. The most difficult lien to discount is the second mortgage. But if the lienholder is out of the area and not able to spend the

Installment Note
Interest Included
(Balance Due Date)

Do Not Destroy This Original Note: When paid, said Original Note, together with the Deed of Trust securing same must be surrendered to Trustee for Cancellation and retention before reconveyance will be made.

$ _____

        (Amount)   (Location)   (Date)

In installments as herein stated, for value received, we jointly and severally promise to pay to

_____

_____

or order, at _____ the sum of

_____ DOLLARS

with the interest from _____ on unpaid

principal at the rate of _____ percent per annum; principal and interest payable in installments of

_____ DOLLARS

or more on the _____ day of each _____ month, beginning on the _____ day

of _____ and continuing until the ____ day of _____

on which day the unpaid balance of said principal sum, with the unpaid interest due thereon, shall become due and payable.

      Each payment shall be credited first on interest then due and the remainder on principal; and interest shall thereupon cease upon the principal so credited. Should default be made in payment of any installment when due, the whole sum of principal and interest shall at the option of the holder of this note become immediately due. Principal and interest payable in lawful money of the United States. If action be instituted on this note we promise to pay such sum as the Court may fix as attorney fee. This note is secured by:

_____   _____

      (Signature)   (Signature)

Figure 12.4   Installment Note for Property Purchase

time necessary to monitor the loan, you have a very good chance of getting a discount.

Follow these important steps to remove liens:

1. Get complete information on all mortgages and liens on the property. Your search can begin with the homeowners, but the most reliable data will come from the county recorder's office. Compile a list of the date each lien was placed, the amount, the terms, the conditions, and the original agreement between the owners and the lienholder. Here again, you must check the laws in your particular state. Above all, check to see if any of the lenders are federally chartered and if any new rulings affect your deal.

2. Work out a plan for each lien involved. In other words, sketch out what will happen to each lienholder under three conditions: (a) if the property goes into strict foreclosure and is sold at auction; (b) if the second lienholder steps in, pays off the amount of the first loan in arrears, and assumes control of the property; and (c) if the lienholder makes some kind of reasonable settlement with you.

Nobody is in a better position than you are to explain the ramifications of these scenarios to the second lienholder. If the property goes into foreclosure, nobody is likely to get the full amount owed, especially not those junior to the first mortgagee. If the second mortgage lienholder takes over the property, he or she will have to do essentially the same things you would do: fix up the property, repair it, and sell it or rent it. Settling with you, on the other hand, will save the second lienholder time and probably leave him or her with more money in the end.

To reinforce your point, tell the second lienholder what you have discovered about the neighborhood and share the same dollars-and-cents data about the property that you gave to the troubled owners. State how much money it will take to bring the loans current and the pitfalls that await. Describe the problems with the property, the repair work needed, and the time and attention necessary to get the property fixed up and a sale completed. The essence of your argument should be that the lienholder would waste time and effort trying to make something of the property. He or she would be better off taking a cash settlement from you. After all, the lienholder undoubtedly has other business and other investments, and making this loan was just another way to put money to work. Stress how much time, money, and interest will be needed to make the property profitable, and the deal will be yours.

The Importance of Discounting Liens

Discounting liens helps you accomplish some very significant things. First and foremost, negotiating good deals on liens and second mortgages lets you double and triple your profit opportunities. (See Case Study 12.1.)

When you negotiate with the troubled owners, use the face amount of the liens in the financial analysis. They are thinking in terms of the full amount owed. They remember the interest and late charges due. So when you are negotiating the final purchase price, the owners are deducting from an already reduced market value the full value of all the liens on the property. The less you pay, the more reserves you have to work with and the more profit you can make.

As for the lienholders, they all want to solve their problem permanently if it doesn't cost them too much. Very few of them really want to get involved in the mess of a foreclosure action. Taking over properties and trying to unload them again is very cumbersome. The people who put money into second and third mortgages don't want to buy other people's problems. They want clean 10 to 15 percent returns with the least possible effort. And the liens placed by vendors and suppliers are usually desperate moves in an attempt to salvage something out of a bad business deal. Very few think they are going to get even fifty cents on the dollar out of their liens. Therefore, most will welcome some kind of effort from someone like you, who will help them recover something.

Negotiating a discount with a second lienholder requires skill. You start out with the same basic sales and negotiating techniques that you used with the troubled borrowers:

"I'm here to see if I can help you and you can help me."

"I do not need this deal."

"I'm working on other deals."

"I'm willing to make this deal if you're reasonable."

"I would like to help everybody concerned."

"I would like the troubled borrowers to preserve their credit."

"I would like you to get something for your money."

Remember that none of this deal was of your making. You are there to see if you can help. If you cannot, you will quite contentedly walk away to another, less complicated, deal.

Case Study 12.1

When home loan rates started soaring for the first time, I decided that a good territory to look in for deals would be a nearby condominium tract of about 300 units called The Village. It lay adjacent to a freeway in the direction of growth. Most of the units were well cared for, and the neighborhood had a mature appearance. More importantly, because I was familiar with this area, I knew that the average sales prices per square foot were less than in the other tracts in the area.

A typical unit in The Village was 1,350 square feet with 3 bedrooms, 2 baths, a two-car garage, air conditioning, a view porch, and several other extras. Comparables at that time were around $90,000.

When the tract opened in 1975, lenders were offering thirty-year loans at 8.5 to 9 percent interest. Most units sold for $49,900, with a $9,900 down payment and a first loan of $40,000.

After I decided to specialize in The Village, I noticed that units were sold within thirty days after listing. I also was aware of both an industrial park and a commercial office park being developed nearby. Adjoining areas had already been built out. The developers had put a lot of good planning and attention to detail into The Village. Now the homeowners association was doing an equally good job of keeping up the tract. All in all, The Village would pass anyone's test for a fine place to live and raise a family.

Within a few weeks after I selected this tract as my territory, I spotted a For Sale by Owner sign on a corner unit in a lovely section. I called the number and left my name on a recording machine. After repeating this about five or six times over the next several days without an answer, I decided to drop in during the evening to see why my calls had not been answered.

The owner of the unit was a former real estate broker who had just finished the legalities of an unhappy divorce. He apologized for not returning my calls, but he felt so depressed that he could not bring himself to attend to his unhappy financial affairs.

I assured him that I was not pressing him. But I said that I had several possible purchases to consider and wanted to consider his unit among them.

Quickly I learned that his unit was typical: 1,350 square feet, 3 bedrooms, 2 baths, two-car

continued on next page

Case Study 12.1 Continued

garage, air conditioning, and other amenities. It was in good shape considering his domestic situation.

But the owner's financial shape was not as good. Using my Financial Analysis form, I discovered the following:

First loan balance	$38,500
First loan principal and interest	$314.50
Taxes	75.50
Association fee and insurance	59.50
Total monthly payments	$449.50

In addition, the owner had a second loan of $20,000 for five years with interest-only monthly payments of $200, a third loan of $12,500 for one year without monthly payments but now due with interest as a single payment, and a lien from a furniture store.

Worst of all, notices of default had been filed several months ago. He now had about two weeks to bring his payments up to date. After that, he'd have twenty-one days before foreclosure, but he'd have to pay off the whole loan and the back payments.

The owner's overall debt picture looked like this:

First loan (at 8.75 percent)	$38,500.00
Four monthly payments in arrears	1,799.20
Second loan (at 12 percent)	20,000.00
Five monthly payments in arrears	1,000.00
Third loan now due	12,500.00
Interest now due at 16 percent	2,000.00
Furniture lien	4,500.00
Total	$80,299.20

The owner knew that the sales price for comparable units was around $90,000. He felt his true remaining equity was between $4,000 and $8,000. His major problem was time and getting someone to come up with the cash that he needed to make himself current on the loans. That cash was as follows:

First loan payments in arrears	$ 1,799.20
Second loan payments in arrears	1,000.00
Principal and interest on third loan	14,500.00
Furniture lien	4,500.00
Estimated cash to seller	6,000.00
Estimated closing expenses	750.00
Total cash needed	$28,549.20

But time was running out on the owner. He had not contacted his creditors, and a strict foreclosure seemed imminent.

For $10 down, he gave me three days to see if I could structure a deal to take over the property and cure his financial problems. At the end of that time, I agreed to buy his unit for $91,000 less a 6 percent broker's fee to myself, or $85,540. After paying debts of $80,299.20,

continued on next page

Case Study 12.1 Continued

he would walk away with $5,240.80 in cash. I would pay him this cash as follows: $240.80 upon execution of a grant deed to me and $5,000.00 within twelve months. We also agreed that any savings I made negotiating with his creditors would be payment to me for my time and effort. He was more than satisfied with the proposal.

First I contacted the furniture store and found that the true amount owed was $3,100, not $4,500. But the store would release the lien and settle for $2,500 cash in six months. I asked for a letter covering this agreement.

Then I proceeded to the third loan owner, who was an out-of-state retired person. I truthfully explained the whole situation and laid out my plan. If the third loan owner agreed to give me six months to work something out, I would contact the second loan owner and renegotiate a new second loan for 85 percent of the fair market value of the unit, or $77,350. For this I would pay 1.5 percent more interest, or 13.5 percent, on a new five-year basis. Part of the second loan, $38,500, would be used to pay off the payments in arrears on the first loan. The remaining $38,850.00 would be disbursed in this manner:

Existing second loan	$20,000
Payments in arrears on second loan	1,000
Payment on existing third loan	6,500
Payments in arrears on third loan	2,000
Furniture lien	2,500
Payment to owner	5,000

This would leave $1,850 to cover closing and miscellaneous expenses. There would then be a new third for only $6,000 (the original $12,500 less $6,500 from proceeds of the new second loan), a straight note at the original 16 percent interest all due and payable in one payment in five years.

With this plan, I would have only $240.80 in cash at risk. But if the third loan holder insisted on being paid in full, my cash required would be $6,240.80. At that point, I would have had to ask myself these questions:

What would the return on my investment be if I sold the property in one, two, or three years?

How does that return on investment compare to other investment choices I have at the moment?

Can I afford to be out $6,000 more at this time?

My analysis showed that the return on $6,000 would have been above average in this case, and I probably would have gone ahead. But the third loan holder and everyone else agreed to my plan, and the dust settled within three months. Here's how my new condominium looked on my balance sheet:

Down payment	$ 240.80
First loan	38,500.00
Second loan	38,850.00
Third loan	6,000.00
Total cost	$83,590.80

continued on next page

Case Study 12.1 Continued

The market value at closing was about $94,000. I had created over $10,000.00 in profit with only $240.80 down. More importantly, my asset was then appreciating at over 15 percent per year. So I was increasing my equity dramatically.

What about cash flow?

Principal and interest on first loan	$314.80
Principal on second loan	437.06
Taxes	90.00
Association fee	63.50
Total	$905.36

My average rent the first six months was $600, which meant a monthly negative cash flow of about $300. I projected rental increases that would bring me to a break-even point in three years.

Over a two-year period I bought three other units at The Village and rented them all out. When the real estate market moved higher, I sold all four of the units at a good profit.

All in all, you should get into the habit of trying to discount liens and second mortgages. Troubled property often is encumbered with them, so you have a greater opportunity to make a bigger profit. Don't fear involvement or complications. The more complicated the deal and the more problems there are, the more ammunition you have to convince lienholders that you're offering them a great opportunity to get out with something.

Don't be surprised if your discounting habit brings new leads to the surface. If you make a satisfactory deal with a lienholder, the chances are that he or she will mention another business opportunity similar to this one. But be careful what you spend time on. Sticking to your own territory gives you a real advantage.

Key Points to Remember About Existing Mortgages

The property with an existing mortgage on it must be handled with care. Most lenders would like to continually rewrite mortgages, always increasing the interest rate, increasing their yield, and making more and more profit from a single loan on an existing unit. As a buyer, however, you want to buy the property subject to the existing loan so you can get the benefit of the older interest rate and the lower monthly payments. This is possible in most states—but you have to take great care with the details. Mortgages with federal savings and loans are especially tricky, because they can enforce due-on-sale clauses.

Here are some tips on handling existing mortgages:

• Always assume that the lender would like to rewrite the mortgage at a higher interest rate with larger monthly payments, and be very careful to do everything correctly when acquiring property. This is especially important in today's financial climate.

• Any property with an existing conventional loan from a non-federal savings and loan can usually be purchased subject to the existing loan, unless specific laws say otherwise.

• When buying property subject to the existing loan, you need be concerned only with the sellers' equity or the sellers' obligations in addition to the first mortgage.

Special Escrow Instructions

If you use an escrow officer, the specially designed Escrow Instructions form in Figure 12.5 is recommended. If you close a deal in any other way, I recommend that you at least review this sheet for the following points:

• Repeat all financial and descriptive information, and be sure it conforms to previous written agreements. Total consistency is a must here.

• Add on all negotiated items (see the Equity Purchase Agreement, Figure 12.1) as final, absolute numbers. There should be no floating unknowns.

• Leave prorated items until last, perhaps as a part of last-minute changes in negotiating strategies.

The Escrow Instructions form included here, like the other sample forms in this book, is designed to be coherent and understandable. It covers all the unknowns that fall into general categories.

Checking for Extras

After the trustee files a notice of default, you may pay off the charges and reinstate the loan any time during the three-month reinstatement period. These charges include delinquent

Escrow Instructions   (Page 1 Of 2)
(Buyer and Seller)

Escrow No. _____

_____ , 20 _____

    The undersigned Buyer and Seller hereby mutually understand and agree that the statements set forth herein shall be construed, by all those concerned, as unconditionally incorporated in these Buyer's and Seller's escrow instructions, to wit:

1. Buyer will hand you $ _____
2. _____
3. Proceeds from loan to be procured by Buyer   _____
4. Buyer has paid outside of this escrow, to Seller
    (with which you are not be concerned) $ _____
5. Broker will hand you, and same shall be returned to Broker if this escrow
    is not consumated $ _____
6. Encumbrance of record, approximate unpaid balance $ _____
7. $ _____
8. Buyer will hand you a new purchase price encumbrance $ _____
9. TOTAL CONSIDERATION $ _____

    and any additional funds and documents required from me to enable you to comply with these instructions, all of which you are authorized to use provided on or before _____
    you can obtain a standard Owner's or Joint Protection Policy or Title insurance, with the usual title company's exceptions, with liabilty to the amount of total consideration, on real property in the County of _____ State of _____
viz;
as per map recorded in Book _____ page _____ of maps of said county, known as _____

Title to Appear Vested In _____

Subject To:

Figure 12.5   Escrow Instructions Form Used with Escrow Officer

(A) _____ installment(s) of general and special county and city taxes, including any special district levies, payments of which are included therein and collected therewith, of the current fiscal year, not delinquent, including taxes for the ensuing year, if any, a lien but not yet payable.

(B) Assessments and bonds of record, unpaid balance **$** _____

(C) Conditions, restrictions, reservations, covenants, rights, rights of way, easements, and the exception of minerals, oil, gas, water, carbons and hydrocarbon substances in, on, or under said land, now of record, and in deed to file, affecting the use and occupancy of said property.

(D) Deed of Trust, now of record, and note secured thereby, approximate unpaid balance of _____ as per their terms; further approval of which is waived through this escrow by Buyer and Seller, except that principal and interest repayable in monthly installments of $_____ including interest _____ % per annum, plus impounds, if any. If unpaid balance shows to be more or less than the said amount shown above then you are to keep the total consideration the same by accordingly adjusting

_____

(E) Deed of Trust, to file (New Loan as stated above) securing an indebtedness in the amount of $ _____

(F) Deed of Trust, to file, as part of the purchase price, on your usual short form, executed by above Vestee(s) in favor of _____

_____

securing a note of $_____ , dated as written, with interest on unpaid principal at _____ % per annum from _____ principal and interest payable in installments of $ _____ or more on the _____ day of each month, commencing on the _____ day of _____ 20 _____ and continuing until _____

In accordance with the manner specified, the following are to be adjusted to prorated to

(_____) Fire Insurance on Property　　(_____) Interest on Encumbrance of Record　　(_____) Taxes

(_____) Impounds Held by Beneficiary　(_____) Interest on Purchase Money Note　　(_____) Rentals

Signature_____   Signature_____

Figure 12.5 Escrow Instructions Form Used with Escrow Officer *Continued*

payments (interest and principal), late charges, and costs and fees incurred during the foreclosure—including payment for professional services rendered by trustees, attorneys, and other advisers; cash disbursements for delinquent obligations, such as taxes and debt service; and the trustee expenses necessary to foreclose.

The borrower is not obligated to pay all the expenses actually incurred in enforcing the terms of the trust deed. Nevertheless, excessive costs are commonly included in the amount of the lien. Since these fees are restricted by statute, beneficiaries and trustees often try to include them in the guise of expenses. To determine if an expense is justifiable, use three simple guidelines:

1. Was the expenditure necessary? Was it actually incurred in enforcing the terms of the trust deed or mortgage?

2. Does state law limit the amount of these charges?

3. Is there a receipt for the expenditure?

Voluntary/Involuntary Sales

In today's difficult financing climate, one of the poorest ways to buy troubled properties is at a sale of properties seized by the IRS. Courts have ruled such sales an involuntary transfer of assets, and in such a case the lender may automatically accelerate the loan and call for full repayment. Thus, you may think you got a great deal in a tax sale, but when you send your payments to the first lender of record, the lender may well call the loan.

The best way to buy a property you may like that has a tax lien on it is before the sale. The courts protect a free or voluntary transfer of equity but usually not an involuntary one.

When you talk to troubled owners who have tax liens on their property, explain these facts:

• If the loan is called after the tax sale (as it most probably will be), their credit rating will be affected in a negative way.

• Any purchaser at a tax auction will bid less than what you're offering, because the purchaser knows that refinancing will be necessary.

A tax sale must be avoided if the owners want to have something left to show for the property.

When the property is encumbered by tax liens, it's better to deal directly with the government before any "IRS-seized" sale.

The owners could freely give you a second trust deed to raise the cash that will satisfy their tax obligations. Or you could take over the payments on the first deed and ensure that the first loan cannot be called in case of a tax sale by making the loan payments current.

The Final Payment

When you are ready to make the final payment to the troubled owners of the property, do it outside the house when they are moving. Never pay them inside the house before they leave. Then it's a good idea to immediately have all the locks changed.

The owners must understand that no game playing is allowed. They cannot get the money and then decide to stay or rip out the appliances and otherwise ruin the house. This deal is strictly business, with both sides sticking to the letter of the agreement.

Make sure they understand that the deal is not consummated until they have vacated the house totally. They must be in their car or truck moving with their furniture before you give them the final payment. But you can stay on friendly terms by reminding them that, when they get back on their feet, you are willing to help in any way possible.

I learned this rule the hard way, on one of my first deals. It was an offering that came to me through a church friend. Mr. and Mrs. S., who had five children, wanted to sell their 4 bedroom, 2 bath home (in a neighborhood I knew very well) before they lost it. After a quick analysis and discussion, I made a fair offer, which they accepted.

The closing was set for Thursday, April 15. Mr. S. had signed all the papers early and was in another state looking for a new job and a new house. Mrs. S. called me on the Monday before closing and asked if she could stay in the house over the weekend. She promised to leave the following Monday. Her reasons had to do with her children's health, a church, and a moving van. I saw nothing wrong with letting her stay for a few more days, but I cautiously suggested moving the closing to Monday. But Mrs. S. said Mr. S. needed the proceeds on Friday to secure both a new home and a moving van, so I agreed to a three-day delay in her vacating.

After the closing, the three-day delay turned into a thirteen-month nightmare. It turned out that Mr. S. was divorcing his wife. Furthermore, three of the five children were foster children, so several layers of state and local bureaucrats became interested in Mrs. S. The welfare department advised me, after three months, that they were "looking into and after Mrs. S. and her children."

Wisely, I waited everyone out and was politely patient. I helped Mrs. S. find another place to rent, and finally I had full possession of my purchase. It was still a good deal for me, but from that transaction on, I determined to close only on vacated and inspected dwellings.

CHAPTER 13

Stage III: Auction Time

In business, when all else fails, there is always the auction block.

—*Anonymous*

When I first became interested in distress properties, I was told that buying at auctions was a waste of time. Most of the reasons I was given had to do with the large numbers of bidders and the lack of terms. I can add a few more reasons not to go, but the truth is that sometimes you can make a better deal bidding at an auction than you can negotiating with the owner. Also, if you missed the property during the earlier stages, your only chance for a deal may be at the auction.

There are several different types of auctions for foreclosure properties. Besides trustee, mortgage, and tax sales, probate and local government sales often take the auction form.

This chapter concentrates on the trustee sale auction, or trust deed auction. If you're from a mortgage state, you'll have to make the appropriate adjustments. My experiences tell me, however, that the two auction procedures are quite similar.

Once I'd decided that auctions might not be so bad, the first thing I did was to try to learn about the trustee sale procedures. As a subscriber to a daily service, I was receiving notices of trustee sales and default postings. For the first week or so I did nothing but read the notices to see if I could understand what they were saying. I noticed the different locations that were covered. I noticed the types of houses. I noticed the amounts of money involved. I noticed all the other things that are an important part of the foreclosure process.

After I felt comfortable with this basic information, I began concentrating on my own area. I listed the cities included in my area, along with the Thomas Guide coordinates or map coordinates that would interest me. Then I decided to concentrate, within my area, on single-family homes in a certain price range and condominiums in a certain price range. I checked out the locations of the trustee sale auctions and decided to attend my first one.

At the auction I mingled with the people who were planning on bidding. I told them honestly that this was my first visit to an auction and that I wanted to learn about the process. One of them mentioned that the service providing my weekly newsletter had a special meeting scheduled for the following week where an attorney would explain auction procedures. Another attendee gave me his version of how things happen at trustee sales. He gave me a couple of tips about things to watch out for. More than once, I heard from people attending that you have to be sure the trustee sale you're bidding on does involve a first trust deed (if that's what you're interested in). Everyone cautioned against making a bid until I was sure of all my facts.

Right on time the auctioneer showed up and began reading the list of postponements and cancellations. For a while I thought there wouldn't be any business transacted that day. But as soon as the paperwork was out of the way, the auctioneer began with the property that practically everyone there was interested in. I don't know too many of the details because the property was out of my area, but I do know that the opening bid was $66,653.12 and the winning bid was $172,300.00 and that the bidding took over half an hour. I thought it was strange that the bidding went so slowly, but I did deduce that considerable strategy was involved in coming up with the right bid. I later developed my own strategy regarding the bidding process.

After a year or so of trial and error, I finally created for myself a pretty satisfactory system for understanding and evaluating deals and bidding on properties at trustee sales. I break the whole process into five phases, which are discussed in the rest of this chapter:

1. Getting information
2. "Snooping"
3. Calculating the bid
4. Going to the auction
5. Winning the bid

Phases 1, 2, and 3 take place in the time between notification of the trustee sale and the actual auction.

Getting Information

You usually have at least two weeks and sometimes as many as four weeks between notification and the auction. When I find a property in my area that I want to bid on, I copy all the information on the Trustee Sale Information form (see Figure 13.1). So that I don't get confused, I highlight in yellow the following information: trustee sale telephone number; address and city of the property; day, time, and place of the auction; the assessors parcel number (APN); legal description; and anything about the property that might make it a little special (like a 4 bedroom house, a condominium, or a newly built property).

At a stationery store, I bought an accordion file with slots numbered from one to thirty-one, and I slip each filled-out form into the slot for the appropriate date. For instance, if the auction is scheduled for the fourteenth of the month, I put it in the file numbered 14.

Once a week, on Thursdays, I schedule the following week's activity, using a form titled This Week's Action (see Figure 13.2). The first thing I do to plan my week is to call the trustee to see if the auction is still scheduled. Usually two out of three are cancelled or postponed. I discard the Trustee Sale Information sheets for the cancelled ones. The postponed ones I simply refile according to the new date. The trustee sales that are still scheduled are listed on the form.

Then I do more research on the properties that are still scheduled. I use the middle columns of the form to check off the sources of information as I consult them. One thing I've found handy is a real estate information service that allows me, through my computer, to tap into the county records. This kind of information is available in most states, but you have to seek it out. I found out about it by asking my title company representative if he knew where I could get quick information at a low cost. He gave me the names of three competing services. From various other sources I get information regarding the present market in that area. How many similar properties are on the market? What have similar properties sold for in the recent past? Putting all this information together as a comparable market analysis, I come up with an idea of what the property would be worth at auction. This is only a preliminary figure, because I have to actually see the property to come up with something more specific to base a bid on.

If the numbers look okay (and usually half of them don't), I then arrange to see the property. Some weeks I may see one or two properties. Other weeks I may see none.

Snooping

When I see a property, I try to see it at the worst possible time. I want to see it when school is out, when it is the busiest, and when

Trustee Sale Information

Phone Number: _____ Date of Sale: _____

Address: _____

City: _____

Trustor: _____

Address: _____

Phone: _____

Owner: _____

Address: _____

Phone: _____

Beneficiary: _____

Address: _____

Phone: _____

Legal Description: _____

APN: _____

TRUST DEEDS	
1st	_____
2nd	_____
3rd	_____
4th	_____
5th	_____
6th	_____
7th	_____

Use: _____

Square Feet: _____

Lot Size: _____

Year Built: _____

Rooms: _____

Loan No.: _____ Trust Deed Sale No.: _____

Sale Date: _____ Location: _____

Time: _____ Approximate Bid: _____

Other: _____

Postponements	Neighborhood Information		House Details
	Good Points	Bad Points	IRS?
			Liens?
			Taxes?
			Vacant?
			Problems?

Figure 13.1 Trustee Sale Information Form

This Week's Action										
MON.		TUES.		WED		THURS.		FRI.		
Date of Sale	Property Address	Type of Property	Time/ Place	MLS	County Records	Title Company	SEE	Other	Result	

Figure 13.2 This Week's Action Form to Schedule Auctions to Attend

all the cars are there. In other words, I want to see it when a possible new buyer might see the property, too.

I get out of the car and walk around. I see whether the utilities are on. I look inside the house if it is possible and if it is safe. I talk to tenants in the area if it is possible and safe. I have a checklist on location factors. Is there enough parking? What is the mix of condos, single-family homes, and stores in the neighborhood? What are the good points? What are the bad points? Are any junk cars around? Are there any graffiti-marked walls? Is the neighborhood being upgraded or going downhill?

This sort of "snooping" is very important. It helps me get a feel for the value of the property. If I'm still interested in it, I look to see if any new homes are being built in the area. If there are new homes, how will they affect the price of the old ones?

A day or two before the trustee sale, I call again to see if the sale is still on. In my experience, about half of the homes I'm still interested in are either cancelled or postponed at this point. If a property is still scheduled for sale, I either do a preliminary title search myself or use a service to get this information.

If I do the title searching myself, I use the following procedure:

1. Check the county records (usually on microfiche) for the appropriate document year and number.

2. Get copies from the record room.

3. Check the title to see if the property is secured by a first trust deed, if it has been bought with an FHA or VA loan, and if the loan has been assumed or is "subject to."

4. If there are any doubts, check the title on the previous owners.

5. Check the General Index or whatever else records IRS liens.

This procedure tells me whether the loan I want to bid on is a first deed of trust, tells me more about the liens (if any) on the property, and tells me if the owners have done anything that would cause me not to be interested.

The day of the trustee sale I call the utility companies to see if the utilities are still connected.

Calculating the Bid

With all this information on hand, I make my final analysis to see how much I can bid. For this I use the Auction Worksheet

shown in Figure 13.3. This is decision-making time, the most critical part of the process.

With all the information I've gathered to date, I come up with
a sales price based on when I think the sale will occur and when it
will close. If the property is occupied, I may have to add two or
three more months for the property to be vacated and fixed up. If
the market values are going up, I can estimate that the market
value of the property will be a little higher six months from now.
Conversely, if the market values are going down, I have to figure a
little lower sales price six months from now.

From years of experience, I know how much a typical closing
costs. I know all the expenses, all the surprise fees, all the garbage
fees. I always put in a full 6 percent for a broker's commission, assuming that I won't be able to sell the property myself. If I sell it
myself, then I get a little extra. I figure the cost of money at the
prime rate plus 2 percent, and I keep that as a separate expense,
even though I usually put up the money myself. Then I have a
minimum profit requirement for a particular area. Although I
usually shoot for a 10 percent profit, my average is greater than
that. Often I would consider taking less profit for special reasons.
Those reasons could range from having surplus funds on hand
that I would like to have working to knowing that the property will
turn over very quickly against a backdrop of possibly dropping
prices in the area.

Now I'm ready to go to the auction. Before I go, I always stop
by to see the property one more time. (See Case Study 13.1.) This
visit is just a safeguard, to verify all my assumptions and conclusions about the property. The one time I didn't stop by for a final
look was almost a catastrophe. I had seen this 4 bedroom home in
City Gardens on a tour that included nine other properties. It
looked like it needed a lot of work, but I didn't see this property at
its worst possible time, so it seemed alright to me. Also, I didn't get
out of the car and walk around because I was in a hurry. So I did
not follow through with the rest of my normal procedures.

On the day of the auction, all the numbers looked fine. But
once again, I was pressured by other matters, so I did not have the
time to stop and review this property. I was very surprised to be
the only bidder. I won it and decided to see it on my way home.

I really got sick when I saw it the second time. First of all, the
neighborhood was not as nice as I originally thought. Second, that
area of the city was recovering from a very bad image. More importantly, the property only had a one-and-a-half-car garage. I
had not realized before that the garage was added on. You had to
walk from outside the garage into the front foyer to get to the
kitchen with the groceries. The existing garage had been con-
verted into a large family room.

Auction Worksheet   Date _____

Address _____ City _____

Sq. Ft. _____ BR _____ BA _____

Overall Grade

Best		Average				Worst
9	8	7	6	5	4	3	2	1

Features _____

Close Streets _____

Map Coordinates _____

Range of Prices _____

Actives _____

Comps _____

New _____

Inside _____   Town Hall _____

Utilities _____   Sales _____

Neighbors _____   Prices _____

"Mix" _____   Parking _____

Good _____   Bad _____

Improved Value _____   Other _____

	Minimum	Probable	Maximum
List	=	=	=
Sell	=	=	=
Inside Repairs	=	=	=
Outside	=	=	=
Arrears	=	=	=
COE Cost	4% =	=	=
Hold Cost	4% =	=	=
Broker	6% =	=	=
Profit	10%=	=	=
Other	=	=	=
Total Cost			
Maximum Bid			

Month	Month	Month	Month	Month	Month	Month

Figure 13.3   Auction Worksheet Used for Financial Analysis of Property Up for Auction

Case Study 13.1

Be on the lookout for neighborhoods that have a large number of rental houses. By large numbers I mean more than one out of six (more than about 17 percent). In these places prices might be very unstable. It's best to avoid areas where a few panicked sellers could depress fair market values for the rest of the owners.

For example, I was tracking a home on White Birch Lane. It was a four-year-old 3 bedroom, 2 bath home of about 1,155 square feet on a 7,000 square foot lot. All my homework was done, and all the numbers were crunched. I was prepared to bid $110,000 based on a re-sale estimate of between $149,000 and $155,000. The opening bid was set at $87,580.22, and I felt like another new deal was about to happen.

On the day of the auction, sticking to the game plan, I revisited the neighborhood. Everything looked good except that I saw two new For Rent signs in addition to the two that had been there on my first trip. This was an automatic "red light." These four rentals were very close together. I stopped at one of the houses and learned that about one in four of the homes in this tract were rentals. Some of the tenants were problem people.

What I learned cancelled my interest in this auction. Even if I could have bought at the opening bid, this property wouldn't be worth the risk. I have no doubt about this as a business decision.

As a follow-up, I learned that two bidders were at the auction and that the winner paid $106,500. The property was rented to troublesome tenants, so it took several months for the whole process to work for the new buyer.

Unfortunately, during this period two of the absentee owners who had their homes listed for sale dropped their asking prices dramatically. The first sold a house similar to the one I was interested in for $139,000 (it was listed for $152,500). The second dropped his price from an original listing of $157,500 to $137,500—a full $20,000, or about 13 percent off the market. By then all prices in this neighborhood were affected. Worse than the lower price was the uncertainty planted in the minds of future buyers. They would naturally ask themselves, "Where is the bottom here? Is something else wrong here that I don't know about?"

I was certainly happy that I stuck to my rules of bidding. You must always remember the basics in real estate. Murphy's law works full speed in distress property sales. But if you stick to the rules and remember the lessons of the past, you'll do alright.

The house had a few good features, so we sold it and made a very small profit. But if I had stuck to my original system and seen it a second time, I would never have purchased it. I probably would not even have considered it if I had spent time looking it over at the beginning. The name of the auction game is to buy the best, to buy "cream puffs," to buy property that you won't have any problems with. You may get fewer properties this way, but you will make more money overall.

Going to the Auction

Before you go to the auction, you have to be prepared. Make sure you know about the bidding procedures. What kind of check do they want? In what increments can the bid be increased? What identification will you need? It's equally important to make sure you know everything about the condition of the property you're bidding for. Know the title history. Know the correct dollar amounts of all encumbrances. Make sure you have the right fair market value for the property as it will be when you sell it. Finally, check the time, location, and date of the sale. And keep checking right up to the morning of the sale. There are often changes and postponements at the last minute. (See Case Study 13.2.)

Before going to the auction, I also call the trustee and ask what the final opening bid will be. Let's say it's $87,220. Let's say I figured the property was worth $130,000 to me. I'd get one certified check for $90,000 and four $10,000 checks, which add up to $130,000. One check will cover me if no one else is bidding and I get the opening bid. The other checks will be enough to take me, in increments, to my maximum bid. If I take one check for $130,000, then I'll have to wait several weeks for a refund. I'd rather save the interest.

When you leave to go to the auction, take the certified checks plus information regarding the properties you're bidding on. Also take a complete list of telephone numbers of the places you might want to call if you think of other questions before you bid.

I always try to get to the auction fifteen to twenty minutes early so I have enough time to rethink my strategy. When it starts, I try to stay alert. I want to be sure I'm bidding on the right property. With a fast auctioneer, I want to be sure to get the right bid in.

When I became a serious bidder, I started avoiding contact with other bidders. For one thing, I want to spend my time thinking about what I'm going to do. For another, I don't want to be swayed by any idle conversation I may hear at the auction. In the past, people interested in the property often went around making comments about problems that might not have been true. Their idea was to discourage the other bidders from bidding.

The best strategy has always been to do your own homework. Be sure of your own conclusions regarding the property. Nor should you play the game of making phony statements. It's better to be as businesslike as possible, to pay attention to your game plan, and stick to it.

Bidder Collusion

Don't ever get involved in collusion with other bidders. Many times during the bidding someone has approached me and said, "Look, there are only two of us bidding. Let's get together and put in one bid."

My answer is standard and forthright: "No, I won't do that be-

Case Study 13.2

Once in a while you get a surprise that makes you money. Mine was the house at 6380 Pleasant Court. On June 10 it was advertised as going to auction on July 17. I knew the neighborhood and liked the area. All the homes were new. Two schools and a big park were close by. The lots were large, and there were never any problems in the neighborhood.

The house at 6380 Pleasant Court had 3 bedrooms, 2 baths, air conditioning, a three-car garage, and a fireplace in the family room. It was 1,471 square feet and sat on an 8,276 square foot lot. It was built in 1986.

I had met the owners, Mr. and Mrs. Pullman, when the first notices of default were filed. They were both working and earning above-average money. But they spent the money faster than they earned it. It was the second marriage for each of them. They each sent money on a regular basis to children from a previous marriage. They also had two children of their own who were well cared for.

When I first met the Pullmans, they had already arranged a large second loan to cover their arrears. They hoped to be caught up within a few months, so they politely declined my offer to buy their home.

I heard no more from them until I read about the scheduled auction of their home. When I tried to telephone them, I found that their phone had been disconnected.

About a week before the sale, I stopped by the house and found it vacant. The neighbor said that the Pullmans had just packed up and moved without telling anyone why. The neighbor had also heard that Mrs. Pullman had lost her job. So it seemed that the new loan never was made and the foreclosure process kept moving on.

I called the trustee and found that the approximate amount owed on the first loan was $130,000. That seemed too high for any bidder to pay. But I never do my comparable price analyses until two or three days before the sale, in case there are any changes.

Then the auction was postponed from June 27 to August 17. The sellers had filed for bankruptcy.

Then it was postponed again to September 6 to allow the trustee to get the proper releases from the bankruptcy court.

continued on next page

Case Study 13.2 Continued

I decided to do my comparables, because the house was vacant and I felt the next date would be the final auction. After much analysis, I concluded that the house could sell for between $139,000 and $145,000. So it seemed that the approximate bid of $130,000 would be too high. I needed to pay between $103,000 and $107,300 to make my usual profit.

Even though it looked hopeless, I followed this sale to the end. I almost always do, no matter how unlikely it may seem that I'll be able to buy the property.

The day of the sale was very busy for me. It would be very hard for me to attend the auction, so an hour beforehand I called the trustee to get the final opening bid of the lender. To my surprise, after analyzing the market and for his own special reasons, the lender set the opening bid at $105,577. I rearranged my schedule, stopped by the bank for a check for $107,300 (my top bid), and showed up at the auction with only a minute to spare. Besides the auctioneer, I was the only one there. I qualified. The bid was opened at $105,577 and closed at my bid of $105,578. I won the bid and owned the house.

Normally there would have been several other bidders for a house as desirable as this one. Two factors probably discouraged them. The first was the price. At $130,000 there would be little room for any profit. The second factor was the several postponements. Almost always, postponements reduce the number of interested buyers.

Five months later, on February 14, I closed the sale of this house for $144,000. After paying all expenses, including a 6 percent sales commission, I made a $16,760 profit.

cause it is against the law. It is not fair to the troubled owners. The purpose of the auction is to get as high a price as possible. That's why we should be bidding against each other." And I mean it. If it were my property on the auction block, I would not want two or three people getting together and keeping the price lower. Normally the troubled owners get what's left from the auction after the lenders are paid back.

Winning the Bid

When you hear "Going once . . . going twice . . . going the third time. . . . Any more bids? . . . Gone" and you are the winning bid, you have mixed feelings. First, you are elated that you won and have an opportunity for profit. But second, you are fearful that you may have made a mistake. At least that's usually how I feel.

All I can say is that if you do all your homework, you won't make a mistake. You'll stay elated, and you'll make good profits. But the "business deal" has only just begun.

Right after I hand my money to the auctioneer, I start working on the following list. These items are not necessarily in order. In fact, most of them must be done pretty much all at once.

• See the occupants ASAP. If the occupants are absent, leave a letter explaining the sale and requesting that they contact you.

• See the neighbors to inform them that you, as the new owner, will be upgrading the property. Leave your card.

• Start legal eviction proceedings.

• Contact your insurance agent for immediate coverage.

• If the property is vacant, change all locks.

• If the property is vacant, transfer all utilities.

• Record a new first lien on the property in the amount of your purchase price plus the amount you intend to spend on the property until its sale to a third party.

• If furniture was left by the previous occupants, post the appropriate notice. Check with the police for the form required in your locality.

• Open escrow.

• Begin your marketing program.

If you've done all your homework, you now have a good profit just waiting to be realized. And since all your expense clocks have just been activated, you must stick to your script and keep everything moving.

CHAPTER 14
Stage IV: REOs and Repos

Good bargains come from bargaining good.

—Emerson

At an auction, when no one bids more than the opening bid, the lucky lender gets the property. I say "lucky" in jest. It's really bad luck, because real estate investors in that area are saying through their lack of interest that the property is overpriced.

Property that is not sold through a foreclosure sale and that reverts to the lender becomes an REO, or "real estate owned," property. REO property is maintained as a separate asset on the lender's balance sheets.

Lenders really don't want REOs. They are visible admissions of having made bad loans. We know that the business world is awash in bad loans. Lenders are going bankrupt by the hundreds because of bad loans.

Banking laws require most lenders to keep higher reserves against REOs than against other types of loans. This is one reason they want to dispose of REOs as quickly as possible. Another reason is that REOs require property management, which is a different type of business. It means more overhead and larger losses (usually).

Lenders will go to great lengths to unload REOs. Each lender has its own special procedure, but they all are willing sellers. The trick for specialists in distress properties is to reach the person who can make the decision to sell at the right time. (See Case Study 14.1.)

Special Conditions That Work

Sometimes it takes a while for REO property to become a bargain. Soon after the lender takes back a property, there's perhaps more hope that the bank might get its money back and maybe

159

Case Study 14.1

I once stopped for lunch in Colton, California, a town west of where I owned some apartments. Nearby was a tract of lovely condominiums. As I was enjoying my burrito on the outdoor patio, I noticed several For Sale by Owner signs tacked onto telephone poles. After lunch I strolled over to the units, walked past a well-maintained clubhouse, pool, and tennis courts, and found the unit that was advertised.

Something had happened to the owners, I guess, because the unit was vacant. A Notice of Trustee Sale sign was taped to the front door. The sale was scheduled for the following day at the San Bernardino courthouse.

This wasn't my territory, but it was close enough for me to feel comfortable about being interested in it. I also believe that there's some kind of reason for everything that happens. I also had the time to work on this suspect.

I walked around the entire tract and discovered two similar units listed through local realtors. Another unit had just been taken over (through foreclosure) by a major California commercial bank. I talked to one neighbor and one worker, and all the input was positive.

Back at my office I went down through my usual procedures. I pulled up the assessor's information on my computer. I verified the taxes and the utilities. I had a title search done, and I called the realtors for current market information.

Through my research, I discovered that the same bank taking over the other unit was the lender foreclosing on this unit. By itself, this fact was no problem, but it was important enough for me to file away the information.

I figured that the unit would easily sell for between $119,000 and $125,000. I could bid up to $90,000 or $92,000. The opening bid was $82,351.17. So far so good.

I expected this sale to be postponed, but it wasn't. So I hurried up to San Bernardino to be at the courthouse steps by 9 A.M. that Friday morning. It was a day of monumental tie-ups on the freeways. I make a habit of tuning in the traffic reports from breakfast on, so I was lucky enough to leave very early and take all the open back roads. I arrived at exactly 8:59. Besides the auctioneer, I was the only person there. Wonderful, I thought. If this particular sale was early on the list, I might still be the only bidder.

Lucky again. The condo was first on the list. The auctioneer opened the bidding at $82,351.17. But before I could make my bid, his pager went off. That meant he had to stop what he was doing and phone his office. Usually the auction is stopped when there is a change in the condition of the trustee sale or in anything having to do with the trustee sale. The auctioneer went to the telephone and called his office. He must have been gone ten to twelve minutes. When he returned, I was still the only one there. He said he had been asked to delay the auction for another ten to fifteen minutes because the lender was negotiating with the owners. They were trying to work something out. The auctioneer then proceeded to read off the postponements and cancellations because apparently the condo was the only sale he had. That is why it was first on his agenda. Reading the cancellations and postponements took him about five minutes. We chatted for another five to ten minutes, and still no one showed up.

The fact that no one showed up could mean many things. It could mean that people were stuck in traffic. It could mean that people in the area called at the last minute and were told that something was going on so they decided not to bother. It could also mean that people in the area who might be interested thought the property wasn't worth the opening bid. Or it could mean that the bidders in the area were planning on bidding on something else during the day. Or it also could mean something was drastically wrong with the neighborhood that I knew nothing about. I guess inwardly I was a little relieved that I now had time to think

continued on next page

Case Study 14.1 Continued

about this situation. But I was resolved to bid if the auction went through because I was satisfied that I had done my homework.

When the auctioneer got back from his second phone call, he was really upset. He said the people at the lender's office didn't know what they were doing. He said they wanted him to postpone the auction until 2:30 that afternoon. He told them he would not be able to come back at 2:30. They said they would find someone else to conduct the auction. I was upset too, because the delay meant I would have to stay there until 2:30 or go back to my office and then return at 2:30. However, situations like this happen sometimes (although very infrequently), and you have to accept them as part of the business.

I rearranged my schedule to be able to go back and bid on the property in the afternoon. With my free time during the day, I reviewed my folder and decided that all the information I had was correct. I also called the town hall to see if something was especially wrong with that neighborhood. There was nothing. It was a good neighborhood. Everything was A-OK.

Again, I left a little early to be at the courthouse by 2:30. Apparently I had used up all my good luck in the morning. In the afternoon I had nothing but bad luck. No matter which road I tried, I lost time. I didn't reach the courthouse steps until about 3 P.M., and by that time the auctioneer was gone. I called his office and finally found out that a new auctioneer had held the sale. No bidders were present, and the property reverted to the lender. I explained to the trustee's office that I had been there in the morning and that I had waited and that I was there in the afternoon and that I really wanted that property and had a certified check and certainly it would be in their interest to get rid of the property. They agreed and were very sympathetic. They said they would discuss my request among themselves and would call me back.

I received a call the following Monday from the trustee's office, and they said they were preparing a letter to the lender. They would explain what happened and suggest that the lender deal directly with me and make the transaction based on what my opening bid would have been. To me, they stressed that they had no say in this matter. But in fairness, they would at least convey the facts to the lender. They thought the lender would be more than happy to get the money rather than the property, seeing that the lender already had property in that tract. To be more helpful, the trustee's office gave me several names of people who worked for the lender and suggested that I call them directly.

During that week I made 17 calls to this particular lender. I spoke to perhaps eight different people. I told my story at least eight times. All the people I talked to said they were interested in helping because they really didn't want the property. But nobody would do anything.

I finally decided that it was too late for me to make anything happen. The property was now on another assembly line. It would be reviewed by appraisers, by committees, by people who were all concerned about covering themselves. Of course they all would like to make money for the bank—but none of them would want to make the wrong decision.

Case histories like this and a few others have sort of discouraged me from attempting to deal directly with lenders on REO properties. Although they are a possible source of business for specialists, they are probably the last one to try.

even make a profit. But after a while reality sets in. The appraiser comes through with a lower-than-expected appraisal. The property managers charge more for their services. A few other things go wrong. At that point, when the lender is really pouring money into this property, you might be able to get a decent deal.

One person I know has developed many friendships over the years at banks with REO accounts. He tells them openly that he's only interested in the property they really are stuck with and want to get rid of at practically any price. He's a favorite with more than a few lenders, because when they call him they know they can unload the property at a reasonable price.

How does my friend make money? Well, he's a broker and a general contractor. He does all the work himself, and he sells the property himself. Best of all, he doesn't have to come up with any of his own money to do this. The lender in trouble provides financing to cover rehabilitation and sale of the property.

Many lenders will make what they call loans to "facilitate," which are loans to take a property out of their REO category. Many of these loans are below existing market rates. The loans themselves have much value. In a way, they're like U.S. Treasury bonds. If you buy a $1,000 bond paying 8 percent and the general interest rates are 8 percent, then your bond is worth $1,000. If interest rates go up to 9 or 10 percent, then your bond is worth less. Nobody would want to buy it from you if a new $1,000 bond could be bought that would pay higher interest. But if interest rates drop to 6 or 7 percent, your bond is worth a lot more. (See Figure 14.1.)

The same reasoning applies to mortgages. If the mortgage interest rate is 9 or 9.5 percent and you get a mortgage for 8 or 8.5 percent, what you are really doing is adding value to the whole property. In a normal real estate market, two similar homes, with the same loan and interest payments, would sell for about the same price. But if one of them had a lower interest rate, its monthly loan payments would be lower. When this happens, the house usually sells for more to give the sellers a "premium" for their lower-interest loan.

Determining just how much a lower-interest loan is really worth is difficult. But the chart shows what happens to the market value of a home with a $100,000 loan at different interest rates (assuming an 80 percent ratio of loan-to-value). The shaded areas represent the maximum change in values.

I know people who work out facilitating loans with lenders and their REO managers. It can take many years to develop such relationships, but once developed they can be very profitable.

The important thing here is for you to determine at what stage of the distress property cycle you want to be active. Each stage has

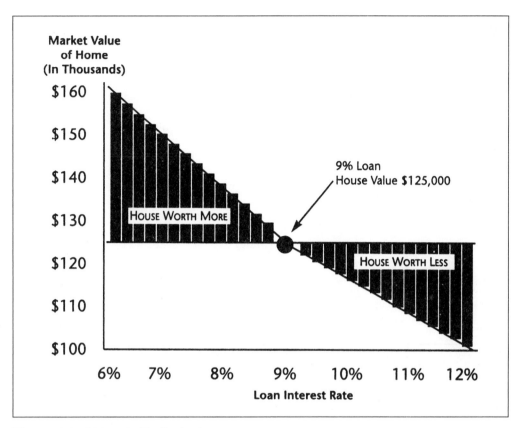

Figure 14.1   Value of a Facilitating Loan

advantages and disadvantages. The choice is a matter of personal preference and perhaps of personal assets as well. Is the ability to make friends with people—and lenders—among your assets? Do you know any REO officers? Are you willing to spend the time and effort to cultivate this type of business? (See Case Study 14.2.)

There is absolutely nothing wrong with dealing in REOs if this is what you are interested in. The outstanding advantage is that you don't have to risk your own capital. Another major advantage is that you might be able to get other concessions from the lender as well, in a package deal. You might be able to get a loan on another property that has nothing to do with this particular REO. Obviously, if the lender wants you to take over an REO, you are usually going to be in a better position to bargain. What makes the whole business very interesting is that the lender is a big organization, with lots of money and property.

Case Study 14.2

The home at 8821 Eagle Pass was a large 4 bedroom, 2 bath home on an acre of land in a very desirable area. There were hardly ever homes for sale in that neighborhood. It was horse country.

The house had been scheduled for auction twice before and cancelled both times. The auction could have been cancelled, instead of postponed, for at least a couple of reasons. Perhaps the owners had removed the reason for the sale. Perhaps, because of a technicality, the auction had to be readvertised.

I knew the house well. The approximate amount owed was $117,224.66. I did all my homework and put a quick sale value on it of $189,000, which meant I could bid up to $140,000.

On the day before the sale, I called the trustee to see if the auction would go on as scheduled. The clerk told me, "It's still scheduled to go, but it looks to me like it will be cancelled again."

She must have told the same story to all the interested buyers. She was wrong. The auction was not cancelled. It was held, but not one bidder was present. Not even me, and I'm the one who says to always stick to the system. That lovely home went back to the lender for the opening bid of $117,237.12. What a disappointment!

As a follow-up, I contacted the trustee again to get the lender's name and other information. Here's where the runaround began. The first lender sold the loan to the second lender, and then the loan was taken over by yet another lender. At the final lender's office, I was referred to the REO department. They told me they had no record of the property reverting back to them yet. I called back twice in the next two weeks and finally found someone who had the file.

I was told to contact the appraiser assigned to make the valuation of the property. The appraiser referred me back to another section of the lender's office. That section asked me to call a real estate broker, who was based out of the area in which the property was located, if I was interested in buying the house. The out-of-area broker had already sold the house to an "interested party" for $169,000, which more than satisfied the lender.

Two points here. First, I should never have assumed that the auction would be cancelled again. Second, I should never waste time and money chasing an REO deal. My experiences have convinced me that, once a property goes back to the lender, if it has any profit left in it at all, it will go to an inside "interested party."

When the VA and FHA Get into the Act

If the VA or FHA has guaranteed the loan, the Veterans Administration or the Department of Housing and Urban Development often gets the final title, or repossesses, after the lender takes back the property. It is very important for you to understand how these government agencies dispose of repo properties. They fall into the REO category, except that they are handled a little differently by these government agencies than they would be by a commercial lender.

In many areas the VA advertises once a week (in the Sunday

newspaper) the list of repo properties it is offering for bid. But it's best to contact the VA office in your district to get exact information. Most recognize licensed brokers as bidders and will give you information on the whole process. You can also get keys that will allow you into the repo properties. In most cases the VA sets a minimum price for a bid and sells the property to the bidder who mails in the highest bid over that minimum. There are many opportunities to get very good values in this manner.

HUD operates quite similarly, except that you have to get on a mailing list before they will send details of their repo properties. I would contact the HUD office in your area and ask about FHA properties. Here again, you'll be given a key to get into the properties so you can make a personal appraisal before you make a bid. Usually HUD lists a suggested bid price, but in some cases they'll accept a bid for less.

Both these bidding procedures are extremely fair and honest. Both government agencies are very cooperative and helpful to brokers interested in bidding on repo properties. The auctions are very well attended, and the bidding is usually pretty competitive. Most of the people at these auctions are brokers who specialize in buying properties for owner-occupant buyers that they already have lined up. I have seen very few speculators or specialists buying property this way.

Special Inspection Forms for Repos

Usually there's enough time to inspect the VA and FHA properties before the deadline for making a bid. The procedure for inspecting and appraising repo properties is a little different. It's much easier in that everyone cooperates. The home is empty, and the whole world knows what's happening.

Most repo units are in need of rehabilitation. To save time, I've prepared a simple Repo Analysis form (Figure 14.2) that incorporates inspection, rehab estimates, and market analysis all in one.

Whether you are dealing directly with lenders who own foreclosed properties or with government agencies, your position improves over time. The longer they keep a property, the more it costs them. And these expenses always show up somewhere. So the pressure keeps mounting for them to make deals and unload.

If you do your homework and are patient, you can negotiate some good deals for yourself. Lenders will always be making some bad loans, so dealing with REOs and repos can turn into a long-term profit-making business for the right people.

Repo Analysis

Address _____

Details _____

Neighborhood
Information

Item	Comments	Rehab Cost
Outside		
Landscaping		
Walks		
Drainage		
Cracks		
Lighting		
Driveway		
Other		
Inside		
Front Door		
Foyer		
Size		
Living Room		
Size		
Carpet		
Fireplace		
Electrical		
Other		
Dining Room		
Size		
Carpet		
Other		
Kitchen		
Size		
Tile		
Cabinets		
Electrical		
Plumbing		
Appliances		
Other		
Bedrooms		
Size		
Carpet		
Other		(Page 1 of 2)

Figure 14.2   Repo Analysis Form Used to Evaluate All Aspects of Repo Property

Item	Comments	Rehab Cost
Bathrooms		
Size		
Floor		
Plumbing		
Cabinets		
Toilets		
Tub		
Shower		
Other		
Laundry		
Heating		
Air Conditioning		
Garage		
Other		
Total Estimated Costs		

Summary

Sales Price	+ $	
Less Sales Expense	-	
Less Cost to Hold	-	
Less Cost to Close	-	
Less Rehab Costs	-	
Total	$	
Less Minimum Profit	-	
Amount to Bid	+	

Comments

Other Factors

Conclusions   **Date**

(Page 2 of 2)

Figure 14.2 *Continued*

The Internet and Other Auctions

The wonder of the twenty-first century, the World Wide Web, is also heavily involved in the troubled properties industry. Any time, day or night, you can pull up details on all kinds of foreclosure activities, including:

Government Foreclosure Reports
Separate Trustee and Mortgage Auctions
Freddi Mac and Fannie Mae Owned Home Reports
REO Seekers
Internet Auction Lists
Separate City Reports on Lis Pendens and Foreclosure Auction Sale Data

As with everything else on the Internet, the pace of this activity is accelerating and soon will cause many other changes in the auction procedures themselves.

CHAPTER 15
Selling for Maximum Profits

*Make every bargain clear and plain that
no man afterwards complain.*

—*Anonymous*

No matter at which stage you buy a property, selling that property will be considerably easier. You have complete control of time. Now you have the choice of making a deal or not. You do not have to convince somebody to go along with your proposal. Selling a home is simply a matter of selling, the same way most homes on the market are sold. More importantly, if you've done your homework, the home you're selling will be in a good area and thus easier to sell. You have put the house in as good a condition as possible to get the highest price. So you can relax and concentrate on maximizing your return.

Selling for maximum returns may be much easier than you think. If you followed the guidelines in this book, you bought the home subject to an existing mortgage, and you might be able to sell it subject to an existing mortgage. There could be a real advantage in selling a house with an older loan. The new buyers might be taking over a lower interest rate, with lower monthly payments than a new mortgage might have. If you also get involved in a second trust deed or mortgage, you could make quite a profit.

In reselling the property, you need to focus on three issues:

1. How much can you get for it?

2. How do you select buyers for a quick sale?

3. How can some residuals be obtained from the sale?

169

A Real Estate License Is Not Needed

When you are ready to resell the home, for the first month or two handle the matter yourself. You won't need a real estate license. The home is private property, and you are acting as a principal. By selling the home yourself, you can save the 5, 6, or 7 percent commission normally paid to a broker and have the advantage of faster action.

If you stick to buying and selling properties in your own name, you have all the rights that other principals have. You can sell subject to existing mortgages and give purchase-money loans on the property you sell. In most cases you won't need a real estate license to buy and sell in your own name. But find out what your rights and responsibilities are in your state so you can carry out the transactions correctly. Call the department of real estate or the licensing authority in your area for complete information.

Advertise in Local Papers

The best places to advertise a home for sale are the local newspapers. This includes the regional paper, the local paper, and the weekly throwaways. Anything that is printed and distributed in the area is a source for good ad response.

It is not wise to skimp here, because people who like to read their newspapers like to read details. They object to abbreviated advertising. Sit down and ask yourself what you would like to read if you were looking for a home. What are some of the good points a buyer would be seeking? Do these apply to the home you're selling?

The headline for the ad should always read *For Sale by Owner.* Real estate agents and brokers call it FSBO ("phisbo"). This is an intriguing phrase that always lures people to the property. Everybody is looking for a chance to save on commissions, so FSBOs are always the first places they look.

Since you are not a real estate agent, you don't have to put down owner-agent. You are an independent principal selling your own home.

Always start out the ad copy by saying "Newly decorated." Then fill in 3 bedroom/4 bedroom; 2 bath/3 bath, the details of existing loans, and so on. Always include the terms of the existing mortgage payment. If the payment is $300 per month including taxes and insurance, say that.

Always list the total sales price. State that the home is available for immediate occupancy. Say there are no qualifications necessary and no escrow delays. Mention other possible savings. Also say that the deal is for owner-occupants only, not for investors.

Mention the cash down payment without specifying any willingness to take back a second mortgage. Most buyers realize that second mortgages are always a bargaining point.

Include the address of the property and your personal phone numbers, home and office. Do everything you can to make contact with you as easy as possible for the buyers.

Here's an example:

> **For Sale by Owner.**
> Newly decorated. All new appliances. 3BR, 2BA, two-story home, $100,000. Only $15,000 down. $85,000 existing 9% mortgage ($883.92 PITI) VACANT. Low closing costs. Close to schools, parks, churches, and shopping. 618 Pleasant Court, Central City. Call owner VAL 381-9511 (B), 391-7703 (H).

You will find you only have to advertise in the papers once, so you need not run the ad on a continuing basis.

Quick action will be forthcoming.

Give the Home Curb Appeal

The important point is timing. While you are negotiating for this property, return to your list of the repairs the property needs. If something is needed to make it more attractive for buyers, allow enough time to do it. In addition to the major problems, you can do a lot of small things before prospects begin arriving. You must improve the home's appearance so it will have curb appeal.

By improving the appearance, you improve your chances of selling the home. People usually decide within the first two to five minutes whether they like a home. That's what curb appeal is all about. A first impression often turns into a lasting impression. It's easy to give a good first impression, which leads to a major positive impression as the buyers walk from room to room.

Start with the outside appearance of the house:

• If painting the house was one of the major requirements you identified when you were buying the house, do it as quickly as possible. More than anything else, a new paint job can work wonders for that first impression.

• Be sure the landscaping looks as good as it possibly can look, with the lawn cut, the shrubs clipped, everything swept away. Do anything needed to create that good first impression.

• Add fertilizer or grass food to make the grass look green and lush.

• Cut back and trim any shrubbery that looks unkempt or unsightly.

• Consider putting extra flowers or shrubbery around the front.

• Consider repainting the front door and the front entrance. Make that area as attractive as possible. Put a new coat of paint on the mailbox.

• Check all outside lighting and fixtures to make sure they give a pleasant and enticing glow to the house.

You should also make a few improvements inside. Since the kitchen is the most important room in the house, check it thoroughly. Make sure it is as attractive and inviting as possible. If new curtains are needed, put them up to add to that welcome feeling. Carefully clean everything, from the kitchen floor to the ventilating fan. Make sure everything smells new and clean.

Also check all bathroom plumbing to make sure everything is working correctly. The prospective buyers will try flushing the toilets and turning on the water. It's nice to keep fresh towels in the bathroom. Many times I add pictures, flowers, and other accessories to create a model home look.

All the living areas benefit from a good freshening up:

• Use special cleaning products to remove stains on walls and floors.

• Immediately repair any plaster that is cracked or in bad shape.

• Immediately repair anything that is visibly improper or in need of correcting, such as missing handles.

• Remove any stains anywhere in the house.

• If your initial rehab list included major interior decorating, do it as quickly as possible.

• Check out the fireplace. Make sure the flue is open. Clean it and lay out some logs to make it look inviting.

• Clean all the windows. Nothing is more inviting than looking out through clean windows to a sun-splashed garden. At the same time, remove or repair any torn screens.

• Be sure every light switch works. When a switch is turned on, something should light up. If necessary, bring in some floor lamps.

• Clean and polish the floors. If there are carpets, clean them; if they are worn, replace them. If there are any creaking boards or stair treads, nail them down.

• Check the closets in all the rooms for odors. Use room deodorizers where necessary to eliminate musty odors.

• Lubricate any sticking or squeaking doors.

• Make sure sliding doors don't stick in their tracks. Rubbing the tracks with a special preparation can eliminate this problem.

• Clean out the basement and the attic.

The route you take to show prospects the home is probably just as important as the way it looks. Show the most advantageous points first. Rehearse the route before you bring people into the house. Have the doors open at the right places.

Keep the house well lit during the showing. Have draperies open to let in the light and make the rooms look larger. In the evening, all the lights should be on, including the outside lights. Never allow children, pets, or strangers in and out while you are showing the property.

Always remember that the house cannot sell itself; it is inanimate. But it can be prepared so the prospect sees its best points. You have to go through all the effort mentioned here and more, depending on the house. Think selfishly. The better the house looks, the more efficient the tour, the better the presentation—the more money you can get.

One Last Point

You are probably not going to live in the houses you acquire as a specialist in distress property. However, you must try to be enthusiastic about the positive aspects of each one. After you acquire a property, you should write down 10 good things you have observed about it. These 10 items may be used as a basis for preparing advertising and a sales pitch. Reexamine them frequently and use them when showing the property to prospects. (See Case Study 15.1 and Figure 15.1.)

Case Study 15.1

A loan broker I work with named Paul lived in a townhouse community near Riverside, California. One day I stopped at his home for some information and met his next-door neighbor, Sandra. Sandra wanted to buy a large hot tub/spa package for her sunroom on the ground floor. She wanted a loan from Paul to cover the hot tub plus some back bills. I went over to Sandra's townhouse with Paul for his appraisal. Her townhouse was beautiful. She had recently remodeled all eight rooms, with beautiful new carpeting throughout both levels. I could see why Sandra needed a second loan on her house.

I forgot about the incident until about six months later when I met Paul again. He reminded me of our visit with Sandra. "Guess what," he said. "Sandra filed for bankruptcy and left for Florida." Paul was upset because his company had made the loan and sold it to an out-of-state lender. We joked about the problems in our industry, but I made a note to follow up on Sandra's townhouse.

Right after Thanksgiving that year, I read about a trustee sale being set for Sandra's townhouse. The first loan was for $81,800, with over $91,000 owing. There were several other loans and liens on the property, but since the first loan was foreclosing, the other loans would fall and be no problem for me.

I made a quick check of values in that tract and found that the last few comparable sales had been for about $130,000. None of the units had a hot tub as did this one. Also, since Sandra lived alone, her townhouse was in move-in condition. The only extra money I would need would be to cover her delinquent taxes.

Since it was the holiday season, I expected this sale to be postponed (it was set for December 22). And since the opening bid was so low, I expected to see many bidders.

When I drove by the unit for one more look, I was surprised to see newspapers covering all the windows from the inside. There was no way to see inside. Apparently Sandra had stayed overnight for a few nights after her furniture (and window coverings) were packed and shipped. For safety's sake she covered all the windows. No problem for me because I already knew her townhouse was in terrific shape.

My guess is that the newspapers on the windows made other interested bidders worried. There was no postponement of the trustee sale. I was the only qualified bidder present. I bid 31 cents over the opening bid of $91,817.69 and won the property for $91,818.

I listed the home for $132,900 and made up a circular featuring the spa (see Figure 15.1). The home sold in three weeks for close to the asking price, and I made a good profit. It just goes to show that you can make money if you buy a good property and market it right.

LOVELY 2-STORY TOWN HOME
WITH FABULOUS SPA ON A PRIVATE PATIO

343 HIGH STREET
CORONA

**Price
$132,900**

3 Bedroom • 2.5 Baths
Breakfast Bar • Fireplace • Two-Story
Central Air/Heating • Brand New Carpeting
Pool • 2-Car Garage

CORNER UNIT WITH PRIVATE ENTRY
AND LOVELY GROUNDS

Presented by: *Geraldine Achenbach*
Office: 780-2124
Home: 359-5733

Figure 15.1   Ad Emphasizing Most Positive Feature of Property for Sale

Discuss the Existing Mortgage Loan

When selling a house with a loan that can be taken "subject to," stress to the buyers that they could have a very difficult time going for a new loan. In addition to paying possibly higher interest rates, they would wait quite a while for the deal to close. They would pay many extra charges. They would pay brokers' commissions. Buying from you would save all these costs. In addition, the buyers would not have to go through a credit check. A large number of families, including those with two wage earners, do not qualify for the homes they want.

Don't argue with the buyers. Don't conceal anything. Just tell them the facts as you perceive them. Either they are buying what is for sale or they are not. Either they are going to get a better value from you than they would anyplace else or they are not. That value includes buying the property subject to a very good existing mortgage, with special terms. Of course, they must understand all the other factors involved so there is never a disagreement. But in all cases, if the dealings are aboveboard and you tell the truth, you will come out on top.

Second Mortgages or Second Trust Deeds

Quite often, new buyers will not have enough money to cover the entire down payment. For example, if the purchase price of the property is $80,000 and the existing mortgage is $50,000, the new buyers may not have the $30,000 necessary to cover the difference. If this is the case, you could take back a $15,000 second mortgage or second trust deed so the deal can be consummated.

These second mortgages or second trusts are commonly called purchase-money loans. They are a very well accepted way of helping both the buyers and yourself. Without the loan, the deal might not be made. The buyers will pay higher interest on the second mortgage, but property appreciates quite dramatically, so the extra expense is worthwhile to them. And even though taking back a second mortgage ties up a large part of your profit, it provides a good return on your money.

When writing a second loan, you may include the following advantageous items:

• *Start-up charges*. These include expenses and a bonus for creating the loan. The extra income here could be as much as 10 percent of the total loan. It usually is all profit, as you will have few real expenses in this transaction (less than $10 for recording the document).

• *Prepayment penalties*. These penalties for paying off the loan early range from a percentage of the loan to six months' (or one year's) interest charges. Secondary loans may bear interest rates as high as 20 percent or more, so these prepayment bonuses can be lucrative.

• *Late charges*. You may charge fees of up to 10 percent of the monthly payment.

Your terms for a purchase-money loan should be similar to those on the first mortgage. You must have well-defined time periods, amounts, interest rates, penalties, and even prepayment conditions. You must also be aware that all states deal differently with purchase-money loans. Many states have usury laws restricting the amount of interest that can be charged. No matter where you live, check the usury or consumer code guidelines about purchase-money mortgages so you can handle the deal properly.

Even if your state imposes a limit on the amount of interest charges allowable, you can substantially increase the effective interest rate by charging points or other expense items that increase the total return on the loan.

Know the Laws concerning Purchase-Money Loans

In every state, you can easily get in touch with the real estate department (or the real estate commissioner or the department of financing or banking or some other powers that be) to get specific information on what is legal or illegal concerning purchase-money mortgages. The information is often available from more than one department. Usually local newspapers also carry information regarding this kind of financing.

At this point you would know what security device is used in your state (a mortgage, a deed of trust, or both) and have some idea what the usury limits and allowable fees are. But you must check with the appropriate agencies to see that you are complying with all the local and state laws. In no way can this book offer advice on the rules in every state or on the legal ramifications of those rules. It can only provide guidance on the various steps necessary to make purchase-money loans.

The Magic of Purchase-Money Financing

Most major financial publications are beginning to tout the attractive returns of purchase-money mortgages. Many states have companies that do nothing but lend money to owners of single-family homes using second or third mortgages or trust deeds. The Wall Street Journal has had several articles stressing how "second mortgages offer investors high yields with apparent safety." Even when the prime rate was over 21 percent and certificates of deposit were yielding more than 17 percent, second trusts were still very popular. Investors realized that the real yield on these instruments when they were paid off was well over 25 percent. That should be reason enough for a seller of a single-family home to consider taking back a purchase-money loan.

How to Develop a Small Fortune

If you have followed the between-two-houses plan, you should be an expert on real estate values in a particular area. Now you know that you can take back purchase-money mortgages safely on property that you are comfortable about. In fact, if you are satisfied with the anticipated growth and appreciation, there is every good reason not to be afraid of purchase-money loans.

In fact, I encourage them. Because profits should be invested rather than saved, it is a good idea to leave the money in the sold property and earn a secure 15 to 20 percent. Another advantage of doing this is that, if the new buyer has trouble making the payments, you will have first crack at getting the property back. If you did your homework correctly and correctly analyzed the territory, the property will still be desirable.

Let the New Buyers Pay All Closing Costs

Tell the buyers that no matter what the precedent is, they are paying all the costs of this transaction. Put that statement right on the table so there can be no misunderstanding.

In return, you are not checking the buyers' credit. Instead you are checking their personality. If you like the buyers and feel comfortable with them, then sell the house. Otherwise find someone else.

Selling Techniques

Whether you work with a professional realtor or handle the sale yourself, I suggest that you consider the following techniques:

• Never accept an offer on the spot. Tell the buyers or their agent that you appreciate the offer and will act on it fast. Then take a few hours or a whole day to read it.

• Understand every word of the offer. Leave nothing to chance. No loose ends are allowed.

• Use the Confidential Offer Analysis form (see Figure 15.2) to cover all the important points in the offer. Be sure your price includes all third-party inspection work. There should be no open-ended fees and expenses; put dollar limits on all of them. Put actual dollar amounts in both the Listing column (for your asking price) and the Offer column (for the buyer's offer).

• Then fill out the column labeled Seller's Counter to cover all the items in the transaction. You could agree on a dollar-amount discount for inspection work. When you compare the bottom lines of

Confidential Offer Analysis					
Date:	Listing	Offer	Seller Counter	Buyer Counter	FINAL
SALES PRICE					
Commissions					
Seller Points					
Termite Inspection					
Lender Fees					
Miscellaneous					
Recording Fees					
Escrow Costs					
Title Costs					
Sub Repairs					
Terms for Fees					
Buyer Warranty					
Other					
Seller's Closing Costs					
Other Costs					
Total Seller Closing Costs					
Left to Seller					
Our Costs					
Gross Profit					
Conditions:					

Figure 15.2   Confidential Offer Analysis Form for Sales Negotiations

the first three columns, you will see what your gross profit could be under your original listing, the buyers' first offer, and your counteroffer.

• Usually the buyers will make one more counteroffer (the next column). After a few changes, you'll both agree on the final deal (the last column).

• Put a time limit on everything. Provide for your right to cancel if anything is not to your satisfaction. Specify when the closing is to occur and what happens if there are delays.

• Have provisions for the deal to go forward even if the appraisal is less than the sales price.

I suggest staying with your favorite escrow company or attorney for all your closings. Make that a condition of your sale. No buyers will walk away from a good deal unless your people are known incompetents (and I'm sure you wouldn't use them if they were). You will always have an extra layer of protection by working all your deals with the same people. And you'll save everyone a lot of time.

Special Opportunities in Lease-Options

Occasionally you might lease a house and give the people an option to buy it later. You would usually use this method for young, first-time buyers who are unable to raise even part of their down payment. Other people who might be interested in a lease-option can carry larger monthly payments but cannot come up with the cash required to close the deal.

In a lease-option, you can arrange the lease conditions in any number of ways. However, the lease payments must always be higher than normal rent payments, at least $75 to $100 more per month. This difference will go toward the down payment. The terms of the lease should be such that if the tenants do not execute the purchase of the property during the purchase period (usually two to four years), then all the monies paid will be considered rent.

With this arrangement you cannot lose. Either the lessees will buy the property at a later date (at the higher-than-market-value figure decided on at the time the agreement is signed) or will return the property. Then you choose again whether to lease or sell. In the meantime, you realize more income than you would get under normal leasing. The problem is your selection of tenants. You will have to thoroughly check them out. But lease-options are definitely an increased-profit opportunity, and you should consider them if the situation arises.

Special Opportunities in Duplexes to Eightplexes

The only other opportunity you might consider in the early stages of investing in single-family homes is a small, multifamily property, such as a duplex, fourplex, sixplex, or eightplex. The same principles apply. The property must be in your chosen territory, the one you are most familiar with. The values must be there. The economic fundamentals must work, and the owners must be in a distress situation. The same strategy prevails when you discuss the transfer of ownership.

After you have acquired one or two single-family properties and leased one or two, you can begin to consider multifamily properties. You will discover that the only significant difference in the transaction is the amount of down payment required. But you can use the same basic strategy if you don't have enough for the down payment: Get a longer option period during which to sell the property. If you have enough money for the down payment, the method is also the same as it would be for a single-family property. Sell it at a higher price down the road, or lease it and realize appreciation and income.

Once you have mastered the fundamentals of buying a property subject to the existing mortgage and once you have become an expert at negotiating liens and mortgages, all kinds of other doors will open. If you concentrate on property that is really for sale rather than property that may or may not be sold, you will create a great deal of business activity.

CHAPTER 16
Upgrading with Major Improvements

If it looks too good to be true, look again.
—*Paul Mellon*

One of the surest ways to make profit in real estate is to improve the value of the property you purchase. You can improve the value by having the zoning changed on the property. You can spend the time and money to convince regulatory agencies that your property should have its use upgraded. For example, you might ask that residential use be changed to commercial. In today's business climate this is very difficult to do. When it is done, it is usually done by people with large organizations and a great deal of staying power—people who can buy property well in advance of when they need it and can hire top-notch consultants to do all the things necessary to make this conversion.

An easier way for the average investor to improve value is to "add on" to existing property. You can do this by adding rooms on the first level. Or, if you feel ambitious, you can add a second floor to a single-story home. I have done this several times, working with general contractors, and it is a very profitable thing to consider. You start by looking for a neighborhood that seems to be improving, and then, within that neighborhood, you look for the least expensive single-story home. It helps if that home is available for sale at a reasonable price and is in a "fixer-upper" condition. I know at least six general contractors who make a very good living looking for fixer-uppers and adding on to the same level or putting on a second story.

There are many ways to improve the value of a fixer-upper. The most popular ways are the following:

• *Enlarge the kitchen.* The kitchen is one of the most important rooms in the house. Usually a fixer-upper is an older house and the kitchen has plenty of room for improvement. If the kitchen is on the outside of the house, you could extend one of the walls out farther. Or if the house has a small dining room, the kitchen could be enlarged to add to the eating area. Most kitchens could use new appliances, new counter tops, and more space to work.

• *Expand the dining room.* Most dining rooms have at least one outside wall. Except where there is no space on the outside to expand, pushing the wall out from 6 to 12 feet is a good idea. Sometimes the room layout is such that you can push the dining room out further and use some of the space left to improve the traffic flow in one of the other rooms. Or part of the dining room could be made into a family room. The dining room is part of the entertaining area and the more you could do to improve the entertaining area the better.

• *Extend the family room.* If the kitchen, dining room, or family room are part of an outside wall, a smart architect or general contractor could come up with a plan to allow you to move the room out and add a lot more space to that room or an adjacent room.

• *Improve the entertainment area.* The kitchen, family room, dining room, and living room together make up a large entertainment area. Usually one or more of these rooms have outside walls. In almost all houses there is an opportunity to add space in these rooms to improve the overall traffic flow and add a lot more appeal to that house.

• *Add to a bedroom.* There is usually one bedroom in the house that has plenty of room for expansion. You could add an extra bath. You could increase the size of closets. You can do any number of things to make bedroom space more saleable.

• *Add a complete bedroom plus patio area.* Sometimes the hallway space is arranged in such a way that you can extend the hallway and add a complete bedroom or two in the back yard. At the same time you have an opportunity to improve the patio arrangement and landscaping. Because it is on the first floor, the expenses are less than second-floor expenses: You simply have to put in a footing and a foundation and extend the existing roof.

• *Convert the garage.* In many cases you have an excellent opportunity to change a one-, two-, or three-car garage into living space. There is usually plumbing already in the garage for a washer or general utility. Also, the garage has excellent access to the outside. It's a prime candidate for upgrading the overall house. But you have to replace the parking space the garage offers. Depending on the configuration of the property, this may mean building a new garage on another part of the property or it may mean adding a garage onto the present garage space.

There are many other possibilities. Depending on the size of the lot and the condition of the house, an imaginative investor can come up with a variety of plans for upgrading a single-family home and adding to its value. A cardinal rule here is never to upgrade one of the highest-priced homes in the neighborhood. It is better to look for one of the lowest-priced homes in the neighborhood for improving the value of an investment property.

Project Upgrade

As a basis for discussing the pros and cons of upgrading with major improvements, as well as the steps involved, I am going to describe a project where I added a second floor to a single-level house. This was not a typical job in that there were many features of this job that were unusual. There were many unexpected events, too. In fact, this project may well have included all the things that can go wrong when you attempt an add-on construction project of this magnitude. In spite of all the problems, however, this job was worth the effort. I made a very small profit on the property, but if my timing had been a little better and if some of these problems had not happened, I would have made a very large profit. When you invest in real estate, you can't be sure that any deal will work out correctly. What you can be sure of is that you are prepared to respond to deals as they come up. If you know the ins and outs of situations like my second-floor add-on and the kinds of problems that can arise when making major improvements, then you will have a better chance of making a good profit when an opportunity presents itself.

Normally I don't pay much attention to second deeds of trust that are going into foreclosure, but in this case I made an exception. The property in question was a very lovely ranch home in a pleasant neighborhood in Mission Viejo. It was across the street from a park and within walking distance to the high school and the library. I spent many hours walking around the area on my many trips to the library. So, when I saw that this property was coming up to trustee sale, I became interested. What interested me the most about this property was that it was one of a very few single-family ranch homes in a neighborhood of larger two-story homes. I made my comparative market analysis and came to the conclusion that I could get a pretty good price for a ranch home here, but I would get a very good price for a home with a second story and more room.

I called a contractor friend of mine and asked him to meet me on the property to discuss the possibility of a second-story addition. The people living in the home were planning on moving to another state and they were very cooperative. They showed me the interior and gave me suggestions about approaching the neighbors if I were interested in doing some remodeling on the house. They also said that many other people were interested in bidding on the property and had come through to see the condition, but that none of them had mentioned adding on to the existing home. Apparently they were only interested in cosmetic improvements and a quick sale. While you can never be sure that some other bidder would not be interested in doing the same thing, I felt pleased with that information.

Considering All the Options

My next step was to evaluate the options available for handling the property. To do that, I used the worksheet shown in Figure 16.1. On this form I listed three different options:

1. Leave it as is with minor cosmetic improvements.

2. Add a room downstairs.

3. Add several rooms upstairs.

This single sheet is a summary of many days of hard work and analysis. The contractor and I met with an architect and we did quite a few sketches and just as many computations. After I did some market research for the area, I was encouraged for the following reasons:

1. There were very few large 4 bedroom homes on the market in this area.

2. All 4 bedroom homes sold quickly and for higher prices.

3. The market appeared to be getting better and if I could sell this home within six months I could probably hit the peak.

4. Mission Viejo had recently become a new city on its own and I felt that I would be able to get all the necessary construction approvals very quickly.

After much analysis, I finally decided that the smartest business decision on this property was to figure my bidding based on adding a whole new second floor.

Winning the Bid

Referring back to the worksheet (Figure 16.1) you can see the advantage that adding a second level would give me at a bidding auction. Notice that if I were planning on doing it as is, I would be able to bid $31,300. If I were planning on adding just one room downstairs, I would be able to bid $46,300. But if I were planning on adding the whole second floor—and selling it at a much larger price—I would be able to bid $68,000 which is much more than the other two bids. So this should give me an advantage at the auction unless someone else was thinking along the same lines.

At the trustee sales auction, I was surprised and disappointed to see over fifty people present. This was the only trustee sale going to auction. The bidding started around $30,000 and went up very slowly. I noticed that the bidding went in waves. The bidders who were interested in the property "as is" stopped bidding at a certain point. Then people who planned on doing a little more went up to a higher point of bidding. But when it got to about sixty thousand dollars, there were only three of us left. I went up to $64,300 which was just a few thousand dollars less than the $68,000 I was prepared to go. When I won the bid at $64,300, I became uncertain again. Half the people left the auction area shaking their heads, thinking that there was a crazy investor among them. Perhaps they were correct. But I quickly went through the analysis in my head again and felt that this was a good deal for me and that I would do well.

Getting the Approvals

I got nothing but cooperation from everybody concerned in this deal. The people living in the home wanted a few extra months before moving but that was no problem because I needed the time to get all the approvals. The first thing I did was go to the town hall and ask for the forms to make the application for construction. For a new city, everybody was very well organized. Unfortunately, I had missed the deadline for filing the application for the appropriate committee. Then, as I looked at all the things that had to be done, I realized I would have further delays because one of the requirements was to get permission from the contiguous neighbors to do what I intended to do. I was not concerned about getting the permission because I had discussed this with the neigh-

WORKSHEET   Date _8/18/88_

CRR _Pepita_ City _MV_ SQ F _1700_ BR _4_ BA _2_

Features _Close to park_

Close Streets _—_

TGNO'S _—_

Actives = _175,000 - 250,000_

Comps = _SAme_

New = _None_

	HOUSE		
Best		Average	Worst
9 (8) 7	6	5 4 3	2 1
See Inside _ok_		Town Hall _yes_	
Utilities _ok_		Sales ↑↓ ↑	
Neighbors _ok_		Prices ↑↓ ↑	
"Mix" _ok_		Parking _plenty_	
Good		Bad	

IMPROVE VALUE	= As Is	OTHER Add One Room +	Add Second Level
LIST	= 199,500	= 250,000	= 330,000
SELL	= 185,000	= 235,000	= 295,000
INSIDE	= 4,000	= 25,000	= } 53,900
OUTSIDE	= 3,000	= 5,000	=
ARREARS	= 0	=	=
COE COST	4%	=	= 70,800
HOLD COST	4% } 24% 44,400	} 24% 56,400	=
BROKER	6%	=	=
PROFIT	10% =	=	=
FIRST D.O.T.	= 102,300	= 102,300	= 102,300
TOTAL COST	= 153,700	= 188,700	= 227,000
LEFT TO BUY WITH	= 31,300	= 46,300	= 68,000

Month =	Month =	Month =	Month =	Month =	Month =	Month =

Figure 16.1 Worksheet Used to Evaluate Different Options for Improving an Investment Property

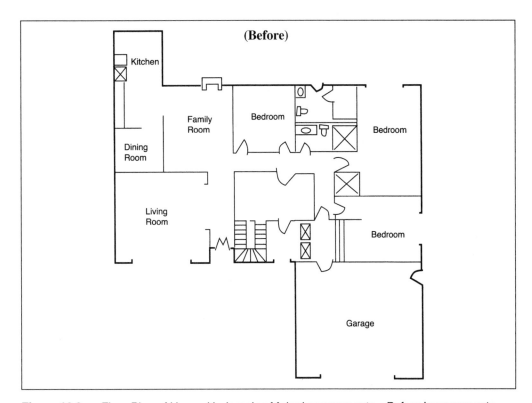

Figure 16.2a   Floor Plan of House Undergoing Major Improvements—Before Improvements

bors and they knew I was going to improve the value of the property. In fact, they were pretty excited about what I was planning on doing, and many of them had good suggestions for me. Nevertheless, I still had to go through a specific procedure of getting all the plans ready, shuffling them back and forth between a few people, and then bringing them to the neighbors for their approval.

The floor plans in Figures 16.2a and 16.2b show the property as it was and as I thought I would build it. In its original form (Fig. 16.2a) it was a very well-designed, compact ranch. You walk through the double-door entrance into a lovely foyer; on the left is a large living room that connects to a large family room and dining area. These connect to a large kitchen with a sliding glass door to the back yard. The bedroom wing is very compact with large closets, two large baths, and a sliding glass door from the master bedroom to the back yard. The large oversized two-car garage has a direct entrance into the laundry room, which leads into the hallway and into the rest of the house. It was one of the better 4 bedroom plans in this whole area. But the rooms were rather tight. There was only a total of about 1,700 square feet for all these rooms. What I planned on doing for the addition (see Fig. 16.2b)

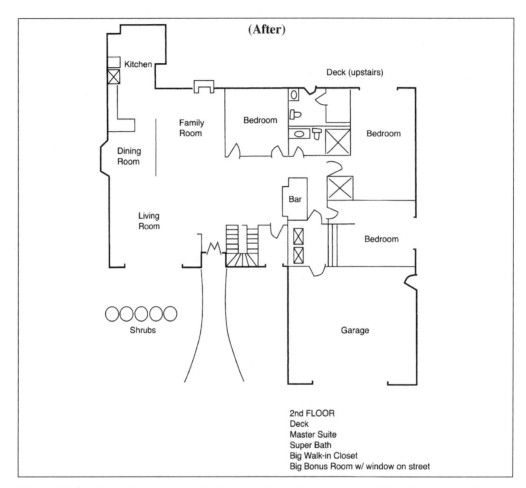

Figure 16.2b Floor Plan of House Undergoing Major Improvements—After Improvements

was to open the foyer area and the family room, tie in the dining room and the living room so that there would be a clear view from the kitchen through the front window. I would add a large master suite upstairs with a super bath, walk-in closets, big bonus room with windows in the front, and a deck off the master bedroom, overlooking the back yard. This would increase the total area to 2,480 square feet. Then I would add all new appliances and all new carpeting.

When I was finally able to get all the exhibits ready and make my application to the different committees, I had smooth sailing. For a new city Mission Viejo was well organized. I had all the approvals I needed by mid-September and I began construction about 30 days later when the property was vacated. Some of the paper work involved includes the Building Permit in Figure 16.3,

CITY OF MISSION VIEJO BUILDING SAFETY DEPARTMENT ## POST IN CONSPICUOUS PLACE ## ON THE JOB			NOTICE You must furnish PERMIT NUMBER and the JOB ADDRESS FOR EACH RESPECTIVE INSPECTION. CALL 582-2489. APPROVED PLANS SHALL BE ON JOB AT ALL TIMES.		

A. P. NO.		DATE ISSUED 9-1988	FINAL INSPECTIONS	Date	Inspector
TYPE	GROUP	PERMIT NO. 1431	28. Electrical Power Meter-Final		
BUILDING ADDRESS 26682 PERTA			29. Final Electric		
TRACT	LOT	BLOCK	30. Final Heating & Air Conditioning		
			31. Final Gas Pipe-Test		
NEW	ADD	ALTER	REPAIR	MOVING	DEMOLISH	32. Final Hood or Canopy		
			33. Final Factory Fireplace		
OWNER ASHLEY · CROWN SYSTEMS			34. Final Plumbing		
USE 2ND STORY ROOM ADDITION			35. Water Service-Final		
WITH DECK			36. Gas Service-Final		
SETBACKS			37. Backflow Preventer — Final		
Front Yd. _____ Side Yd. L _____ R _____ Rear _____			38. Handicap Regulations — Final		
_____ Side Yd. L _____ R _____ Rear _____			39. ZONING — FINAL		
			40. ENGINEERING — FINAL		

CONSTRUCTION AND PLANNING APPROVALS Permit # 1431	Date	Inspector
		41. HEALTH DEPT. — FINAL
1. Temporary Electrical Service or Pole		42. STRUCTURE & BUILDING FINAL
2. Soil Pipe-Undrgrnd.		FIRE DEPT. REQUIREMENTS APPROVALS Permit #
3. Water Pipe-Undrgrnd.		43. Underground Hydro
4. Electrical Conduit-Undrgrnd.		44. Product Piping ☐ Gas ☐ Oil
5. Electrical UFER Grnd.		45. Underground Flush
6. Footings & Steel		46. Undergrnd. Storage Tank ☐ Gas ☐ Oil
7. Pre-Slab		47. Overhead Hydro
8. Steel Reinforcement		48. Dry Chemical
9. Structural Floor System		49. Dry Standpipe
10. Property Sewer Line & House Connection		50. FIXED SYSTEM FINAL
11. Sewer Cap		51. FIRE PREV. FINAL
12. Roof Drains & Over Flows		POOL & SPA APPROVALS Permit #
13. Rough Plumbing		52. Pool & Equipment Location
14. Rough Electrical-Conduit		53. Steel Reinforcement
15. Rough Electric Wiring		54. Electrical Bonding
16. Rough Electrical T Bar Ceiling		55. Rough Plumbing & Pressure Test
17. Rough Heating & Air Conditioning		56. APPROVAL TO COVER-GUNITE
18. Rough Factory Fireplace		57. Electrical Conduit-Undrgrnd.
19. Ducts, Ventilation		58. Gas Pipe, ☐ Undrgrnd., Test
20. Gas Pipe-Rough & Test		59. Backwash Lines, P-Trap, ☐ Undrgrnd.
21. Roof Sheathing		60. APPROVAL TO DECK
22. T-Bar Ceiling (Structural) & Monocoat		61. Heater & Vent-Final
23. Frame and Flashing		62. Plumbing System - Final
24. Lathing & Siding		63. Electrical-Final
25. Insulation		64. Fencing & Access Approval
26. Drywall Nailing		65. APPROVED FOR PLASTERING
27. Plaster Brown Coat		66. POOL/SPA SYSTEMS FINAL

Notes:

Figure 16.3   Getting Approval for Construction: *Building Permit*

the Certificate of Compliance in Figure 16.4, and the Engineer's Certificate in Figure 16.5

Problems and More Problems

Murphy's Law hit this project with a vengeance in the form of delays, supply errors, and miscommunications. On my first trip to town hall to get approval forms, I could see immediately that two or three months would slip by before I could actually begin construction. I would not be concerned about a delay like that in an up market, but it began to appear that the market we were in had sort of exhausted itself. It looked like it might be approaching a peak, and once it hits a peak, prices usually waffle and go down. I began getting concerned that I would miss the peak and be on the down side of the market. However, there was nothing I could do about it at this point in time. I had paid too much for the property simply to do some minor cosmetics and put it on the market again. So I was stuck with the course I had chosen. The only thing I could do was to get the appraiser as quickly as possible and then try to do the construction with equal speed.

The next round of delays involved construction. I had decided to put a completely new roof on the property since I thought this would be a good sales feature. Two thirds of the old roof was being removed anyway, so having that small part of an old roof certainly would not look good. This meant opening the house for a while before it could be covered and protected. It meant taking the roof off and putting some kind of protective covering on until the new roof could be put on. A logistics problem to begin with, it was compounded by intermittent rain for a whole month. Every time it looked like the roof could be done, it rained, and the installers would go to other jobs. Then, when the roof could come off, the framers were unable to do their work. It became a comedy of errors as far as timing was concerned. I had no problem with financing. I even offered to pay the subcontractors on a daily basis just to get them to do the work. However, at that time there was so much work around and so many other commitments that early payments didn't entice them.

There were additional delays caused by supplier errors. For example, I had problems with having the right quantity of shingles for the roof delivered. The supplier sent only two thirds of the amount needed and we had to wait a week or so longer to get the right shingles to finish the job. Next, the wrong appliances were sent for the kitchen. Then the wrong tile was sent for the bathrooms and for the floors. Finally, there was the carpet. As an added treat, I had decided to put in Berber carpeting throughout

SADDLEBACK VALLEY UNIFIED SCHOOL DISTRICT

CERTIFICATE OF COMPLIANCE

Log/
Receipt # _____3719_____   (Government Code Section 53080)

Government Code Section 53080 authorizes a School District to impose certain fees or other requirements for construction or re-constuction of school facilities. By execution of this certificate, the undersigned School District certifies that the development project described below has met any requirements imposed by the District pursuant to Government Code Section 53080.

Applicant Name: _____Howard Marcus_____   Daytime Phone _____892-4726_____

Address: _____P. O. Box 1627_____ Laguna Beach, Ca. 92652_____

Subject Property: Study Grid No. _____00762_____

Tract: _____ Lot: _____ Address: _____26682 Pepita_____

# of units: _____   Mission Viejo, Ca. 92691_____

(if different than above)

Sales Office Name _____

Check one only:

A __x__   Additions - Residential Fees: $1.53 per sq. ft. x---744.5--- sq. ft.

= $ _____1139.09_____ fee paid (project less than 500 sq.ft. are exempt from fee payment per AB1919)

B _____   Residential Fee: $1.53 per sq. ft. x _____ sq. ft.

= $ _____ fee paid

C _____   Commercial/Industrial Fee: .25 per sq. ft. x _____ sq. ft.

= $ _____ fee paid

D _____   Fee to be paid under Developer Fee Agreement number _____ dated prior to 1/1/87

upon Certificate of Occupancy OR _____ Fee attached

E _____   No fee paid - Other District/Developer Agreement (Mello Roos)

This certificate is valid for ---744.5------square feet only.

Note: If the square footage calculation on the final building permit application for this unit exceeds the square footage listed on this certificate, this certificate shall become void and must be re-issued.

(District Seal)

By: _Mary Lou Smith_
Mary Lou Smith, Facilities Planning Specialist

Date: _____September 19, 1988_____

* B,D,E - attach sq. ft. & address

jr 1/38 - 6/15/88

Figure 16.4   Getting Approval for Construction: *Certificate of Compliance*

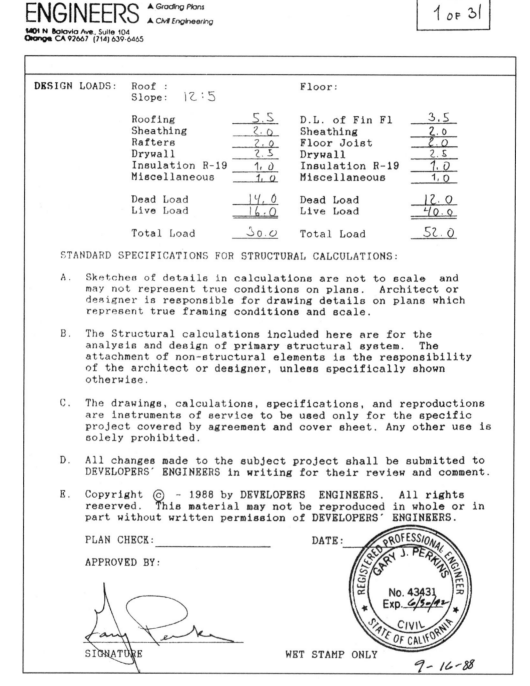

Figure 16.5   Getting Approval for Construction: *Engineer's Certificate*

the whole house. I had several problems with this. Even though I took great pains to select a particular shade of Berber carpeting, the first roll that was sent was the wrong color. That had to go back and the right color Berber sent out. Then the carpet installers made some poor decisions about the cuts in the carpeting, and as a result, I saw too many of the seams throughout the house. Fortunately, the installer and the carpeting people were reputable: They came back and made adjustments that didn't eliminate the problem but did minimize it so that there was no sales resistance from prospective buyers.

This project was unbelievably bad as far as scheduling was concerned. This doesn't happen all the time. I've had other jobs where everything went smoothly and on schedule. On this job timing was critical because we were missing the peak of the sales curve. On a weekly basis I noticed that property values had stopped climbing. The number of sales per week had slowed down. The market seemed to be cooling off. Looking ahead, I became very concerned. No one ever knows for sure how far a market will go down or up. I knew I had plenty of room on the project for a reasonable profit, but I did not want it delayed for too long.

But delay followed delay. I even tried to sell the property while it was under construction. That was just a waste of time: Buyers going through the house got very confused because they could not visualize where the rooms would start and stop. Also, some framers walked off the job at one point because I was showing the property.

Finally I called an urgent meeting for everybody working on the property in order to analyze all the problems we had and come up with a last-ditch strategy to finish the job once and for all. By now everybody was sick of the job. There were disputes between tradespeople over who did what and when and who caused what extra expense and why. At this meeting I sat in the middle and resolved every problem we had and laid out a strategy to finish. The strategy worked and the house was ready to show at the end of March—one of the slowest months of the year.

Realtors to the Rescue

At first I tried to sell the house myself and prepared the flyer shown in Figure 16.6. I thought I might get lucky. Perhaps somebody watching the property being remodeled would be interested and would come directly to me. If so, I would be able to work a deal at a better price. In fact, there were a lot of people interested in the property, and I had several offers, but none of them was near my asking price. By that time I was so busy with a few other

In A First Class Established Neighborhood
Almost All New Home - Across from Park

photography & brochures by **ADVANCED** (714)768-4076

- 4 Bedrooms, 3 Baths (About 2480 Sq. Ft.)
- New Master Bedroom Suite with Oversized Separate Shower - His and Hers Vanities, Walk-In Closet
- 105 Sq. Ft. Sun Deck off Master Bedroom Suite
- New Fire Retardent Wood Shingle Roof
- New Berber Scotch Guard Stain Resistant Carpeting Entire House
- Family Room with Fireplace
- Formal Dining Area
- New Dishwasher
- New Oven and Microwave
- Arched Clear Story Window in Stairwell
- Zoned Heating
- Italian Ceramic Tile Entry - Kitchen & Bath
- Extra Cozy Spaces Both Levels
- Sheetrocked and Painted Garage
- New Brick Planters in Front Yard
- Hard Wired Fire Alarms - Battery Back-Up

Presented By
Crown Realty
(714) 924-7337
22952 Alcalde
Laguna Hills

Style and Value At: $330,000

Figure 16.6 Advertising Flyer Prepared by Owner

deals that I neglected to pay attention to this one. Two months later I realized that nothing had transpired on this property and I began to panic. I made two decisions: (1) this would be the last time I tried to sell any property myself because my expertise was not in selling property, but in creating the deal; and (2) I would look for the best realtor in the area to represent me on this property.

Next, I evaluated all the realtors in the area who had listings in this location. I checked to see which of the brokers had the most listings and which of the brokers sold the most listings. Then I checked to see which of the brokers sold the most of their own listings. After I selected the broker, I considered the various sales agents within that brokerage firm. I decided on the two top salespeople and called each of them to arrange to meet with them. During the meeting I explained what I was doing and that I wanted to get the best sales agent possible to list this property and to sell it for me. Since I was not negotiating down the listing commission, I wanted to be convinced that I had the right party. It was a very tough call.

Finally, I selected a husband and wife team who suggested that I add a lot more curb appeal to the house in order to sell it for my asking price. They were very aggressive in their recommendations. And they were correct. After they got through with what they wanted to do, the house had more of a homelike appearance. It had better shrubbery in front. It had a lot of throw rugs, towels, flowers and other decorating touches inside. It looked like a home that somebody was living in and enjoying.

The property sold very quickly. They prepared a new flyer, shown in Figure 16.7, and held open houses every weekend until we had a satisfactory offer. We met with the agent who represented the buyer and worked out a quick close and move-in deal that pleased everybody.

The Bottom Line

I was very glad to sell the property at the price we got because it was a fair price for that point in time. Nevertheless, we had clearly missed the market. The final price was nowhere near the price I projected early on in my worksheet (see Figure 16.1). The final price was nowhere near the price I set when I tried to sell it myself (see Figure 16.6). I wasn't too eager to put the final figures together to see how much money we made or lost, but that was the next, and last, step.

Figure 16.8 shows my closing statement for this project. At the top, I wrote the sales price of $270,700. Then I listed all of the ex-

photography & brochures by ADVANCED (714)768-4076

Light - Bright - Big - Beautiful!
Shows Like A Model
Established Neighborhood - Perfect Family Home - Steps To Park, Walk To School & Shopping, Curb Appeal, Charm & Pool Size Private Backyard
26682 Pepita Dr., Mission Viejo

- 4 Bedrooms, 3 Baths (About 2480 Sq. Ft.) Not Taped per Arch. Plan
- New Upstairs Master Bedroom Suite with Oversized Separate Shower - His and Hers Vanities, Walk-in Closet - in Addition To Downstairs Master Suite
- 105 Sq. Ft. Sun Deck off Master Bedroom Suite
- New Fire Retardent Wood Shingle Roof
- New Berber Scotch Guard Stain Resistant Carpeting Entire House
- Family Room with Fireplace
- Formal Dining Area
- New Dishwasher
- New Oven and Microwave
- Arched Clerestory Window in Stairwell
- Zoned Heating
- Italian Ceramic Tile Entry - Kitchen & Bath
- Extra Cozy Spaces Both Levels
- Sheetrocked and Painted Garage
- New Brick Planters in Front Yard
- Hard Wired Fire Alarms - Battery Back-Up
- Assoc. Fees $13.50/month Lake Mission Viejo

Style and Value At:
$279,900

Vacant - Easy To Show!
Supra Lock Box - Waterpipe
T.G. # 29 DB2

* All Model Accessories & Decor Shown with Home Included with Sale ... 1 Year Warranty.

Figure 16.7   Advertising Flyer Prepared by Realtors

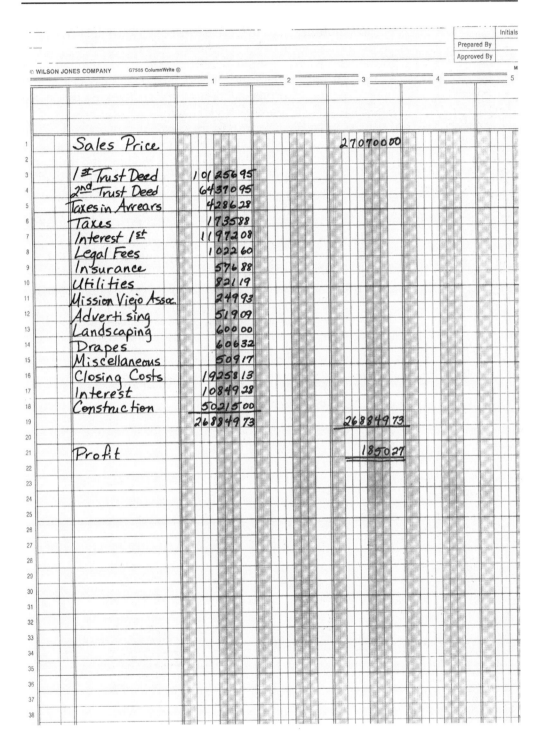

	1	2	3	4	5
Sales Price			27070000		
1st Trust Deed	10125695				
2nd Trust Deed	6437095				
Taxes in Arrears	428628				
Taxes	173588				
Interest 1st	1197208				
Legal Fees	102260				
Insurance	57688				
Utilities	82119				
Mission Viejo Assoc.	24993				
Advertising	51909				
Landscaping	60000				
Drapes	60632				
Miscellaneous	50917				
Closing Costs	1925813				
Interest	1084928				
Construction	5021500				
	26884973		26884973		
Profit			185027		

Figure 16.8   Closing Financial Statement for Upgraded Property

penses, from trust deeds to construction costs to interest on the money I had put up front. The bottom line is an $1,850 profit. In reality this wasn't profit at all, because there is nothing in these figures for my time and effort. Even though I hadn't been spending all my time on this one project, if I charged the time I did spend at an hourly basis, it would have been a clear loss.

As I said at the start, you can never be sure that any deal will end up the way you planned. Every deal is an opportunity or a learning experience. On the one hand, I did have the possibility of making a substantial profit if timing had worked in my favor— if I had gotten the approvals sooner, if the work had been started earlier, if the work had gone according to schedule. If I had been able to get this property on the market in December instead of March, then I might have been able to sell it for $330,000—the market price at that point in time—or at least for the $319,000 that I was figuring on. In that case I would have had a very big profit. But all those "ifs" did not happen and I didn't make the profit I had hoped for. On the other hand, I did learn a lot from this job. Since that time the experiences I got on this job have helped me on many other jobs I have been involved in.

CHAPTER 17

Being a Real Estate Investor

You can't take it with you? Why not,
I'm only going as far as the bank.

—*Jack Benny*

Once you've made a deal on a property, you have several choices. If you don't have enough money to carry the property, you must sell it immediately. If you don't have enough money for a down payment, you must sell within the "option" period. But in the event you have enough money to acquire the property, you can consider leasing it rather than selling it.

The Sell or Lease form shown in Figure 17.1 allows you to completely analyze what you should do with a property. Once you complete the form, the numbers will tell you whether the property will provide the best return as a sale or as a lease. The form assumes that you have observed the between-two-houses fundamentals, that you did a careful study of property values in your special territory, and that you have a pretty good grasp of what will happen there in the future.

If you decide to lease the property, you need to be very committed. You must maintain the property just as if you were going to live in it. Keep it neat and clean. Keep up the landscaping. Put the place in the best possible shape before showing it to any prospective tenants, and make sure they understand that this is the way they must maintain the property. It isn't difficult to keep the property in good shape, and it is very important to do so because you can attract better tenants that way. Also, you can keep your overall repair bills down. By keeping your property in good shape, you will be able to continue improving its value.

Sell or Lease

B.T.H. No. _____ _____
(lot)   (block)

Facts

Cash needed before sale or lease: _____

Projected monthly carrying costs if leased: _____

Projected monthly income from leasing: _____

Cash that sale of this property would generate: _____

Questions   Yes   No

1. Do I need the cash this sale would generate for
my next "specialist" deal?   _____   _____

2. On a monthly basis, will I need to put more of
my own cash into the property?   _____   _____

3. Do I forsee any "surprises" during the next
twenty-four months that could cost more out-of-pocket
cash than the tenants would pay in?   _____   _____

4. Do I forsee any "surprises" in the next twenty-four
months that could adversely affect the market
value of this property?   _____   _____

Only if you answered all four questions **no** should you **not** sell. That means **leasing** is the best decision on this property to maximize your financial gains.

If any answer is yes, **sell.**

Figure 17.1   Sell or Lease Form Used to Determine Best Return

How Sell-or-Lease Decisions Are Made

One of the properties I acquired from a troubled owner was located near a Marine air base. Property values had held up very well during the previous five years, so I had no reason to believe they would not continue to hold up. I filled out the Sell or Lease form, and all my answers were no until question 4: Do I foresee any "surprises" during the next twenty-four months that could adversely affect the market value of the property?

Then I remembered that the county had set up a task force to seek locations for a major new commercial airport. One of the suggested sites was this Marine air base. But since the Marines were opposed to surrendering this location, I suspected that the existing activities on the base might change in some manner. Then the property values would be affected (probably in a negative way). I decided that yes was the best answer.

Any yes answer on the form is a sell signal. Within six months I sold the property for a profit of over $20,000, which was 20 percent of the sales price and over 10 times the $2,000 cash I had put into the property. That $20,000 gave me the cash to make several more deals I hadn't counted on earlier that year.

Nothing happened at the air base to hurt property values during the next twelve to eighteen months. But then a builder entered the area and began building large numbers of competitively priced homes, which did have a negative effect on prices. Although I didn't know this was specifically what would happen, the Sell or Lease form stimulated me to consider all aspects of the future financial situation.

Most properties I have purchased recently have been hold-and-lease deals, but remember that everything changes. You must review your sell-or-lease decisions at least once a year. There is an optimum time to sell most properties.

As a specialist in your area, you will be the first to recognize the following "sell" signals:

• Some adverse happening in the area that might hurt the value of the property

• General economic conditions that would combine to reduce your values

• Unexpected expenses that would hurt your cash flow

In addition, your personal tax situation may weigh heavily in sell-or-lease decisions. Or the cash realized from a sale might bring a higher return in another deal or two. Consider all these factors when you use the Sell or Lease form. (See Case Study 17.1.)

Acquiring Prospective Tenants

To attract the best tenants, you need to show the property the way it should look when the tenants leave. The inside must be clean, the lawn must be cut, the house must be painted. To attract better-than-average tenants, your property must look better-than-average and be in better-than-average condition.

The best way to get tenants is to advertise in all the regional and local newspapers. The larger and more eye-catching your ad and the more circulation it gets, the faster the home will be leased. As soon as you figure the monthly payment you want, place an effective ad as quickly as possible. As a general rule, most people have better success running ads during the week rather than on weekends.

Put both a home and a work phone number in the ad so people can call at their convenience. Make the ad comprehensible and enticing to prospective tenants. Include all the home's good points. Previously you listed ten good points for every house you were thinking of purchasing. This is the time to review that list, select the top three or four points, and feature them in the ad. Use all the positive adjectives and phrases that you can truthfully use to make the house sound appealing.

Selecting Tenants

Usually a good ad produces more than enough qualified prospective tenants. You will not have enough time to see everybody, so you must be as selective as possible over the phone. Quite a bit can be learned about a person during a phone conversation.

The best thing to discuss is your basic requirements. Ask about their income, the number of people in the family, and how often they move. Thus you can make a judgment about their qualifications before you actually see them. Then ask them questions that will cover some or all of the following points:

• Are they negative about their previous landlord?

• Are they negative about the area they are living in?

• Are they reluctant to give credit references?

• Do they seem to be on the upswing of a career or on the downswing?

Case Study 17.1

This lovely condo in Orange County, California, was owned by two real estate brokers who had a falling out and stopped speaking to each other. I was called in by a mutual friend to help them dissociate themselves from this deal. I also picked up a good rental unit with only $2,000 cash down.

Market value	$86,000
First loan ($30,000 at 8 percent)	$220.13
Second loan ($15,000 at 10 percent, interest only)	125.00
Third loan ($15,000 at 15 percent, interest only)	187.50

Adding taxes of $60 a month and association fees of $40 a month, their total carrying charges were about $635. They had it rented for only $490, but the fair market rental was at least $590 a month.

I proposed a purchase price of $82,000. (Being real estate people, they readily agreed that a deduction of about 5 percent for fees was reasonable.) I agreed to pay $1,000 cash to each one and to give each a $10,000 personal note at 10 percent interest, all due and payable in three years. After much negotiating, we settled on 12 percent ballooning in five years. The ex-partners preferred this plan, because it deferred any reportable gain they had for five years.

I immediately raised the rent to $600 a month and within a year was renting the unit for $650 a month. Thus I had a positive cash flow after investing less than $400 in negative payout.

Within two years after my purchase, comparable condos in this tract were selling for $107,500. Shortly after my note expired, after owning it for five years, I sold my unit for over $130,000 and made a good profit.

When they talk, really listen. If your applicants are negative about any of the above points, they may turn out to be problem tenants. And listen for angry or disturbing noises in the background that might betray problems.

After this prequalifying conversation, meet the people you're interested in and get a feel for how they might take care of the property. Before meeting prospective tenants, formulate some idea of your minimum requirements for such things as income and credit experience. You have a right to set up restrictions, as long as they aren't based on race, creed, color, national origin, gender, or marital status. Lately state legislatures have been passing new laws, making it harder for owners to rule out possible tenants for specific reasons. Just get to know your local laws so you won't encounter problems. Usually, however, you can check items like employment history, pets, ability to come up with your security deposit, banking references, and landlord references. The Tenant Information form (see Figure 17.2) includes most of these things.

What you're looking for are responsible people who understand what you mean when you say the property must be kept in good condition. Desirable people should make good money, so they know its value, and should have a good credit rating and wish to maintain it. These people should be able to understand your problems.

Some of the Most Important Qualifications

If tenants are going to pay $900 a month on lease payments, they need to earn more than $2,200 a month on the job. Most lenders insist that home buyers earn at least three and a half times their total shelter payments in gross income. Some lenders even require more. If you insist on a three-to-one ratio, you can feel reasonably sure that the tenants will be able to pay. At least make sure they would have enough left from their gross salary after paying the lease and other payments to equal about $1,000–1,500 a month depending on the cost of living in your state for a family of four.

Check the employment record of prospective tenants. If they are "job jumpers," you could have problems. But if they have spent more than a year each on at least two of the last three jobs, the chances are good that they will be responsible.

One of the better ways to check people's credit is to call their bank references. Ask all the usual leading questions about their ability to pay: Have they written any bad checks? Have they had other financial problems? This is an easy way to avoid the expense and time of getting credit bureau reports.

Tenant Information

Anticipated length of occupancy		

PERSONAL DATA

	Date of	Social Security No.	
Name	Birth	Drivers Lic. No.	Expir. Date
Name of cotenant		Social Security No.	
Present address		Drivers Lic. No.	Expir Date
City/State/Zip		Res. phone	Bus. phone
How long at present address		Landlord or Agent	Phone
Previous address	How long?	Landlord or Agent	Phone
City/State/Zip			

Occupants: }	Relationships:	Pets?
	Ages:	

Car Make	Year	Model	Color	License No.

OCCUPATION

	PRESENT OCCUPATION	* PRIOR OCCUPATION	COTENANT'S OCCUPATION
Occupation			
Employer			
Self-employed d.b.a.			
Business Address			
Business Phone			
Type of Business			
Position held			
Name and Title of Superior			
How long?			
Monthly Gross Income			

*if employed or self-employed less than two years,
give same information on prior occupation.

REFERENCES

Bank reference		Address		Phone	

CREDIT REFERENCE	ACCOUNT NO.	ADDRESS	HIGHEST AMOUNT OWED	PURPOSE OF CREDIT	ACCOUNT OPEN OR DATE CLOSED

PERSONAL REFERENCE	ADDRESS	PHONE	LENGTH OF ACQUAINTANCE	OCCUPATION

NEAREST RELATIVE	ADDRESS	PHONE	CITY	RELATIONSHIP

Figure 17.2 Tenant Information Form for Evaluating Potential Lessees

The best check on prospective tenants is to go back to their last residence and talk to their previous landlord and neighbors. If the people live anywhere within an hour's drive, this step is well worth the effort. You want to be sure they are not losers or troublemakers. Obviously, if the tenants are from out of state or live in an area too difficult to reach, then a phone call or letter would be in order. The best way to check, however, is for you to go personally to see how the prospective tenants are living. Observe how they keep their property. Time spent now can save you hundreds of dollars later.

The Security Deposit

Before you give tenants possession of the property, collect the first and last month's payments in advance to be used against any repair or cleaning costs. Most people expect to pay this kind of deposit. If a person doesn't have this kind of money available before occupancy, that's a sure sign of trouble. Somebody who agrees to pay $500 a month but is unable to come up with $1,000 for a security deposit will probably not be able to make the payments over the term of the lease.

Impress upon tenants that you do not intend to use the deposit for the last month's payment. You want it for security in case the property has been deliberately or accidentally damaged. Tell the tenants that any expenses to repair the property will be deducted from the security deposit. If they leave the property as it is now, all the money will be returned.

The Lease Agreement and Contract

Put all understandings between you and the tenants in writing. In most states oral agreements are not enforceable. Putting agreements in writing can eliminate many headaches later. Few tenants will renege on a written agreement. More importantly, they know the terms are more enforceable and will do their best to comply to the letter.

Figure 17.3 is a sample Lease Agreement used in many different states that can be modified to suit your particular situation. Note that it provides for a $10 penalty if the lease payment is overdue by five days. As long as the agreement is in writing, you can include a penalty for late payments. At all costs, include in the lease provisions for the economic conditions that might prevail in the next year or two.

Any agreement you use should also include details about breaking the lease if something doesn't happen as planned. Sometimes tenants must move before the lease runs out, or you may want

---

THIS IS INTENDED TO BE A LEGALLY BINDING AGREEMENT—READ IT CAREFULLY.

Owner leases to Tenant and Tenant hires from Owner premises described as:

_____

together with the following furniture, appliances if any, and fixtures:

_____
_____
with the maximum number of tenants being (including children) _____
The terms of this lease shall be month-to-month beginning on the first day of _____ ,20 _____
1. Tenant is to pay $ per month which is due and payable on the first day of each month for the duration of this lease.
2. The rent shall be paid at P.O. Box 7594: Laguna Niguel, CA 92657 or at any address designated by the owner in writing. The rent is payable in advance on the first day of every calendar month to Owner or to his Agent.

IF RENT IS UNPAID AT THE SECOND DAY OF THE MONTH, A 5% LATE CHARGE SHALL BE ADDED TO THE ABOVE RENT AND THE OWNER RESERVES THE RIGHT TO TERMINATE THIS AGREEMENT.

3. $_____ as a security/ $_____ cleaning fee/ $_____ pet deposit has been deposited. Owner may use therefrom such amounts as are necessary to remedy Tenant's defaults in the payment of rent, any legal service needed by Owner to recieve rent owed, to repair damages caused by Tenant, and to clean premises upon termination of tenancy. If used toward rent or damages during the term of tenancy, Tenant agrees to reinstate said total security deposit upon five days written notice delivered to Tenant in person or by mailing. Balance of security deposit, if any, together with a written itemized accounting shall be mailed to Tenant's last known address within 14 days of surrender of premesis.
4. Tenant agrees to pay for all utilities and services based upon occupancy of the premises and the following charges:
_____ except which shall be paid for by Owner.
5. Tenant has examined the premises and all furniture, furnishings and appliances if any, and fixtures contained therein, and accepts the same as being clean, in good order, condition and repair, with the following exceptions:
6. The premises are leased for use as a residence by the following persons

_____	SS# _____	TENANT
_____	SS# _____	TENANT
_____	SS# _____	COSIGNER

and no other and may not be subletted. Occupancy by guests staying over 15 days will be in violation of this provision unless written consent is given by Owner.
7. No animal bird or pet except _____
shall be kept on the premises without Owner's prior written consent.
8. Any holding over at the expiration of this lease shall create a month-to-month tenancy at a rate of120% payable in advance. Rental is from the first of the month to the last of the month. Notices for move-out must be given 30 days prior. All move-outs after the first of the month must pay the full month's rent. All other terms and conditions herein shall remain in full force and effect.
9. Tenant's absence from the premises for five (5) days while all or any portion of the rent is unpaid shall be deemed an abandonment of said premises. Owner may at his option terminate this agreement, and regain possesion in the manner prescribe by law. Tenant shall be liable for the entire rent due for the remainder of the term or the cost of re-renting the premises including rent loss; the cost of restoring the premises to the condition at the time it was rented, and reasonable fees for re-renting the premises Unless otherwise notified in writing prior to departure, all property left upon the premises by Tenant upon vacating jor abandoning the premises, shall be deemed abandoned and may be disposed of by Owner as he sees fit and without accountability to Tenant.

TENANT(S) AGREES TO THE FOLLOWING:
B. Tenant shall not disturb, annoy, endanger or interfere with other tenants of the building or neighbors, nor use the premises for any unlawful purposes, nor violate any law or ordinance, nor commit waste or nuisance upon or about the premises.
C. To keep from making loud noises or disturbances and to keep from playing music and broadcasting programs loudly so as not to disturb other people's peace and quiet.
D. Not to paint, wallpaper, or alter interior or exterior of said premises in any way that may be objectionable without prior written consent from Owner.

Figure 17.3   Sample Lease Agreement Subject to Modifications

E. To park their motor vehicle in their assigned space and to keep that space clean of oil drippings.

F. Not to repair their motor vehicle on the premises.

G. Upon not less than twenty-four hours advance notice, Tenant shall make the demised pemises available during normal business hours to Owner or his authorized agent or representative for the purpose of entering (1) to make neccessary agreed repairs or cleaning, decorations, alterations or improvements or to supply neccessary or agreed services, and (2) to show the premises to prospective or actual purchasers, lenders, tenants, workmen or contractors. In an emergency, Owner or authorized agent or representative may enter the premises at any time without securing prior permission from Tenant for the purpose of making corrections or repairs to alleviate such emergency.

H. Not to keep any liquid-filled furniture in this dwelling.

I. To pay rent by money order made out to ____ or by cash. NO PERSONAL CHECKS are accepted in payment of rent. If an exception is made and the check is returned for any reason, Tenant is responsible for all bank charges and a 5% late fee.

J. To pay for repairs of all damages, including drain stoppages, they or their guests have caused.

K. To pay for any windows broken in their dwelling while they live there.

L. Tenant agrees to comply with all reasonable rules or regulations posted on the premises or delivered to Tenant by Owner or his agent.

M. Time is of the essence. The waiver by Owner or Tenant of any breach shall not be construed to be a continuing waiver of any subsequent breach.

N. Tenant agrees to keep public ways, such as sidewalks, driveways, garage areas and stairwells free of toys, bicycles, any type of motorized vehicles, or any obstacle that may be a safety hazard to others. Bicycles should be kept in the rear car-port/garage or assigned parking.

O. Owner is not liable for any damage done to food or personal property of tenants caused by failure of leased appliances. Tenant is not to try to fix or call a repair service on his/her own without prior consent from the Owner. If Tenant decides to call a repair service on his/her own, the Owner is not held liable for such repairs.

Violation of any part of this agreement or nonpayment of rent when due shall be cause for eviction under appropriate sections of the applicable code, and the prevailing party shall recover court costs and reasonable attorneys fees involved.

If Owner is unable to deliver possession of the premises as agreed, Owner shall not be liable for any damage caused. Tenant shall not be liable for any rent until possession is delivered. Tenant may terminate this agreement if possession is not delivered as agreed above.

Owner shall not be liable for any damages or losses to person or property caused by other Tenants or other persons. Owner shall not be liable for personal injury or damage or loss of Tenant's personal property (furniture, jewelery, clothing etc.) from theft, vandalism, fire, water, rain, hail, smoke, explosions, sonic booms, or other causes whatsoever, unless the same is due to the negligence of Owner. Owner strongly reccomends that Tenant secure insurance to protect himself/herself against the above occurrences. If any of Owner's employees are requested to render any services such as moving automobiles, handling of furniture, cleaning, delivering packages or any other service not contemplated in this contract, such employee shall be deemed the agent of Tenant, regardless of whether payment is arranged for such service and Tenant agrees to hold Owner harmless from all liability in connection with such services.

No failure of Owner to enforce any part of this agreement shall be deemed a waiver, nor shall any acceptance of a partial payment of rent be deemed a waiver of Owner's right to the full amount.

The undersigned Tenant acknowledges having read the foregoing prior to execution and receipt of a copy hereof.

Owner: _____   Tenant: _____

Owner: _____   Tenant: _____

Figure 17.3   Sample Lease Agreement Subject to Modifications   *Continued*

them to move out before the lease expires because you've decided to sell the property. There should be a provision in the lease agreement for a penalty when the tenants break the lease. Even though they are liable for the full term of the lease should they move out, you are legally bound to lease the property as quickly as possible.

It's easy to lease properties because there is usually a shortage of good rentals. Your position is more difficult when you want the tenants to move and they have time left on the lease. You need a protective clause in the lease agreement, and you need to present it as an opportunity for the tenants. Tell them that they can break the lease by paying only two or three months' rent. Tell them this clause is their best protection against getting stuck for the entire balance of the lease if circumstances force them to move. In return, you can break the lease (and evict them) by giving them two or three months' notice. By tying such an agreement to the security deposit, you can make it much more enforceable.

Be aware, however, that a legal hassle with tenants, trying to evict or force them out of the property, is very expensive and highly aggravating. So try to select tenants who are compatible with your needs and plans. Then be a good landlord. Anything else takes too much time, effort, and energy away from your main activity of securing new properties. Legal action also creates ill will and bad feelings. The right tenants won't want legal action either.

Advantages of No Lease

The landlord laws are so tough in many states that it is almost impossible to enforce the terms of a lease. Under those conditions, it's better to have no lease but still collect the first and last month's rent plus a security deposit. In fact, with no lease you can raise your rents more often if market conditions are favorable. Stating "no lease requirement" in your ad for the property may also bring you more desirable applicants. If the laws of the state make leases hard to enforce anyway, this may be the way for you to operate.

When the Tenants Leave

Unless the tenants have thoroughly cleaned the house before leaving, someone will have to come in and do a cleaning job that could cost between $50 and $200. Your agreement with the tenants was that the property would be left in the same condition as it was when they moved in. Deduct the cleaning bill from the security deposit if it isn't.

Figure 17.4 is a sample Checkout List for departing tenants that shows all the items to be covered. It is an excellent means of communication between you and the tenants. It helps sidestep arguments about how much money should be deducted from the security deposit. In many cases tenants would prefer that the landlord have the work done and deduct the money, to save them time

Deductions from the security deposit will be made based on the need to bring this dwelling back to the condition it was in at the time you moved in. Please review all the rooms. This list was used to prepare the dwelling for your occupancy and will be used to prepare it for the next family's occupancy.

A. Bedrooms and Living Room
1. Clean all closets, doors, doortracks, and baseboards.
2. Vacuum rugs or carpets.

B. Kitchen
1. Clean refrigerator inside, outside, behind, and underneath.
2. Clean stove inside, outside, racks, broiler and top drip pans. Clean fan.
3. Clean cabinets inside and outside. Remove all paper.
4. Clean dishwasher inside and outside. Clean light fixtures.
5. Clean floors–remove wax or shampoo carpet.

C. Bathrooms
1. Clean shower stalls, walls, chrome, fan and medicine cabinet.
2. Clean floors, baseboards, mirrors and light fixtures.

D. All Areas
1. Clean all windows inside and out. Dust screens.
2. Clean and replace all light fixtures.
3. Vacuum wall heater and air conditioner.
4. Clean all baseboards and wood paneling, if any.
5. Sweep and wash, if neccessary, all balconies and patios.
6. Remove all trash, clippings and debris from the premises.
7. Repair anything that is broken or damaged.

Figure 17.4 Sample Checkout List for Departing Tenants to Follow

and effort. If the property has been inspected with the tenants in the beginning and again when they leave, you should all completely agree, especially if you use the checklist. You might even say at the outset that most tenants average a $50 to $200 deduction from their security deposit for extra cleaning and repair work. By warning tenants of the likelihood of the deduction at the beginning, you make it easier to obtain later.

Make Friends with the Tenants

There are three R's of leasing, just as in learning. They are Repeat, Referral, and Reputation. If you're going to continue being a landlord, you need to have repeat business, referral business, and reputation business.

It's important to have a good relationship with tenants, because you will be doing business with them again. If you were correct in selecting a desirable territory and correct in believing home values will increase there, then the tenants you select probably will feel the same way. Thus they will be future customers who might be interested in buying another home you have in the area. In addition, they will recommend you to their friends—or perhaps they will tell people bad things about you and make things more difficult later on. Tenants, former tenants, and their friends and relatives may be the neighbors you will go to when you try to acquire other troubled property.

There is every reason to believe that you can have a good relationship with tenants because you are linked in a simple business transaction. You have a property available for lease, and they are looking for a place to live. Each party gives the other value. There is no reason for antagonism. If you look for the right kind of people, you can end up with new friends who will soon become old friends.

Basic Economic Law

Remember that inflation is increasing at an average rate of about 4 percent per year. Double-digit inflation appears every seven years or so. Some parts of the economy, and some areas of the country, have inflation rates higher than others.

If you have selected your area properly, property values there will increase faster than the national average. That may be 8 percent per year or more. If the rate is 8 percent, every nine years the property will double in value. Most properties in many areas have increased at just about that rate in the last six years. This being the case, maintain your chosen property as well as you can so its rate of appreciation will be more than the average.

Bear in mind that you could perhaps realize an effective 18 to 20 percent return on your investment under the following conditions:

- If the property value is increasing at 8 percent annually

- If there is a cash flow from its lease

- If you are paying off the mortgage principal

- If you are deducting from taxes your expenses and interest on the loan

The most important thing to remember is that a single-family rental property is a money-making machine. It should be well cared for so that it works better, stronger, harder, and more productively.

The Secret of Success

Once you find the magic formula, never let it go. Once you have acquired the knack of securing properties and leasing them so they continue to appreciate while producing income for you, keep on trying to improve the formula so it will work better. If you develop good relationships with people in your chosen territory, this is a system for making money. If one property works, two will work; if two work, then four or six will work. There is no real limit to the number of properties you can have making money for you in an area.

It is possible, however, that you may start feeling that a good area has too many risks. If so, you can do several things instead of simply increasing your exposure in one area:

- Hire someone to work with you, so you can expand to another area.

- Invest in other types of income-producing property in your main area.

- If you are more sure of the territory than you are afraid of the risks, substantially increase your percentage of holdings in that area.

If you follow this last course, be positive there are no "knockout drops," nothing that could seriously impair the value of properties in the area. These could range from the relocation of a major employer to the planned building of several "new towns" that could cause an oversupply of housing. There is no sense in having too many eggs in one basket. However, if you are sure that your area is going to prosper and if you know the area well, you could have a virtual monopoly in this business.

CHAPTER 18
The Time of Your Life

*Without enterprise none can be rich and
with it few can be poor.*
—Samuel Johnson

Full-page ads are now appearing in many newspapers around
the country about free seminars on how to make money on foreclosure properties. These introductory seminars describe courses
held at a later date, which then give full details on buying and selling foreclosure properties in a chosen area. The fees for these
courses run from $65 to $450, and the seminars are usually given
from 9 A.M. to 4 P.M. on a Saturday.

Here are some of the quotes from newspaper advertisements
selling some of these programs:

*"Other people . . . just like you . . . have learned to make big profits buying and
selling . . . foreclosure property. . . . Let me show you how."*

*"Every homeowner, real estate investor, apartment renter, too, should attend this
revealing program."*

*"You can earn 20 percent to 100 percent cash returns by learning how to buy
and sell foreclosure properties."*

Many more seminars of a similar nature are given by well-
known lawyers, brokers, authors, syndicators, and the like.

They Are All Worth Considering

You can gain many benefits by attending these local seminars.
Not only can you get valuable data on who county and state offic-

ers are and the correct procedures in your specific locality, but you can learn some of the shortcuts that the pros in this field have been practicing for years.

By asking questions, you can learn the names and addresses of local publishers of default notices. You can discover which title and escrow companies are easiest to deal with.

Many people attending these seminars can be turned into valuable contacts who may help later with ideas and advice.

Any questions you have come across during your efforts to make deals might be answered by the course instructor or by a referral.

In short, these courses can help you do the very thing for which you bought this *Goldmining in Foreclosure Properties*. Take it along, and make notes in it that pertain to your personal program.

Testimonials Abound

Because hundreds of deals are being made daily throughout the United States, it is easy to find testimonials encouraging participation. Here are a few that appear regularly in advertisements:

"Our first deal just closed for a net profit of $3,700."

"On my first deal I made twice what it took me all of last year to make. I have since bought and sold six more properties."

"Now I have a house with $15,000 equity. We have both left our jobs to work full time."

"Two weeks after the seminar my first deal was in escrow, and after closing it gave me a profit of $17,000."

"We are indebted to you for the home we moved into—we bought it the way you taught and saved lots of money."

"My second sale is closing and will produce a net return of $7,800."

"We can't believe it. From just our small home to over a half-million dollars in rental homes in one year—$75,000 net."

And many, many more. All true, all documented and verified.

Anyone, Anywhere Can Participate

This is one of the best times in recent history for anyone to make money in real estate. Today's circumstances may never happen again. Credit and financial conditions keep changing, and new debt instruments may appear on the financial scene that could alter the picture permanently. Now is the time to act. Review *Goldmining in Foreclosure Properties* and your notes one more time, and then resolve to forge ahead. Follow the steps below to get started:

1. Choose your place in the Distress Property Cycle.

2. Decide on a between-two-houses area for your own.

3. Be a specialist, and know property values in your area better than anyone else.

4. Keep informed on all real estate transactions.

5. Collect a suspect list.

6. Narrow it down to good prospects and evaluate them.

7. Meet and negotiate with your prospects before legal action starts.

8. Go to an auction better prepared than your competitors.

9. Work with lenders and government agencies to help them unload their repos.

10. Close the deal.

11. Decide whether to resell or keep the property.

This is the time to start. You have a real and continuing opportunity to mine gold from your chosen area. And being a specialist in distress properties will fill a need in the exciting world of real estate.

CHAPTER 19

Dealing with Bankruptcy Cases

As mentioned in Chapter 10, the threat of bankruptcy can generate considerable leverage when the time comes to negotiate with a lender. In this chapter we'll examine bankruptcy in greater detail—and you may decide that the threat of bankruptcy is better than the reality of bankruptcy, since it complicates things for the lender, the debtor, and for you.

But while bankruptcy filings are a source of possible problems for anyone hoping to profit from distress property, they do not put you out of business. That is because bankruptcy involves unsecured debt, such as credit card bills or personal business debt. Mortgages are secured debt, and filing for bankruptcy does not erase what's owed on a mortgage. Basically, it just complicates the legal status of the property.

In fact, when it comes to foreclosure, the best a debtor can hope for by filing bankruptcy (as explained later) is that, after submitting the right papers, presenting a financial plan that passes muster with a judge, and making catch-up payments, three to five years down the road he or she may be able to get a defaulted mortgage reinstated by the lender.

Short of that, a foreclosure can still proceed, although under circumstances controlled by the bankruptcy court. The most that a debtor is going to do by filing for bankruptcy protection is delay a foreclosure—briefly.

Bankruptcy: The Big Picture

As stated, bankruptcy really only covers unsecured debts. But even with unsecured debts, the debtor does not get to just walk away—some attempt at payoff is required. But after a debtor files for bankruptcy, he or she is protected from further collection efforts by creditors. Then, at the end of the bankruptcy process, which may involve a liquidation of assets or a repayment effort, the debtor's unsecured debts are discharged (i.e., forgiven, wiped clean). Creditors are barred from ever again taking any action to collect the discharged debts, including legal action, phone calls, and personal visits.

Meanwhile, there are exceptions—certain unsecured debts cannot be discharged under the Bankruptcy Code, as we'll explain later.

Otherwise, freed from impossible debt, the honest debtor can become a productive member of the economy again, while the creditor suffers for having irresponsibly loaned money to someone who could not pay it back.

At least, that's the theory. In practice, the prevalence of personal bankruptcy has gone up by almost a factor of five in the last two decades, from about 288,000 cases in 1980 to 1.4 million in 2001. The rate of business bankruptcies, on the other hand, has shown no fundamental change—there were about 40,000 in 1980 and there were about 40,000 in 2001. (Actually, the number of business filings peaked in 1987 at 82,000 and bottomed in 2000 at 35,000.)

In response, various efforts have arisen to amend the Bankruptcy Code basically to make personal bankruptcy less attractive and harder to obtain. These efforts may or may not ever become law. If they do, the proposed changes (explained later in this chapter) may or may not lead to a decline in the rate of personal bankruptcy filings.

But either way, bankruptcy has become part of the landscape, and you will need to become familiar with the topic if you plan to work with distress property.

Caveat

This chapter can help you understand what the participants are talking about in a case involving bankruptcy, but it cannot pretend to replace the advice of an attorney-at-law. Aside from the fact that the law is being tinkered with at the time of this writing, the Bankruptcy Code is chock full of grace periods, filing deadlines, and picky exceptions. Meanwhile, there are technical issues (such as multiparty cases, cosigners, divorce cases, and homestead exemptions) whose handling and consequences differ between jurisdictions.

Overview: The Bankruptcy Chapters

Bankruptcy in the United States is entirely a matter of federal law. There are no state bankruptcy laws, and all bankruptcies are filed through the federal court system under the Federal Bankruptcy Code. (The states do have some input concerning homestead exemptions, which we'll get to later.)

The Bankruptcy Code of the United States is divided into chapters. Different kinds of bankruptcies are commonly referred to by the chapter that controls that kind, so once you understand the chapters you'll also have a grasp of bankruptcy law. We'll look at them in the order of their importance to a distress property specialist:

• *Chapter 7.* This chapter deals with liquidations, both individual and corporate. The assets of the debtor—including real estate—are turned over to the court, where together they become the bankruptcy estate. The court sells each asset (or allows repossession, or decides it's worthless and abandons it by giving it back to the debtor) and divides the proceeds among the creditors. The debtor loses that property, but gets to walk away debt free.

• *Chapter 13.* This chapter concerns personal bankruptcy, where the debtors reschedule or renegotiate their debts. Obviously, it applies to people who retain a steady income despite their problems and is often called *wage-earner bankruptcy.* Unlike Chapter 7, the debtor has some hope of retaining his or her property. The court oversees a repayment plan and monitors the debtor's budget during the course of the plan, which may run three to five years. Unsecured debts that cannot be repaid over that period may be discharged. If the debtor catches up on the mortgage during the plan period, the lender must reinstate the loan. However, only about a third of filers manage to work out their plans, and the others may end up worse off than before. Companies and partnerships cannot use Chapter 13, although sole proprietorships can.

• *Chapter 12.* Family farmers who also have a regular income can use this chapter for debt protection, allowing them to reorganize under a repayment plan. Basically, it's very similar to Chapter 13. The pending revision of the law makes Chapter 12 a permanent part of the Bankruptcy Code—it would have expired otherwise. (The revision will also add coverage for family fishing boats.)

• *Chapter 11.* This famous chapter lets businesses reorganize in order to settle their debts. The business may remain under the control of its management or the court may assign a trustee.

• *Chapter 9.* This chapter deals with municipal bankruptcies (i.e., the bankruptcy of a taxing entity, be it a large city or a toll bridge). There are not many such bankruptcies, and you will probably never be concerned about Chapter 9.

• There are also Chapters 1, 3, and 5, which deal with back-office issues like application and jurisdiction.

Notice that all the chapters have odd numbers except 12. This is the result of a century of tinkering with the original act in 1898, especially the major revisions of 1938 and 1978. Also, notice the use of arabic numerals. Officially, roman numerals refer to chapters in the Bankruptcy Code before it was overhauled in 1978. Updating to arabic numerals, picky as it may seem, removed a source of confusion, since the Bankruptcy Code is, more correctly, Title XI of the U.S. Code. Yes, thanks to the use of arabic numerals, lawyers can now readily distinguish between Title XI and Chapter 11.

Chapter 7 versus Chapter 13

For most individuals, the choice (when it comes to bankruptcy) is between Chapters 7 and 13. There are major differences in the way things are handled, so you need to fully understand the difference.

As stated, under Chapter 7, the debtor walks away with neither property nor debt—except for assets that are exempt and debts for which the law makes an exception, as we'll discuss later. The process can be completed in four to six months.

Under Chapter 13, the debtor may keep everything and may, in fact, pay off everything. But the process may take five years. Meanwhile, Chapter 13 distinguishes between priority and nonpriority debts. Priority debts must be paid in full. These include unpaid wages, spousal or child support, and recent taxes. On the other hand, payment of nonpriority debts under a court-approved repayment plan can amount to as little as 10 percent— but everything hinges on what the judge thinks is reasonable when the repayment plan is drawn up. When the plan is written, the creditors must receive at least as much (by the end of the plan) as they would have gotten had the debtor liquidated under Chapter 7. And all of the debtor's disposable income must be fed into the repayment plan during the three- to five-year reorganization period.

Of course, in the real world, further trouble often arises during the reorganization period since the underlying cause of the financial problems didn't suddenly vanish. As for the mortgage, the debtor was likely mortgaged to the hilt before filing, and catching up on the payments, much less reinstating the mortgage, is probably not a realistic option.

But in a Chapter 7 personal bankruptcy, if there is no equity that can be used to pay the creditors, and if—and that's a big if—the mortgage is not in default, the trustee may abandon the house to the debtor. So in this situation the bankrupt homeowner gets to keep the house—and the mortgage that goes with it, which of course remains in force.

Meanwhile, thanks to local exemptions (explained later in this chapter) it may be that the house will be treated as if it had no equity.

There are also major differences in the kinds of exceptions that Chapter 7 and Chapter 13 allow, as explained later in this chapter. These differences can be the deciding factor when a debtor decides which form of bankruptcy to use.

But with either chapter, filing for bankruptcy protection, in and of itself, does not cause a debtor to lose a house—if there is no default and the mortgage payments continue to be made.

Exemptions

Some assets are exempt from the bankruptcy procedure, and the creditors are barred from getting at them. Exemptions can become an issue with distress real estate because the debtor's home may be added to the bankruptcy estate if there is equity in it that exceeds the exemption limit. The owner could lose the house in a bankruptcy sale, retaining only the exempt equity. (However, as we'll see, in some cases the exemption can be, in practice, unlimited.)

The idea behind asset exemption is that the debtor ought to be able to have a fresh start after emerging from bankruptcy, and for that purpose, certain things are left out of the bankruptcy estate. They are not available for settling debts, and the debtor gets to keep them. Exemptions typically include household goods, the means of daily living, tools of a trade, the contents of most pension plans, and, in some cases, a certain amount of the equity in the debtor's house.

And this is where things get complicated, because while the U.S. Bankruptcy Code stipulates its own list of exemptions, bankruptcy exemptions are actually set at the state level. (This is the only area of bankruptcy procedure that involves state law.) Fifteen states (Arkansas, Connecticut, Hawaii, Massachusetts, Michigan, Minnesota, New Jersey, New Mexico, Pennsylvania, Rhode Island, South Carolina, Texas, Vermont, Washington, and Wisconsin) plus the District of Columbia allow their citizens to use either the federal exemptions or their local state exemptions. The rest of the states set their own exemptions, and the federal exemptions cannot be used by their citizens.

The federal exemptions include $15,000 equity in the debtor's residence; another $2,400 equity in one car; household goods, clothes, appliances, musical instruments, and so forth not exceeding $8,000 total; $1,500 in tools of the trade or professional books; and prescribed health equipment. The debtor also has the right to continue to receive most benefits, pensions, annuities, and favorable court judgments.

Some of the state exemptions are much more liberal. As mentioned in Chapter 10 of this book, Californians can claim a homestead exemption of $100,000 if they are over sixty-five years old. Floridians can declare their homesteads exempt without regard for equity or market value. Similarly, a Texan in a rural area can exempt—regardless of equity or market value—a homestead of up to 200 acres with its associated farming or ranching equipment and a list of household goods that includes one motor vehicle for each person in the family who claims to need one and two firearms.

On the other hand, New Yorkers can only exempt equity up to $10,000, plus a list of personal goods that includes food, forage, and heating fuel for 60 days. In Illinois, a debtor can exempt only $7,500 of equity, plus a short list of personal goods.

Obviously, in bankruptcy cases where there is actual equity, you'll need the advice of someone with local legal expertise.

One final note: In a Chapter 13 case, the exemptions must be arranged so that the nonexempt assets are equal to what the creditor could get at if it were a Chapter 7 (liquidation) case. Of course, in many personal Chapter 7 cases there are no assets, nonexempt or otherwise.

Liens

A discussion of exemptions brings us to a discussion of liens, since one affects the other. Liens, like mortgages, can pass through a bankruptcy intact. This is because a lien is attached to the property, rather than the debtor, and amounts to another form of secured debt. But to the extent that a lien eats into the exempt portion of the equity of the property, the debtor can ask the court to avoid that lien. That (whole or partial) lien then becomes unsecured and subject to discharge under both Chapter 7 and 13.

Of course, a mortgage is another kind of lien, but the law says that a voluntary lien secured by the debtor's residence—a standard mortgage—cannot be avoided.

Lien stripping (as the process is called) is more of an issue with cars than with houses, since owing more on a car than it is worth is not uncommon and car loans are not covered by the exception that covers residential mortgages. The process is used to reduce the amount owed so that it is equal to the amount that the car is worth.

Liens are not stripped automatically. The debtor must file a motion stating exactly how the statutes entitle him or her to avoid the lien, and the creditor must be served with papers.

Exceptions

Meanwhile, there are debts that cannot be discharged under bankruptcy. Secured or unsecured, the law will not let you walk away from them. As stated, there are different exceptions defined by Chapter 7 and Chapter 13, and those exceptions can make a world of difference to individual debtors.

Debts that are not dischargeable in Chapter 7 include recent tax claims; spousal support, child support, or alimony; debts for willful or malicious injuries; government-imposed fines and penalties; debts incurred by fraud or intentional wrongdoing; government-backed student loans; condominium or cooperative housing fees; debts for personal injury caused by the debtor's operation of a motor vehicle while intoxicated; and most debts that did not show up on the bankruptcy petition.

Of course, fraud or intentional wrongdoing can be interpreted to mean charging sky-high credit card debts just before filing for Chapter 7 bankruptcy protection. Credit card companies are known to file adversary proceedings in Chapter 7 cases, saying that the filer's credit card debts were the result of fraud and therefore should be nondischargeable. Various events are known to rouse a credit card company to action, such as massive charging by an unemployed person who had no hope of repayment but who had recently visited a bankruptcy lawyer.

Chapter 13 is a little more liberal, and the debtors are discharged of all debts covered in their reorganization plans, except spousal support, child support, or alimony; government-based education loans; recent taxes, criminal fines, or court-ordered restitution; and drunk-driving injuries. Debts incurred through fraud or intentional wrongdoing can be discharged if the debtor can convince the judge that the repayment plan is a good faith effort. Therefore, adversarial proceedings by credit card firms are not an issue. Mortgages, of course, are not discharged, but, as mentioned previously, a defaulted loan can be reinstated.

Bankruptcy and Foreclosures

Remember, bankruptcy involves unsecured debt. Secured debts are not discharged. Mortgages, you'll recall, are secured debts—the house itself is the collateral for the mortgage loan, and in the event of a default the lender can seize it through a foreclosure process. Filing bankruptcy does not entirely prevent that from happening.

Filing for bankruptcy does, however, trigger an injunction called an *automatic stay* that halts all collection activity, such as lawsuits and garnishments, as well as foreclosures. (Collection activities connected with criminal proceedings, spousal or child support, and tax matters are the exceptions.)

A foreclosure can still proceed, but court permission is needed—the lender just needs to get a court order called a *relief from stay*. Relief is granted only after a hearing before the bankruptcy judge. Such hearings can be arranged on what the legal profession calls short notice, but in the real world that's two or three weeks. The lender has to file a written motion, and so he or she will probably need a lawyer. This involves additional expense, but the judge can have the attorney's fees charged to the bankruptcy estate or made part of the debtor's repayment plan.

In a Chapter 7 case the debtor is usually trying to delay the inevitable, while in a Chapter 13 case the debtor may be trying to avoid foreclosure altogether. In either case, the lender will have to show cause, since relief is not given automatically. The law recognizes two basic reasons for granting a relief of stay:

• The debtor does not have any equity in the house and the property is not necessary for the planned reorganization. (In other words, the foreclosure might as well go ahead since the house adds nothing to the bankruptcy estate.)

• "For cause," generally meaning that the debtor is not adequately taking care of the property.

A judge can grant a preliminary stay without a hearing if it is argued that the property faces irreparable harm before a hearing can be scheduled. But a real hearing must then follow.

If the debtor has some equity in the house, the court may decide to leave the stay in effect as long as the debtor continues to make payments to the lender and can rapidly catch up on the defaulted payments.

If the debtor is not actually in default but the lender still files for a relief of stay, the judge may not be amused, unless the lender can show that the bankruptcy filing was made in bad faith.

Meanwhile, if you're dealing with commercial owners or multi-unit properties, you might encounter something bankruptcy lawyers call the new debtor syndrome. With foreclosure imminent, the debtor might transfer the property to a new corporate entity that then declares bankruptcy. The new entity has only one asset—the distressed property—which presumably isn't generating enough revenue to cover its mortgage and upkeep. The debtor, oddly enough, retains control over the new entity.

Sensing abuse, Congress in 1994 added another ground for relief of stay. This exception covers cases involving real property that generates substantially all of the debtor entity's income and in which the debtor has no business involvement except to run the property, and the indebtedness is not greater than $4 million. If it is residential property, it has to involve more than four units. Under the new rule, the debtor has 90 days to come up with an appropriate reorganization plan or to start making reasonable monthly payments to the lender. Otherwise, the court will grant a relief of stay, and foreclosure can proceed.

Meanwhile, with ordinary residential property, there are cases where someone facing foreclosure will transfer at least partial ownership to someone else, who then declares bankruptcy. The court will not be fooled, and may treat it as a case of bankruptcy abuse or fraud.

In the final analysis, while foreclosures and bankruptcies are both indicators of financial distress, they are two very different things. There can be a foreclosure without there being any bankruptcy. A debtor can file bankruptcy and not suffer a foreclosure. And filing bankruptcy in the face of a foreclosure may not prevent the foreclosure.

Proposed Changes

As stated, the rate of personal bankruptcy filings has ballooned. In fact, so many people have been filing bankruptcy that pundits have begun calling bankruptcy a social welfare program overseen by the courts. Conservative commentators have pondered why most of the population doesn't file for bankruptcy, since the alleged advantages are so great.

In response, Congress came back with the Bankruptcy Abuse Prevention and Consumer Protection Act (pending in 2003). Under its terms, if bankruptcy is still a social welfare program, it will become one that Charles Dickens would feel at home with. It would not exactly bring back debtors' prisons or workhouses for the poor, but it does add more hoops for the debtor to jump through and generally assumes that anyone filing for bankruptcy protection is trying to shirk responsibilities, rather than a victim of economic hardship.

The end result may be that the threat to declare bankruptcy will generate less leverage with lenders, who will assume that the debtor is bluffing. But on the other hand, the deal you offer the debtor may look correspondingly more attractive, since the debtor probably will actually be bluffing.

The changes have been heavily backed by the credit card lobby, since most unsecured debts in personal bankruptcies involve credit card purchases. If you, too, get several unsolicited credit card offers per week in the mail, you might wonder if the credit card companies are asking the government to save them from the adverse results of their own marketing efforts. Nevertheless, the bill's chief opponents have rarely been so bold as to cite that conundrum, instead complaining that the revisions would (somehow) punish anti-abortion demonstrators.

Proposed Chapter 7 Changes

Before filing for Chapter 7 (liquidation) bankruptcy, the debtor will have to show eligibility. In most cases of personal bankruptcy the debtor is not eligible if his or her disposable income (based on the income of the preceding 6 months) is sufficient to pay 25 percent of the unsecured debt over a five-year period. Being able to amass a disposable income of more than $10,000 over the same period also makes the filer ineligible. The portion of the income that is disposable (as opposed to necessary for upkeep) would be defined using the same guidelines that the Internal Revenue Service (IRS) uses when it decides how much wages to garnish from tax cheats.

Assuming the filer has proven eligible, he or she must then go through some kind of court-approved consumer credit debt counseling to see if the debts can be paid outside of bankruptcy. (Presumably, this will delay the process at least a month.)

Having finally satisfied the requirements, the filer can enter into Chapter 7 bankruptcy, but a condition of final discharge is that the debtor must finish an instructional course on personal financial management.

Meanwhile, any so-called party at interest (in other words, a creditor) may move to dismiss the bankruptcy or convert the filing to Chapter 13 on the grounds that the filer's budget or income makes him or her ineligible. But such an abuse motion will only be granted if the filer's income is above the median income in that state for a family of the same size.

It gets better: While, previously, the judge could dismiss a bankruptcy filing after finding substantial abuse, the new law removes the word "substantial." Meanwhile, there will be a presumption of abuse if the debtor's monthly income is more than a certain figure, such as $10,000, or a certain ratio of the unsecured debts.

Chapter 13 Changes

Like Chapter 7, Chapter 13 filers will have to undergo court-approved consumer credit debt counseling to see if the debts can be paid outside of bankruptcy, and (before discharge) must complete a course on personal financial management.

If the debtor's income is above the median for that state for a family of the same size, the debtor must use a five-year payback plan. This means he or she must pay back all the debts that can be paid back in five years, based on the disposable income available during that time. The payment plan will be based on the previous 6 months' income and will use IRS guidelines to decide what part of the income is disposable. Those with lesser income may use three years as the limit.

Other Proposed Provisions

The homestead exemption will be fixed, probably at $100,000 or $125,000, overriding the option to use the limit (if any) set by the state. The debtor will have to have lived in the house longer to get the exemption, probably two years instead of 180 days.

The automatic stay that is granted upon filing for bankruptcy will no longer prevent a rental landlord from evicting a defaulted tenant. But as for getting paid, the landlord becomes another unsecured creditor.

Lien stripping would be severely restricted.

Reaffirmation agreements would have to be approved by the court. These are agreements by the debtor to go ahead and pay specific debts despite the bankruptcy filing. In the past they have been pressed upon debtors by creditors who said that it would help the debtors' credit ratings. And this provision appears to be the sole justification for putting the words "consumer protection" in the bill's title.

Final Argument

Basically, you don't want distress property owners to file for bankruptcy while you are dealing with them, because the one thing that a filing is certain to do is to complicate your efforts, since suddenly there is an extra party to the transaction: the bankruptcy court.

So it may be important to explain the basics of bankruptcy when negotiating with distress property owners. The owners need to understand that, without astute legal and financial guidance, there is no guarantee that they will improve their long-term situation by filing for bankruptcy protection. But, in the short term, they are very likely to complicate your efforts to help them, since their house becomes part of the bankruptcy estate after they file. Meanwhile, a foreclosure can still proceed. This is especially true for people who have tried to fix their financial situations with second or third mortgages, so that they no longer have any equity in their homes.

Of course, there are situations (such as a personal business bankruptcy) where paying the mortgage is not their chief headache, and your arguments will find no traction. And there will be people who will cling to the idea of bankruptcy as their hope for salvation—even if the revisions pass, with their multiple sticking points.

So you might remind them that, under federal law, a bankruptcy filing can show up on their credit reports for 10 years and that there has always been a stigma attached to bankruptcy.

Alas, these arguments may carry no weight either. After all, most people need credit only for buying a house, buying a car, and for working capital (i.e., credit cards). When contemplating bankruptcy, they may have heard that most mortgage lenders will ignore a bankruptcy filing that is more than two years old. They may have seen ads jamming their newspaper from car dealers touting their willingness to work with people with bad credit. And they may have heard of secured credit cards, which someone with bad credit can get by posting a cash deposit. As for the stigma attached to bankruptcy, many people don't even know what their neighbors do for a living these days and will attach no importance to their neighbor's reactions.

The result is that you may occasionally find yourself dealing with people who have no fear of bankruptcy. If they are aware of complexities of the Bankruptcy Code, they figure they can navigate them and, after doing so, they won't owe anything to anyone. Their credit report is already a disaster, so the addition of bankruptcy will hardly matter. As for their house, they were probably going to lose it anyway, so why should they care about what problems they are creating for you or for the mortgage holder?

But there is one final aspect of bankruptcy that may sway them: Property management firms rely heavily on credit reports to decide who they will be willing to rent to, and the presence of a bankruptcy filing is not going to generate a positive reference. As for distress property owners contemplating bankruptcy, they are probably going to have to move out of their houses, but they are almost certainly not in a position to immediately buy another one. Tell them that if they file for bankruptcy they will probably end up living with relatives for several years, since they may be unable to immediately rent or lease a place to live.

Glossary of Real Estate Terms

*Brief Dictionary of Terminology
Most Commonly Used in the
Distress Property Business*

Of the several hundred terms being used daily in the real estate industry, the following are perhaps the most important for the newcomer to understand.

Abstract of Judgment. Summary of a Court's judgment. When recorded in a county, it creates a general lien upon all real and personal property owned by the judgment debtor in that county.

Abstract of Title. A summary or digest of the conveyances and any other facts relied on as evidence of title, together with any other elements of record.

Acceleration Clause. This clause in a note and trust deed permits the lender or beneficiary to declare the entire unpaid balance immediately due and payable when a given condition occurs. Such a condition can be the sale of the land. This clause is sometimes called an *alienation clause.*

Alienate. To transfer the title to real property from one person to another.

Alienation Clause. A special type of acceleration clause which demands payment of the entire loan balance upon sale or upon other transfer of title to the property.

Amortized Loan. A loan that is completely paid off, interest and principal, by a series of regular payments that are equal or nearly equal. Also called a level payments loan.

Appraisal. Estimate or opinion of value.

Appreciation. Increase in value due to any cause such as inflation, repair, modernization, or supply and demand factors.

Assessed Value. Value placed on property by the County Tax Collector for the purpose of computing real property taxes. For California properties that have sold since 1978, it is the fair market value of the property; it is determined from the last sale price or else from the assessor's appraisal.

Assumption of Mortgage. The taking of title to property by a grantee, wherein he assumes liability for payment of an existing note that may be secured by a mortgage or deed of trust against the property. The grantee becomes a coguarantor for the payment of a mortgage or deed of trust note.

Attachment. Seizure of property by court order, usually to have it available in case a judgment is obtained in a pending suit.

Balloon payment. A final installment payment on a note that is greater than the preceding installment payments and pays the note in full.

Bankruptcy. A legal proceeding that allows a debtor to discharge certain debts or obligations without paying the full amount, or that allows the debtor time to reorganize his financial affairs so he can fully pay his debts. A bankruptcy does not discharge obligations secured by a deed of trust.

Beneficiary. One entitled to the benefit of a trust. Also, the lender on the security of a note and deed of trust.

Beneficiary's Demand. Instructions by a beneficiary (usually in writing) under a deed of trust stating and demanding the amount necessary for issuance of a reconveyance.

Beneficiary's Statement. A written report from the lender setting forth the terms and conditions of a recorded loan, such as amounts still owed, interest rate, monthly payments, and so on.

Caveat Emptor. "Let the buyer beware." The buyer must examine the goods or property and buy at his own risk.

Certificate of Sale. A certificate issued to a buyer at a judicial sale (e.g., foreclosure of a mortgage).

Certificate of Title. A certification of the ownership of land. A forerunner to title insurance.

Closing. The final accounting of a sale given by escrow to the buyer and the seller.

Closing Statement. The final accounting of a real estate sale.

Comparative Analysis. A method of appraisal in real estate in which selling prices of similar properties are used as the basis for arriving at the value estimate. It is also known as the Market Data Approach.

Condition Precedent. A condition that must be fulfilled before title can be transferred.

Conditional Sale Contract. A contract for the sale of property stating that delivery is to be made to the buyer, title to remain vested in the seller until the conditions of the contract have been fulfilled.

Condition Subsequent. A condition providing that if the owner fails to do something, his title may be defeated and he may lose.

Consideration. Something of value.

Constructive Eviction. A disturbance of a tenant's possession by the landlord.

Contingent. Dependent upon conditions or events specified but not yet accomplished. Property may be sold contingent upon the seller or buyer meeting specific predetermined conditions.

Contract. A promise to do or not to do certain things.

Conventional Loan. A loan made without government backing.

Conveyance. A written document that transfers title from one person to another. A deed, bill of sale, and an assignment are all conveyances.

Corporation. An artificial person created by law. This so-called person has many powers and duties normally given to an individual.

Debtor. This is the party who owns the property that is subject to the security interest. Previously this party was known as the mortgagor, the pledgor, and so forth.

Declaration of Homestead. Document recorded to establish a homestead to protect the owner against judgment liens.

Deed. Written instrument that, when properly executed and delivered, conveys title.

Deed of Trust. An instrument used in many states in place of a mortgage. Property is transferred to a trustee by the borrower (trustor), in favor of the lender (beneficiary), and reconveyed upon satisfaction of all conditions.

Default. Failure to fulfill a duty or promise or to discharge an obligation; omission or failure to perform any act. Forfeiture.

Deficiency Judgment. A judgment given when the security pledge for a loan does not satisfy the debt upon its default.

Deterioration. Impairment of condition. One of the causes of depreciation. Reflects the loss in value brought about by wear and tear, disintegration, use in service, and the action of the elements.

Discount. To sell a promissory note for less than its face value.

Documentary Transfer Tax. A tax on the transfer of all real property.

Earnest Money. An amount of money given as part of the property's purchase price to bind the agreement between buyer and seller.

Encumbrance. Anything that affects or limits the fee simple title to property, such as mortgages, easements, or restrictions of any kind. Liens are special encumbrances which make the property security for the payment of a debt or obligation, such as mortgages and taxes.

Equity. The interest or value that an owner has in real estate over and above the liens against it; branch of remedial justice by and through which relief is afforded to suitors in courts of equity.

Equity Purchase. Buying the equity of a residential property. The sales price less all debt and encumbrances.

Escrow. The deposit of instruments and funds with instructions to a third neutral party bonded by law to carry out the provisions of an agreement or contract. When everything is deposited to enable carrying out the instructions, it is called a complete or perfect escrow.

Eviction. The physical removal of a person from a property.

Exclusive Right to Sell. A listing in which the owner may sell his property but with the payment of a commission.

Federal Housing Administration (FHA). The federal government agency that administers FHA insured loans.

Federal Tax Lien. An obligation to the U.S. government as a result of non-payment of taxes.

FNMA. Abbreviation for the Federal National Mortgage Association. It is an agency that buys big blocks of loans from banks, thus enabling the banks to loan more money. The FNMA gets its money by selling securities in the market to investors. The securities are guaranteed by the loans behind them.

Forced Sale. An involuntary sale of real property. The owner is forced, usually by law, to sell a property for whatever it will bring. Usually the sale will occur within a short period of time. Often the actual sale is carried out by someone other than the owner, such as a trustee, a sheriff, a judge, or another official.

Foreclosure. Procedure in which pledged property is sold to pay a debt. In California there are three steps in the foreclosure of a Trust Deed.

1. A 90-day notification of default. Time during which the trustor may reinstate by paying the delinquent payments.

2. A 21-day publication. If the trustor has not reinstated within the 90-day period, the beneficiary must publish the time, place, and date of the sale and wait 21 days. During this publication period, the trustor may reinstate by paying the entire balance due.

3. Trustee's sale. The sale is conducted by the beneficiary but in the name of the trustee who has the title. The successful bidder at the sale receives a trustee's deed.

Foreclosure Consultant. Anyone familiar with foreclosure laws and procedures who offers his services to either borrower, lender, or both. Credentials usually include real estate brokers license and mortgage brokering experience.

Fraud. The intentional and successful employment of any cunning, deception, collusion, or artifice, used to circumvent, cheat, or deceive another person, whereby that person acts upon it to the loss of his property and to his legal injury.

General Index. County recorder's record of documents filed, organized alphabetically by names of parties involved.

Grant Deed. A deed conveying the title. It has two implied warranties: that the grantor has not previously conveyed the property, and that he has not encumbered the property except as already disclosed.

Grantee. The buyer.

Grantor. The seller.

Guarantee of Title. Opinion of title condition backed by a fund to compensate in case of negligence. A forerunner of title insurance.

Highest and Best Use. That use which is most likely to produce the greatest net return to the land and/or building over a given period of time.

Home Equity Sales Contract. Purchase agreement between owner and buyer spelling out the terms and conditions of sale. See Figure 12.1 for sample contract. State laws govern form, content, and even size of type to be used for printing. See Appendix for copy of the California law.

Homestead. A home upon which the owner or owners have recorded a declaration of homestead, which protects the home against judgments up to specified amounts.

Impound Account. A compulsory bank account demanded of a borrower by the lender to ensure the payment of taxes and insurance of the property on which the loan was made.

Institutional Lender. Financial institutions whose loans are regulated by law. The category includes such groups as banks, savings and loans, thrift and loans, insurance companies, credit unions, and commercial loan agencies.

Involuntary Lien. A lien imposed against property without consent of an owner; taxes, special assessments, federal income tax liens, and so forth.

IRS. Internal Revenue Service, the tax-collecting arm of the U.S. government.

Joint and Several Note. A note signed by two or more persons in which they are liable jointly and individually for the full amount of the loan.

Joint Tenancy. Joint ownership by two or more persons with right of survivorship; all joint tenants own equal interest and have equal rights in the property.

Junior Lien. A lien that does not have first priority to make property security for the payment of a debt or discharge of an obligation. Examples: judgments, taxes, mortgages, deeds of trust, and so forth.

Lease. A contractual agreement whereby possession and use of land is transferred for a limited period under certain specified conditions.

Legal Description. A proper and formal method of describing a parcel of real estate that is recognized by law. There are several methods used.

Lien. An encumbrance that uses a property as security for the payment of a debt or obligation of the property owner.

Lis Pendens. Suit pending, usually recorded so as to give constructive notice of pending litigation.

Market Value. The price for which property can be sold on the open market if there is a willing seller, a willing buyer, and a reasonable time to make the sale. The seller and buyer are not under pressure to sell or buy quickly.

Mechanic's Lien. A lien placed on property by laborers and material suppliers who have contributed to a work of improvement.

Mutual Consent. Offer and acceptance by which the parties exchange their promises. A unilateral agreement containing a promise of the signer to a named person or bearer of a definite sum of money at a specified date or on demand. Usually provides for interest and is secured by a mortgage or trust deed.

Notarize. To witness a signature on a document and to place a Notary Public's seal on that document.

Note. A unilateral agreement containing a promise of the signer to give a named person or bearer a definite sum of money at a specified date or on demand. The note usually provides for interest, and it is often secured by a trust deed or a mortgage.

Notice of Default. A notice filed to show that the borrower under a mortgage or deed of trust is in default (behind on the payments).

Notice of Trustee's Sale. The last step before the foreclosure auction. Recorded in the county recorder's office, the document is advertised and posted. It gives the time and location of the trustee's sale. It also contains the legal description of the property to be sold.

Offset Statement. Also referred to as a beneficiary's statement. A statement requested of the lender in a mortgage or trust deed, showing the history and present status of the loan.

Option. A right given a person to buy or lease property within a stated period and given under certain specified terms. The person has the right to buy or sell, but is not required to do so.

Points. A charge made by a lender. One point equals one percent of the loan.

Postponement. A verbal announcement made at the time and place of the scheduled trustee's sale. The announcement establishes the new time for the trustee's sale.

Power of Sale. Notarized document conferring a power of attorney status on a third party for the purpose of legally representing either party in a buy/sell transaction.

Preliminary Title Report. A report from a title company of present condition of title made prior to the issuance of a title policy.

Prepayment Penalty. An agreement to pay a penalty for the payment of a note before it actually becomes due.

Principal. A person who is acting for himself in a transaction. Also, the full amount of a loan, note, or debt, exclusive of interest.

Promissory Note. Following a loan commitment from the lender, the borrower signs a note, promising to repay the loan under stipulated terms. The promissory note establishes personal liability for its repayment.

Purchase Money Encumbrance. Any mortgage or trust deed given by buyer to seller as all or part of the purchase price.

Qualifying. The person conducting a foreclosure auction asks potential bidders to prove that they have enough money to purchase the property. The person will do this before allowing them to bid at the sale.

Realtor. A broker or sales agent who is a member of a local real estate board that is affiliated with the National Association of Real Estate Boards (NAREB).

Recording. Recording is called constructive notice. If you want to record a deed, it must be acknowledged by the grantor in the presence of a notary. The deed must be recorded in the county where the property is located. The fee for recording is paid by the persons benefiting by the recording. The grantor delivers the deed, but the grantee wants to record it.

Rehabilitation. The restoration of a property to satisfactory condition without drastically changing the plan, form, or style of architecture.

Reinstatement Period. An interval of three calendar months following the recording of a notice of default. During this period, a default may be cured when the owner pays whatever is owed to the lender.

Rent. Consideration paid for the occupancy and use of real property. When a tenant is to be evicted the lessor must give a three-day notice to quit, then institute an unlawful detainer action and the court will order the sheriff to physically evict. You will also get a judgment for back rent and damage to the property.

REO. The abbreviation for Real Estate Owned. The term is used to describe properties owned by institutional lenders after foreclosing on loans secured by the properties.

Repo. Short for repossession. A property that a lender owns after a foreclosure sale. The lender has repossessed that upon which they loaned money.

Request for Notice of Default. A recorded notice requesting that a person be notified in the event that foreclosure proceedings are commenced on a specific trust deed by a party of interest to that trust deed. Any person can request this notice for a small fee. It is used most often by a junior lien holder so he can act to protect his interest should a senior lien be delinquent and start foreclosure action.

Rescission. The mutual agreement of the parties to a contract to release each other.

Restraint of Bidding. An agreement by two or more people to not raise the bidding on a property being sold at a foreclosure auction. Such an agreement is illegal.

Right of Survivorship. Right to acquire the interest of a deceased joint owner; distinguishing feature of a joint tenancy.

Secondary Financing. Junior trust deeds or mortgages.

Security Interest. A term designating the interest of the creditor in the property of the debtor in all types of credit transactions. It thus replaces such terms as the following: chattel mortgage; pledge; trust receipt; chattel trust; equipment trust; conditional sale; inventory lien; and so forth.

Separate Property. That which is not community property.

Sheriff's Deed. Deed given by court order in connection with sale of property to satisfy a judgment.

Steal. A popular term for a very good purchase. Similar to a super bargain; however, less clearly defined. Not all steals are truly super bargains.

Subject To. Usually referred to as the condition of title that exists at the time of acquisition by the buyer, such as subject to a deed of trust of record.

Subordination Clause. A clause in a trust deed or mortgage by which the lender relinquishes his priority to a subsequent trust deed, mortgage, or other lien. It benefits the borrower.

Tax Shelter. A factor (such as a special depreciation allowance) that reduces taxes on current earnings.

Tenancy in Common. Ownership by two or more persons who hold undivided interest, without right of survivorship; interests need not be equal.

Title. Evidence that owner of land is in lawful possession thereof; an instrument evidencing such ownership.

Title Insurance. Insurance written by a title company to protect property owner against loss if title is imperfect.

Trustee. One who holds property in trust for another to secure the performance of an obligation.

Trustee's Deed. A deed by which the trustor conveys his title to a trustee to be held in trust as security to borrow money.

Trust Deed. A deed by which the trustor conveys his title to a trustee to be held in trust as security to borrow money.

Trustor. One who deeds his property to a trustee to be held as security until he has performed his obligation to a lender under terms of a deed of trust.

Unlawful Detainer Action. A lawsuit to evict a tenant or former owner who unlawfully remains in possession of real property.

Usury. An illegal rate of interest.

Vendee. A purchaser; buyer.

Vendor. A seller; one who disposes of a thing in consideration of money.

Voluntary Lien. Any lien placed on property with consent of, or as a result of, the voluntary act of the owner.

Warranty Deed. A deed used to convey real property that contains warranties of title and quiet possession, and the grantor thus agrees to defend the premises against the lawful claims of third persons.

Wrap-around Mortgage. Involves the borrower entering into a second mortgage. This arrangement represents the means by which he can add to his borrowing without refinancing the first mortgage at substantially higher current rates.

Appendix: Selections from the California Civil Codes

CHAPTER 2.5. HOME EQUITY SALES CONTRACTS

§ 1695. Legislative findings and declarations

(a) The Legislature finds and declares that homeowners whose residences are in foreclosure have been subjected to fraud, deception, and unfair dealing by home equity purchasers. The recent rapid escalation of home values, particularly in the urban areas, has resulted in a significant increase in home equities which are usually the greatest financial asset held by the homeowners of this state. During the time period between the commencement of foreclosure proceedings and the scheduled foreclosure sale date, homeowners in financial distress, especially the poor, elderly, and financially unsophisticated, are vulnerable to the importunities of equity purchasers who induce homeowners to sell their homes for a small fraction of their fair market values through the use of schemes which often involve oral and written misrepresentations, deceit, intimidation, and other unreasonable commercial practices.

(b) The Legislature declares that it is the express policy of the state to preserve and guard the precious asset of home equity, and the social as well as the economic value of homeownership.

(c) The Legislature further finds that equity purchasers have a significant impact upon the economy and well-being of this state and its local communities, and therefore the provisions of this chapter are necessary to promote the public welfare.

(d) The intent and purposes of this chapter are the following:

(1) To provide each homeowner with information necessary to make an informed and intelligent decision regarding the sale of his or her home to an equity purchaser; to require that the sales agreement be expressed in writing; to safeguard the public against deceit and financial hardship; to insure, foster, and encourage fair dealing in the sale and purchase of homes in foreclosure; to prohibit representations that tend to mislead; to prohibit or restrict unfair contract terms; to afford homeowners a reasonable and meaningful opportunity to rescind sales to equity purchasers; and to preserve and protect home equities for the homeowners of this state.

(2) This chapter shall be liberally construed to effectuate this intent and to achieve these purposes.

§ 1695.1. Definitions

The following definitions apply to this chapter:

(a) "Equity purchaser" means any person who acquires title to any residence in foreclosure, except a person who acquires such title as follows:

(1) For the purpose of using such property as a personal residence.

(2) By a deed in lieu of foreclosure of any voluntary lien or encumbrance of record.

(3) By a deed from a trustee acting under the power of sale contained in a deed of trust or mortgage at a foreclosure sale conducted pursuant to Article 1 (commencing with Section 2920) of Chapter 2 of Title 14 of Part 4 of Division 3.

243

(4) At any sale of property authorized by statute.

(5) By order or judgment of any court.

(6) From a spouse, blood relative, or blood relative of a spouse.

(b) "Residence in foreclosure" and "residential real property in foreclosure" means residential real property consisting of one- to four-family dwelling units, one of which the owner occupies as his or her principal place of residence, and against which there is an outstanding notice of default, recorded pursuant to Article 1 (commencing with Section 2920) of Chapter 2 of Title 14 of Part 4 of Division 3.

(c) "Equity seller" means any seller of a residence in foreclosure.

(d) "Business day" means any calendar day except Sunday, or the following business holidays: New Year's Day, Washington's Birthday, Memorial Day, Independence Day, Labor Day, Columbus Day, Veterans' Day, Thanksgiving Day, and Christmas Day.

(e) "Contract" means any offer or any contract, agreement, or arrangement, or any term thereof, between an equity purchaser and equity seller incident to the sale of a residence in foreclosure.

(f) "Property owner" means the record title owner of the residential real property in foreclosure at the time the notice of default was recorded.

§ 1695.2. Written contract; size of type; language; signature and date

Every contract shall be written in letters of a size equal to 10-point bold type, in the same language principally used by the equity purchaser and equity seller to negotiate the sale of the residence in foreclosure and shall be fully completed and signed and dated by the equity seller and equity purchaser prior to the execution of any instrument of conveyance of the residence in foreclosure.

§ 1695.3. Contents; survival of contract

Every contract shall contain the entire agreement of the parties and shall include the following terms:

(a) The name, business address, and the telephone number of the equity purchaser.

(b) The address of the residence of foreclosure.

(c) The total consideration to be given by the equity purchaser in connection with or incident to the sale.

(d) A complete description of the terms of payment or other consideration including, but not limited to, any services of any nature which the equity purchaser represents he will perform for the equity seller before or after the sale.

(e) The time at which possession is to be transferred to the equity purchaser.

(f) The terms of any rental agreement.

(g) A notice of cancellation as provided in subdivision (b) of Section 1695.5.

(h) The following notice in at least 14-point boldface type, if the contract is printed, or in capital letters, if the contract is typed, and completed with the name of the equity purchaser, immediately above the statement required by Section 1695.5(a):

NOTICE REQUIRED BY CALIFORNIA LAW

"Until your right to cancel this contract has ended,

_____
(Name)
or anyone working for

_____
(Name)
CANNOT ask you to sign or have you sign any deed or any other document."

The contract required by this section shall survive delivery of any instrument of conveyance of the residence in foreclosure, and shall have no effect on persons other than the parties to the contract.

§ 1695.4. Right of cancellation; time and manner of exercise.

(a) In addition to any other right of rescission, the equity seller has the right to cancel any contract with an equity purchaser until midnight of the fifth business day following the day on which the equity seller signs any contract or until 8 a.m. on the day scheduled for the sale of the property pursuant to a power of sale conferred in a deed of trust, whichever occurs first.

(b) Cancellation occurs when the equity seller personally delivers written notice of cancellation to the address specified in the contract or sends a telegram indicating cancellation to that address.

(c) A notice of cancellation given by the equity seller need not take the particular form as provided with the contract and, however expressed, is effective if it indicates the intention of the equity seller not to be bound by the contract.

§ 1696.5. Right of cancellation; notice of right; form

(a) The contract shall contain in immediate proximity to the space reserved for the equity seller's signature a conspicuous statement in a size equal to at least 12-point bold type, if the contract is printed, or in capital letters, if the contract is typed, as follows; "You may cancel this contract for the sale of your house without any penalty or obligation at any time before _____

_____
(Date and time of day)

See the attached notice of cancellation form for an explanation of this right." The equity purchaser shall accurately enter the date and time of day on which the rescission right ends.

(b) The contract shall be accompanied by a completed form in duplicate, captioned "notice of cancellation" in a size equal to 12-point bold type, if the contract is printed, or in capital letters, if the contract is typed, followed by a space in which the equity purchaser shall enter the date on which the equity seller executes any contract. This form shall be attached to the contract, shall be easily detachable, and shall contain in type of at least 10-point, if the contract is printed, or in capital letters, if the contract is typed, the following statement written in the same language as used in the contract:

NOTICE OF CANCELLATION

_____
(Enter date contract signed)

You may cancel this contract for the sale of your house without any penalty or obligation at any time before _____
(Enter date and time of day)

To cancel this transaction, personally deliver a signed and dated copy of this cancellation notice, or send a telegram to _____
(Name of purchaser)

at _____
(Street address of purchaser's place of business)

NOT LATER THAN _____
(Enter date and time of day)

I hereby cancel this transaction _____
(Date

_____
(Seller's signature)

(c) The equity purchaser shall provide the equity seller with a copy of the contract and the attached notice of cancellation.

§ 1695.6. Contract requirements; responsibility of equity purchaser; prohibited transactions; bona fide purchasers and encumbrancers; cancellation; return of original documents; untrue or misleading statements; encumbrances

(a) The contract as required by Sections 1695.2, 1695.3, and 1695.5, shall be provided and completed in conformity with those sections by the equity purchaser.

(b) Until the time within which the equity seller may cancel the transaction has fully elapsed, the equity purchaser shall not do any of the following:

(1) Accept from any equity seller an execution of, or induce any equity seller to execute, any instrument of conveyance of any interest in the residence in foreclosure.

(2) Record with the county recorder any document, including, but not limited to, any instrument of conveyance, signed by the equity seller.

(3) Transfer or encumber or purport to transfer or encumber any interest in the residence in foreclosure to any third party, provided no grant of any interest or encumbrance shall be defeated or affected as against a bona fide purchaser or encumbrancer for value and without notice of a violation of this chapter, and knowledge on the part of any such person or entity that the property was "residential real property in foreclosure" shall not constitute notice of a violation of this chapter. This section shall not be deemed to abrogate any duty of inquiry which exists as to rights or interests of persons in possession of the residential real property in foreclosure.

(4) Pay the equity seller any consideration.

(c) Within 10 days following receipt of a notice of cancellation given in accordance with Section 1695.4 and 1695.5, the equity purchaser shall return without condition any original contract and any other documents signed by the equity seller.

(d) An equity purchaser shall make no untrue or misleading statements regarding the value of the residence in foreclosure, the amount of proceeds the equity seller will receive after a foreclosure sale, the equity seller's rights or obligations arising out of the sale transaction, the nature of any document which the equity purchaser induces the equity seller to sign, or any other untrue or misleading statement concerning the sale of the residence in foreclosure to the equity purchaser.

(e) Whenever any equity purchaser purports to hold title as a result of any transaction in which the equity seller grants the residence in foreclosure by any instrument which purports to be an absolute conveyance and reserves or is given by the equity purchaser an option to repurchase such residence, the equity purchaser shall not cause any encumbrance or encumbrances to be placed on such property or grant any interest in such property to any other person without the written consent of the equity seller.

IF YOUR PROPERTY IS IN FORECLOSURE BECAUSE YOU ARE BEHIND IN YOUR PAYMENTS, IT MAY BE SOLD WITHOUT ANY COURT ACTION, (14-point boldface type if printed or in capital letters if typed) and you may have the legal right to bring your account in good standing by paying all of your past due payments plus permitted costs and expenses within the time permitted by law for reinstatement of your account, which is normally five business days prior to the date set for the sale of your property. No sale date may be set until three months from the date this notice of default may be recorded (which date of recordation appears on this notice).

This amount is _____ as of _____
                                              (Date)

and will increase until your account becomes current.

While your property is in foreclosure, you still must pay other obligations (such as insurance and taxes) required by your note and deed of trust or mortgage. If you fail to make future payments on the loan, pay taxes on the property, provide insurance on the property, or pay other obligations as required in the note and deed of trust or mortgage, the beneficiary or mortgagee may insist that you do so in order to reinstate your account in good standing. In addition, the beneficiary or mortgagee may require as a condition to reinstatement that you provide reliable written evidence that you paid all senior liens, property taxes, and hazard insurance premiums.

Upon your written request, the beneficiary or mortgagee will give you a written itemization of the entire amount you must pay. You may not have to pay the entire unpaid portion of your account, even though full payment was demanded, but you must pay all amounts in default at the time payment is made. However, you and your beneficiary or mortgagee may mutually agree in writing prior to the time the notice of sale is posted (which may not be earlier than the end of the three-month period stated above) to among other things, (1) provide additional time in which to cure the default by transfer of the property or otherwise; or (2) establish a schedule of payments in order to cure your default; or both (1) and (2).

Following the expiration of the time period referred to in the first paragraph of this notice, unless the obligation being foreclosed upon or a separate written agreement between you and your creditor permits a longer period, you have only the legal right to stop the sale of your property by paying the entire amount demanded by your creditor.

To find out the amount you must pay, or to arrange for payment to stop the foreclosure, or if your property is in foreclosure for any other reason, contact:

_____
(Name of beneficiary or mortgagee)

_____
(Mailing address)

_____
(Telephone)

If you have any questions, you should contact a lawyer or the governmental agency which may have insured your loan.

Notwithstanding the fact that your property is in foreclosure, you may offer your property for sale, provided the sale is concluded prior to the conclusion of the foreclosure.

Remember, **YOU MAY LOSE LEGAL RIGHTS IF YOU DO NOT TAKE PROMPT ACTION.** (14-point boldface type if printed or in capital letters if typed)"

Unless otherwise specified, the notice if printed, shall appear in at least 12-point boldface type.

If the obligation secured by the deed of trust or mortgage is a contract or agreement described in paragraph (1) or paragraph (4) of subdivision (a) of Section 1632, the notice required herein shall be in Spanish if the trustor requested a Spanish language translation of the contract or agreement pursuant to section 1632. If the obligation secured by the deed of trust or mortgage is contained in a home improvement contract, as defined in Sections 7151.2 and 7159 of the Business and Professions Code, which is subject to Title 2 (commencing with Section 1801), the seller shall specify on the contract whether or not the contract was principally negotiated in Spanish and if the contract was principally negotiated in Spanish, the notice required herein shall be in Spanish. No assignee of the contract or person authorized to record the notice of default shall incur any obligation or liability for failing to mail a notice in Spanish unless Spanish is specified in the contract or the assignee or person has actual knowledge that the secured obligation was principally negotiated in Spanish. Unless specified in writing to the contrary, a copy of the notice required by subdivision (c) of Section 2924b shall be in English.

(2) Any failure to comply with the provisions of this subdivision shall not affect the validity of a sale in favor of a bona fide purchase or the rights of an encumbrancer for value and without notice.

(c) Costs and expenses which may be charged pursuant to sections 2924 to 2924i, inclusive, shall be limited to the costs incurred for recording, mailing, publishing, and posting notices required by Sections 2924 to 2924i; inclusive, postponement upon the written request of the trustor pursuant to section 2924g made to either the beneficiary or trustee not to exceed fifty dollars ($50) per postponement and a fee for a trustee's sale guarantee or, in the event of judicial foreclosure, a litigation guarantee.

(d) Trustee's or attorney's fees which may be charged pursuant to subdivision (a), or until the notice of sale is deposited in the mail to the trustor as provided in Section 2924b, if the sale is by power of sale contained in the deed of trust or mortgage, or, otherwise at any time prior to the decree of foreclosure, are hereby authorized to be in an amount which does not exceed two hundred dollars ($200) with respect to any portion of the unpaid principal sum secured which is fifty thousand dollars ($50,000) or less, plus one-half of 1 percent of the unpaid principal sum secured exceeding fifty thousand dollars ($50,000) up to and including one hundred fifty thousand dollars ($150,000), plus one-quarter of 1 percent of any portion of the unpaid principal sum secured exceeding one hundred fifty thousand dollars ($150,000) up to and including five hundred thousand dollars ($500,000), plus one-eighth of 1 percent of any portion of the unpaid principal sum secured exceeding five hundred thousand dollars ($500,000). Any charge for trustee's or attorney's fees authorized by this subdivision shall be conclusively presumed to be lawful and valid where the charge does not exceed the amounts authorized herein.

(e) Reinstatement of a monetary default under the terms of an obligation secured by a deed of trust, or mortgage may be made at any time within the period commencing with the date of recordation of the notice of default until five business days prior to the date of sale set forth in the initial recorded notice of sale.

In the event the sale does not take place on the date set forth in the initial recorded notice of sale or a subsequent recorded notice of sale is required to be given, the right of reinstatement shall be revived as of the date of recordation of the subsequent notice of sale, and shall continue from that date until five business days prior to the date of sale set forth in the subsequently recorded notice of sale.

In the event the date of sale is postponed on the date of sale set forth in either an initial or any subsequent notice of sale, or is postponed on the date declared for sale at an immediately preceding postponement of sale, and, the postponement is for a period which exceeds five business days from the date set forth in the notice of sale, or declared at the time of postponement and shall continue from that date until five business days prior to the date of sale declared at the time of the postponement.

Nothing contained herein shall give rise to a right of reinstatement during the period of five business days prior to the date of sale, whether the date of sale is noticed in a notice of sale or declared at a postponement of sale.

Pursuant to the terms of this subdivision, no beneficiary, trustee, mortgagee, or their agents or successors shall be liable in any manner to a trustor, mortgagor, their agents or successors for the failure to allow a reinstatement of the obligation secured by a deed of trust or mortgage during the period of five business days prior to the sale of the security property, and no such right of reinstatement during this period is created by this section. Any right of reinstatement created by this section is terminated five business days prior to the date of sale set forth in the initial date of sale, and is revived only as prescribed herein and only as of the date set forth herein.

As used in this subdivision, the term "business day" has the same meaning as specified in Section 9.

ARTICLE 1.5 MORTGAGE FORECLOSURE CONSULTANTS

§ 2945. Legislative findings and declarations

(a) The Legislature finds and declares that homeowners whose residences are in foreclosure are subject to fraud, deception, harassment, and unfair dealing by foreclosure consultants from the time a Notice of Default is recorded pursuant to Section 2924 until the time of the foreclosure sale. Foreclosure consultants represent that they can assist homeowners who have defaulted on obligations secured by their residences. These foreclosure consultants, however often charge high fees, the payment of which is often secured by a deed of trust on the residence to be saved, and perform no service or essentially a worthless service. Homeowners, relying on the foreclosure consultants' promises of help, take no other action, are diverted from lawful businesses which could render beneficial services, and often lose their homes, sometimes to the foreclosure consultants who purchase homes at a fraction of their value before the sale.

(b) The legislature further finds and declares that foreclosure consultants have a significant impact on the economy of this state and on the welfare of its citizens.

(c) The intent and purposes of this article are the following:

(1) To require that foreclosure consultant service agreements be expressed in writing; to safeguard

the public against deceit and financial hardship; to permit rescission of foreclosure consultation contracts; to prohibit representations that tend to mislead; and to encourage fair dealing in the rendition of foreclosure services.

(2) The provisions of this article shall be liberally construed to effectuate this intent and to achieve these purposes.

§ 2945.1. Definitions

The following definitions apply to this chapter:

(a) "Foreclosure consultant" means any person who makes any solicitation, representation, or offer to any owner to perform for compensation or who, for compensation, performs any service which the person in any manner represents will in any manner do any of the following:

(1) Stop or postpone the foreclosure sale.

(2) Obtain any forebearance from any beneficiary or mortgagee.

(3) Assist the owner to exercise the right of reinstatement provided in Section 2924c.

(4) Obtain any extension of the period within which the owner may reinstate his or her obligation.

(5) Obtain any waiver of an acceleration clause contained in any promissory note or contract secured by a deed of trust or mortgage on a residence in foreclosure or contained in any such deed of trust or mortgage.

(6) Assist the owner to obtain a loan or advance of funds.

(7) Avoid or ameliorate the impairment of the owner's credit resulting from the recording of a notice of default or the conduct of a foreclosure sale.

(8) Save the owner's residence from foreclosure.

(b) A foreclosure consultant does not include any of the following:

(1) A person licensed to practice law in this state when the person renders service in the course of his or her practice as an attorney at law.

(2) A person licensed under Division 3 (commencing with Section 12000) of the Financial Code when the person is acting as a prorater as defined therein.

(3) A person licensed under Part 1 (commencing with Section 10000) of Division 4 of the Business and Professions Code when the person makes a direct loan or when the person (A) engages in acts whose performance requires licensure under that part, (B) is entitled to compensation for the acts performed in connection with the sale of a residence in foreclosure or with the arranging of a loan secured by a lien on a residence in foreclosure, (C) does not claim, demand, charge, collect, or receive any compensation until the acts have been performed or cannot be performed because of an owner's failure to make the disclosures set forth in Section 10243 of the Business and Professions Code or failure to accept an offer from a purchaser or lender ready, willing, and able to purchase a residence in foreclosure or make a loan secured by a lien on a residence in foreclosure on the terms prescribed in a listing or a loan agreement, and (D) does not acquire any interest in a residence in foreclosure directly from an owner for whom the person agreed to perform the acts other than as a trustee or beneficiary under a deed of trust given to secure the payment of a loan or that compensation. For the purposes of this paragraph, a "direct loan" means a loan of a real estate broker's own funds secured by a deed of trust on the residence in foreclosure, which loan and deed of trust the broker in good faith attempts to assign to a lender, for an amount at least sufficient to cure all of the defaults on obligations which are then subject to a recorded notice of default, provided that, if a foreclosure sale is conducted with respect to the deed of trust, the person conducting the foreclosure sale has no interest in the residence in foreclosure or in the outcome of the sale and is not owned, controlled, or managed by the lending broker; the lending broker does not acquire any interest in the residence in foreclosure directly from the owner other than as a beneficiary under the deed of trust; and the loan is not made for the purpose or effect of avoiding or evading the provisions of this article.

(4) A person licensed under Chapter 1 (commencing with Section 5000) of Division 3 of the Business

and Professions Code when the person is acting in any capacity for which the person is licensed under those provisions.

(5) A person or his or her authorized agent acting under the express authority or written approval of the Department of Housing and Urban Development or other department or agency of the United States or this state to provide services.

(6) A person who holds or is owed an obligation secured by a lien on any residence in foreclosure when the person performs services in connection with this obligation or lien.

(7) Any person licensed to make loans pursuant to Division 9 (commencing with Section 22000), 10 (commencing with Section 24000), or 11 (commencing with Section 26000) of the Financial Code, subject to the authority of the Commissioner of Corporations to terminate this exclusion, after notice and hearing, for any person licensed pursuant to any of those divisions upon a finding that the licensee is found to have engaged in practices described in subdivision (a) of Section 2945.

(8) Any person or entity doing business under any law of this state, or of the United States relating to banks, trust companies, savings and loan associations, industrial loan companies, pension trusts, credit unions, insurance companies, or any person or entity authorized under the laws of this state to conduct a title or escrow business, or a mortgagee which is a United States Department of Housing and Urban Development approved mortgagee and any subsidiary or affiliate of the above, and any agent or employee of the above while engaged in the business of these persons or entities.

(c) "person" means any individual, partnership, corporation, association or other group, however organized.

(d) "Service" means and includes, but is not limited to, any of the following:

(1) Debt, budget, or financial counseling of any type.

(2) Receiving money for the purpose of distributing it to creditors in payment or partial payment of any obligation secured by lien on a residence in foreclosure.

(3) Contacting creditors on behalf of an owner of a residence in foreclosure.

(4) Arranging or attempting to arrange for an extension of the period within which the owner of a residence in foreclosure may cure his default and reinstate his obligation pursuant to Section 2924c.

(5) Arranging or attempting to arrange for any delay or postponement of the time of sale of the residence in foreclosure.

(6) Advising the filing of any document or assisting in any manner in the preparation of any document for filing with any bankruptcy court.

(7) Giving any advice, explanation or instruction to an owner of a residence in foreclosure which in any manner relates to the cure of a default in or the reinstatement of an obligation secured by a lien on the residence in foreclosure, the full satisfaction of that obligation, or the postponement or avoidance of a sale of a residence in foreclosure pursuant to a power of sale contained in any deed of trust.

(e) "Residence in foreclosure" means a residence in foreclosure as defined in Section 1695.1.

(f) "Owner" means a property owner as defined in Section 1695.1.

(g) "Contract" means any agreement, or any term thereof, between a foreclosure consultant and an owner for the rendition of any service as defined in subdivision (d).

§ 2945.2. Owner's right to cancel contract with consultant; time and manner of cancellation

(a) In addition to any other right under law to rescind a contract, an owner has the right to cancel such a contract until midnight of the third "business day" as defined in subdivision (e) of Section 1689.5 after the day on which the owner signs a contract which complies with Section 2945.3.

(b) Cancellation occurs when the owner gives written notice of cancellation to the foreclosure consultant at the address specified in the contract.

(c) Notice of cancellation, if given by mail, is effective when deposited in the mail properly addressed with postage prepaid.

(d) Notice of cancellation given by the owner need not take the particular form as provided with the contract and, however expressed, is effective if it indicates the intention of the owner not to be bound by the contract.

§ 2945.3. Written contract; contents; language, date, and signature; notice of cancellation; form

(a) Every contract shall be in writing and shall fully disclose the exact nature of the foreclosure consultant's services and the total amount and terms of compensation.

(b) The following notice, printed in at least 14-point boldface type and completed with the name of the foreclosure consultant, shall be printed immediately above the statement required by subdivision (c):

NOTICE REQUIRED BY CALIFORNIA LAW

_____ or anyone working for him or her
(Name)

CANNOT:

(1) Take any money from you or ask you for money until

_____
(Name)

has completely finished doing everything he or she said he or she would do; and

(2) Ask you to sign or have you sign any lien, deed of trust, or deed."

(c) The contract shall be written in the same language as principally used by the foreclosure consultant to describe his services or to negotiate the contract; shall be dated and signed by the owner; and shall contain in immediate proximity to the space reserved for the owner's signature a conspicuous statement in a size equal to at least 10-point bold type, as follows: "You, the owner, may cancel this transaction at any time prior to midnight of the third business day after the date of this transaction. See the attached notice of cancellation form for an explanation of this right."

(d) The contract shall contain on the first page, in a type size no smaller than that generally used in the body of the document, each of the following:

(1) The name and address of the foreclosure consultant to which the notice or cancellation is to be mailed.

(2) The date the owner signed the contract.

(e) The contract shall be accompanied by a completed form in duplicate, captioned "Notice of Cancellation", which shall be attached to the contract, shall be easily detachable, and shall contain in type of at least 10-point the following statement written in the same language as used in the contract:

NOTICE OF CANCELLATION

_____
(Enter date of transaction)   (Date)

You may cancel this transaction, without any penalty or obligation, within three business days from the above date.

To cancel this transaction, mail or deliver a signed and dated copy of this cancellation notice, or any other written notice, or send a telegram to

_____
(Name of foreclosure consultant)

at _____
　　(Address of foreclosure consultant's place of business)

NOT LATER THAN MIDNIGHT OF _____
　　　　　　　　　　　　　　　　　　　Date

I hereby cancel this transaction _____
　　　　　　　　　　　　　　　　Date

_____
(Owner's signature)

(f)　The foreclosure consultant shall provide the owner with a copy of the contract and the attached notice of cancellation.

§ 2945.4. Prohibited practices

It shall be a violation for a foreclosure consultant to:

(a)　Claim, demand, charge, collect, or receive any compensation until after the foreclosure consultant has fully performed each and every service the foreclosure consultant contracted to perform or represented he would perform.

(b)　Claim, demand, charge, collect, or receive any fee, interest, or any other compensation for any reason which exceeds 10 percent per annum of the amount of any loan which the foreclosure consultant may make to the owner.

(c)　Take any wage assignment, any lien of any type on real or personal property, or other security to secure the payment of compensation. Any such security shall be void and unenforceable.

(d)　Receive any consideration from any third party in connection with services rendered to an owner unless such consideration is fully disclosed to the owner.

(e)　Acquire any interest in a residence in foreclosure from an owner with whom the foreclosure consultant has contracted. Any interest acquired in violation of this subdivision shall be voidable, provided that nothing herein shall affect or defeat the title of a bona fide purchaser or encumbrancer for value and without notice of a violation of this article. Knowledge that the property was "residential real property in foreclosure," shall not constitute notice of a violation of this article. This subdivision shall not be deemed to abrogate any duty of inquiry which exists as to rights or interests of persons in possession of residential real property in foreclosure.

(f)　Take any power of attorney from an owner for any purpose, except to inspect documents as provided by law.

(g)　Induce or attempt to induce any owner to enter a contract which does not comply in all respects with Sections 2945.2 and 2945.3.

§ 2945.6. Action against consultant; judgment; cumulative remedies; limitation of actions

(a)　An owner may bring an action against a foreclosure consultant for any violation of this chapter. Judgment shall be entered for actual damages, reasonable attorney's fees and costs, and appropriate equitable relief. The court also may, in its discretion, award exemplary damages and shall award exemplary damages equivalent to at least three times the compensation received by the foreclosure consultant in violation of subdivision (a), (b), or (d) of Section 2945.4, in addition to any other award of actual or exemplary damages.

(b)　The rights and remedies provided in subdivision (a) are cumulative to, and not a limitation of, any other rights and remedies provided by law. Any action brought pursuant to this section shall be commenced within four years from the date of the alleged violation.

§ 2945.7. Violations; punishment; cumulative remedies

Any person who commits any violation described in Section 2945.4 shall be punished by a fine of not more than ten thousand dollars ($10,000), by imprisonment in the county jail for not more than one year, or in the state prison, or by both that fine and imprisonment for each violation. These penalties are cumulative to any other remedies or penalties provided by law.

§ 2945.8. Severability

If any provision of this article or the application thereof to any person or circumstance is held to be unconstitutional, the remainder of the article and the application of such provision to other persons and circumstances shall not be affected thereby.

Index